"Whether you're a se ever dinner party, *Invited* will draw you in with the warm welcome, genuine voice, and Southern charm of the author. And then, once you're settled in, you'll find inspiring truth about the ministry of hospitality and the many ways we can love one another through celebration. With story after story, Price shares her own experiences with events and parties, demonstrating how to plan and enjoy lovely events while also reminding readers that life will never be perfect—but, with Christ, it can be beautiful and something worth celebrating."

~ MARY CARVER
author of *Choose Joy: Finding Hope and Purpose When Life Hurts* and
Plan a Fabulous Party {Without Losing Your Mind}

"*Invited* could be my story. Christen Price gets me. She understands a woman's drive for perfection and how that drive so often just drives her over the edge. If that also describes you, don't miss Christen's new book, *Invited: Live a Life of Connection, Not Perfection*. Through real life illustrations and practical, biblical wisdom Christen digs out the roots of our need to be "perfect" and guides us to experience real connectedness with others through everyday hospitality."

~ KATHY HOWARD
speaker and author of *Unshakeable Faith*, www.kathyhoward.org

"This book, oh my! It's like a bubble bath for the frazzled woman's soul. All my adult life I've been envious of friends who can whip up a five-star event without breaking a sweat. *Invited* has freed me from the shame of my party deficiencies, my dust bunnies, and burnt pie crusts. It invites us, through delightful stories, practical tips, and biblical insight, to explore God's heart for hospitality—one that's far less about perfection than it is about love. And we all know love can be messy sometimes. Why shouldn't our parties be, too?"

~ BECKY KOPITZKE
author of *The SuperMom Myth: Conquering the Dirty Villains of Motherhood*

"In today's world where social media is the mainstay of human interaction, Christen Price reminds us the gift of hospitality is about loving others up close and personal—nothing fancy, just a warm invitation to the table. Christen reminds us to live a life of connection, not perfection, and it's this refreshing remedial lesson we all desperately need to hear."

~ JOANNE KRAFT
author of *The Mean Mom's Guide to Raising Great Kids* and *Just too Busy—Taking Your Family on a Radical Sabbatical*

"Hospitality is not one of my spiritual gifts. I love being around people. I just tremble at the thought of letting them inside my messy house or my messy life. It feels too vulnerable. I'm afraid of being judged. Christen lovingly and transparently challenges me—and you—to get over ourselves. Because hospitality is not about perfection. It's about connection. It's about opening the doors of our homes and our hearts to the beauty of relationship. It's about making people feel loved. It's the same beautiful invitation Jesus extends to us: to be accepted and loved, just as we are, in all our messiness."

~ MELINDA MEANS
speaker and author of *Invisible Wounds: Hope While You're Hurting*, www.melindameans.com

"In *Invited: Live a Life of Connection, Not Perfection*, Christen Price literally invites the reader to embrace the power and beauty of relationships ignited and nurtured through the lost art of imperfect and authentic hospitality. *Invited* is woven with biblical insight, infused with doable ideas, and chock full of delightful recipes in the back. I highly recommend *Invited* for individuals and women's small groups as well."

~ STEPHANIE SHOTT
author, Bible teacher, and founder of The MOM Initiative

"A refreshing breath of hope and hospitality, *Invited* reminds us that rich relationships are far more important than a Pinterest-perfect life. Christen encourages us to embrace the grace-filled life of connection rather than the distracted hustle of perfection, and inspires us to look to Christ as we continue the hard, rewarding work of loving our people. "

~ KAYSE PRATT
www.IntentionalMoms.com

"With her southern hospitality charm, Christen Price makes plans to connect with and celebrate her people, but she's learned the hard way those gatherings don't always go according to plan. In *Invited*, Christen encourages people to never see a party in the same way again. This book has a biblical foundation and ushers readers into the freedom that comes with letting go of perfection and striving for genuine connection with your people instead."

~ KRISTIN HILL TAYLOR
www.kristinhilltaylor.com

"If you have ever struggled with anxiety or its cousin perfectionism, this book will gently release you from fear to love your people, place, and purpose through the art of perfectly imperfect celebration. This book is full of Southern charm and real stories and was an absolute joy to read."

~ AMANDA CONQUERS
blogger at www.amandaconquers.com

invited

live a life of connection,
not perfection

Christen Price

AMBASSADOR INTERNATIONAL
GREENVILLE, SOUTH CAROLINA & BELFAST, NORTHERN IRELAND

www.ambassador-international.com

Invited

Live a life of connection, not perfection

ISBN: 978-1-62020-604-1

eISBN: 978-1-62020-677-5

Cover Design and Typesetting by Hannah Nichols

eBook Conversion by Anna Riebe Raats

Photography by Ashley Skinner Photography

AMBASSADOR INTERNATIONAL
Emerald House
411 University Ridge, Suite B14
Greenville, SC 29601, USA
www.ambassador-international.com

AMBASSADOR BOOKS
The Mount
2 Woodstock Link
Belfast, BT6 8DD, Northern Ireland, UK
www.ambassadormedia.co.uk

The colophon is a trademark of Ambassador

For Raleigh

With you, I'm home.

SPECIAL THANKS

How could I have known when I sat next to Alison Lowry at Allume in 2014 that our conversation would lead to me writing a book with Ambassador International three years later? Only God could have arranged that divine appointment, and I am forever grateful for the chance to sit beside her and share my idea about writing a book that celebrates our people, place, and purpose. I'd like to thank Alison for introducing me to her husband, Tim, who has championed this project from the beginning. Tim, thank you for being a visionary and for guiding me throughout the early stages of writing this book. I'd also like to thank Anna Raats for coordinating the final stages of production and Brenda Covert for being so patient with my perfectionistic tendencies when it came time to edit. Thank you, Hannah Nichols, for designing a beautiful cover that brought the book to life. Without this team, *Invited* would still just be an idea in my head. Thank you, Ambassador International, for helping me write my first book.

Invited could not have been written without the support of my family and friends. To my parents, thank you for believing in me and for allowing me to share some of our family's story with my readers. You've taught me the value of home, and whenever I smell barbecue over a charcoal grill, I will think of you. Thanks for always welcoming me and our tow of children at any time of the day and for any length of time. Also, I'd like to thank my in-laws, John and Sondra, for including me in their family traditions. Since becoming a Price, I've learned the importance of making time for weeknight meals with family and Friday Night suppers at Nan Nan's. You all have taught me that it's not about what we eat or do but about the time we spend together. Thank you. Throughout this book, I've had the chance to share many family recipes, and I'd like to thank our grandmothers, Patsy Creel and Okalee Gunter, for allowing me to document their recipes. I have loved learning to cook from the two of you, and I thank you for being such wonderful examples of the Proverbs 31 woman to your families. To Courts, Leslie, Gunter, and Kari Beth, thank you for being both family and friends. Raleigh and I are so grateful for the memories that we all have shared together.

So many friends have prayed for me and my crazy dreams to write a book, but I'd like to especially thank Ashley, Susanne, Stephanie, K.C., Leah, Courtney, Ashlea, and my small group girls (Megan, Michelle, Hannah, Heather, Catherine, Jamie, Kayla, and Tabitha) for allowing me to use your stories of friendship in this piece of writing. Thank you to Michelle, Jennifer, Emily, Ashley, Dana, Abby, and Baily for shooting the promo video for *Invited*. Your transparency and love for Christ was so undeniable, and I thank you for helping me support this book. To my Covenant family, thank you for cheering me on as I wrote this book, and to my pastors Hays and Kyle for your advice and wisdom. I'd also like to thank my prayer warriors—Jessica, Barbi, Rachel, Ashley, and Mrs. Pam—as well as my team at Undivided Women for helping me cling to the promises of God when trouble has come my way. A very special thanks to the readers of my blog, the women who have purchased items from Christen Price Studio, and for my street team—this book is for you!

Words can't express how much I love my people, but I'd like to thank Raleigh for asking me to share life with him. I've treasured being your wife, and I thank you for always being there for me. Thank you for wiping away my tears, giving me courage, and for doing the laundry so I could write this book. You are an amazing husband and dad. I truly am so blessed to have you by my side. Adeline, Maralee, and Ridley, you munchkins mean the world to us! Thank you for drawing Mommy pictures to put at my writing desk, and for being the favorite part of my day. I know you don't understand this whole book thing, but I hope one day you will find inspiration from this experience to follow the desires that God has placed within your hearts. I love each of you to the moon and back, and I pray that you will always know the true meaning of home.

Contents

INTRODUCTION

"To do great and important tasks, two things are necessary:
a plan and not quite enough time."

~ Anonymous

MY FRIEND MICHELLE HAS MAD design skills and just renovated a house that was in dire need of love. Even though she had just moved into her house and still had several odds-and-ends items to complete, she wanted to throw our friend Hannah a baby shower at her home. When she asked me to help, we met for lunch to discuss the shower, and Michelle began to show me her ideas for decorating, which involved loads of flowers in shades of bright fuchsia, pale pink, and lavender. A few days before the party, I stop by Michelle's to drop off some of my items and find her busy painting her front door and hanging pictures while her husband mows the front lawn. She jokes that the party has given them motivation to finish getting their home in perfect condition and shoos me away until the party on Sunday. Getting in my car, I say a little prayer for my friend and promise to be back a few hours before the party begins to help set up.

On Sunday, I pull up to her home and feel like I've just been part of an episode of *Fixer Upper*. Her landscape is in immaculate condition, the front door is painted a beautiful mint, and the inside of her home is decorated to perfection. Her house is ready for a party!

Michelle had hung a flowery door hanger in the center of her fireplace mantle with Hannah's little girl's name scrolled across it, with dangling ribbon and flowers. Over her kitchen table hung a stunning mobile made from two natural grapevine wreaths of different sizes and dried flowers. With two packs of three-for-twelve-dollars flowers from the grocery store and the help of another hostess, we arranged the flowers in adorable glass vases, which were placed all around Michelle's house. Pink balloons welcomed guests from the mailbox and were also placed in bunches around the room. On Michelle's kitchen island, we fixed a spread of veggie pizza, chicken salad, homemade cheese straws, fruit and yogurt dip, pimento cheese pinwheels, and chocolate mousse brownies with fresh strawberries. For drinks, we mixed together my favorite pink punch recipe and sliced lemons and limes in a big Mason jar container with water. Michelle's house had been transformed into a flower wonderland, ready for a party.

When Hannah walked into the room, she cried.

Parties give us opportunities to celebrate the people we love. Hannah's reaction to the party was priceless, worth all the planning and preparation. Later, she told us that even if Michelle's front door was still painted its original color and her house did not have pictures hung perfectly, she still would have cried because she felt such love from her family and friends.

The idea behind this book is that we are called to celebrate, be in community, and believe that connection is far better than perfection. As women, we so often let the hurdles of perfection stop us from practicing hospitality, but God invites us to release our anxieties, receive others in love, and rejoice in the moment. We can spend our whole lives trying to practice hospitality perfectly, but God simply wants us to accept His invitation and extend His love to the people we cherish most. How we practice hospitality is a direct way for us to put love into action. God invites us into community with Him through opportunities to live in community with others. We learn how to be patient, kind, and welcoming—all the qualities of a hostess—through parties. Deep gratitude resides in our hearts after we've experienced the sweetness of celebrating. When we finally learn to accept our imperfections, we better love ourselves. Hospitality isn't about perfection; it's about connection.

It's true; to do great and important tasks, two things are necessary: a plan and not quite enough time. I've been an event planner for over ten years and have planned every kind of non-profit event imaginable—women's conferences, fancy galas, community walks, golf tournaments, crawfish boils, silent auctions, motorcycle rides, art auctions, fashion shows, canned goods contests, pageants, pep rallies—you name it, I've planned it. These events, while they differ in theme from an event I'd plan for loved ones, like birthday parties and baby showers, are still all about creating an experience that is meaningful to a specific group of people. These fundraising events celebrate life, honor loved ones, and give people hope for their futures.

While a party is simply a social gathering of invited guests and typically involves eating, drinking, and entertainment, it's so much more. Planning and attending parties are a beautiful way for us to show Christ's love to others and live out the gift of salvation that we were all created to receive. God is the Perfect Party Planner, wooing us into a life everlasting with Him in heaven through His Son. Jesus is perfect, so we don't have to be. He offers us a new way to live, one where we don't have to stress out about planning; preparing, and performing perfectly . . . He invites us to just *be* in Him. What a gift!

Parties are not always going to go as planned, but my hope is that you will find joy as you read these pages and invite people not only into your home but also into your life's-not-going-according-to-my-plan day. The words scribed on these pages are the lessons that I've learned over the years, not just in party planning, but in my relationship with Christ. Parties have taught me to expect the unexpected and to trust that God has a plan, even when mine fails. Practicing hospitality has not always come easily for me, but I believe it's changed my life for the better.

May we be like Michelle and plan a party even if it takes extra time and preparation. Let us love our people well, so they know just how thankful we are to have them in our lives. As we plan our parties, I pray that we experience the deep and gratifying joy that comes from celebrating.

Part One:
Connection

Chapter 1:

A CALL FOR CONNECTION, NOT PERFECTION

Being confident of this, that he who began a good work in you
will carry it on to completion until the day of Christ Jesus.

~ Philippians 1:6 NIV

GROWING UP SOUTHERN, I QUICKLY learned that hospitality connects people.

My family lives in Alabama. Every year we traveled to New Orleans to visit my dad's parents and sisters. We would ride I-10 for six hours until the rhythm of the roads changed from smooth interstate to a bumpy two-lane canal street. When we arrived at my grandparents' house past bedtime, Grandpa would always welcome us with his amazing chocolate sheet cake. He created the sponge for his chocolate cake with lots of cocoa powder and hints of cinnamon. When all of the ingredients are combined and cooked, the cake emerges from the oven puffy in the sheet pan and the color of soft brown leather. He would mix his icing on low heat over the stove using more cocoa, butter, condensed milk, confectioners' sugar, and vanilla. My favorite part of the cake was the icing, and I'd always ask him to serve me second, so I could scrape up all the extra icing that drizzled on the bottom of the pan after he'd cut my brother's piece. We'd sit at his round kitchen table, and under the warm glow of the overhead light, we'd feast on ooey-gooey cake and wash it down with a tall glass of milk. Those nights in the kitchen made me feel welcome in his home and taught me that hospitality is love, simply served one slice of chocolate cake at a time.

Cupcakes on the floor were not exactly part of my party plan.

Moments before my son's first birthday, I'm scrambling in the kitchen to plate party food. I'd taken off work that day, but I'd been working non-stop cleaning up our home, putting together last-minute party decorations, and making his smash cake from scratch. I'd been planning Ridley's first birthday party since before he was born, and now that it was here, I wanted it to be perfect, just like him. Years earlier, I had saved an "Up, Up, and Away" party invitation in my inbox, hoping to purchase it if I ever had a boy. The invitation had a vintage hand-drawn hot air balloon on it in colors of turquoise and yellow, and I found lots of ideas on Pinterest for ways to tie the theme together throughout the party. I ordered iced sugar cookies shaped like hot air balloons and clouds, and I stuck a couple to the sides of his smash cake with icing. Blue and yellow polka dot balloons were filled with helium and tied on each side of a wicker basket, and we placed Ridley inside the basket wearing a matching appliqued outfit with his name on it for pictures. On our wall I hung his monthly growth pictures, and each picture had tiny balloons floating above it, anchored with tape and string. He sat in a vintage white high chair that I borrowed from a friend, and more balloons—the giant 36" ones—were tied to the back of his high chair with tassels hanging down. Clouds were cut out of cardboard to place on the walls with streamers, and little pots that held paper kites served as my table centerpiece.

My mom is in the kitchen with me, and even though she means well, she's in my way. Without thinking, I pick up my cupcake storage container by the top handle, ignoring my note written in a black Sharpie pen that instructed whoever carried this container to "pick it up from the bottom." When picked up from the handle, the cupcakes would sometimes be too heavy, which would cause the container to pop open (a side note—who makes a storage container that doesn't secure itself properly?!). With cupcakes in route to be plated, the handle gives. Suddenly, my vanilla cupcakes with homemade chocolate buttercream icing (and sprinkles!) begin falling toward the floor. Trying to save them from splattered doom, I attempt to rescue my art from destruction. It's like I'm in the movies and the camera is on slow-motion, watching me scream "Nooooo" while doing my best to catch a dozen cupcakes in mid-air. Instead of making the most amazing save of television history, the camera zooms in to epically capture the cupcakes crashing on the floor in a crumbled mess. All sound in the kitchen comes to a halt. Everyone—my mother, my husband, my children, my in-laws, and my grandparents—watches me in silence. Standing above the mess, my brain instructs me to remain calm. I know I should be the hostess who keeps it together, doesn't cry over spilled milk, and makes a joke about the unfortunate accident. But I can't be that girl. Not today.

I let the tears fall, and I don't try to wipe them away as I race out of the room. No longer caring that my family has witnessed my breakdown, I run to my closet. My closet is more than a space that holds my clothes and rows of shoes; it is my hiding place, and once inside, I slide the pocket door closed to be alone. It is at this moment that the heat from within me surfaces so fast that I can hardly breathe. Short breaths, in and out, in and out, made haste in my chest, and I fall to the floor, unable to control what my body so desperately needed to release. Crouched in my party clothes with mascara rolling down my cheeks, all I can do is ask God why this is happening to me.

This kind of episode was nothing new to my mother, and when I left the kitchen, she knew where to find me. I heard the door roll open and smelled her Chanel #5 before I opened my eyes. When I was a young girl, she would bend down next to me in my closet at home. I would lean my head into the warmth of her chest, crying tears of shame. My mother would let me cry for what seemed like hours. Her embrace brought me comfort and made me feel less afraid. Now, in my thirties, I just wanted to cry with my mama and explain that this was about more than the cupcakes. I wanted to tell her that I didn't know how to be a mom of preschoolers and a soon-to-be toddler and a dreamer and a wife and an employee. I wanted to tell her that all of the house renovations had caused our income to be extremely tight and how I wished that we could have a house that looked like it came out of a magazine. I wanted to tell her that I was jealous of other moms, and I wanted to ask her how she had maintained hope during her thirty-five-year marriage when things had happened incredibly different from what she expected. I wanted to tell her about everything

I feared, how afraid I was of not being good enough, and how much I just wanted to be okay.

Instead, my mom came into my closet and told me to dry my eyes and return to the party.

Standing in silence, I smoothed my clothes and emerged from my closet. Staring at my reflection in my bathroom mirror, I reapplied my makeup and fixed my hair. Taking a deep breath and one last look, I plastered on my "everything's fine" smile before leaving my place of solitude. Opening my bedroom door, I walked into the kitchen, scooped my baby into my arms, and tried to pretend like that moment never happened. We went outside in the February cold and took family pictures with Ridley in the basket, and we sang "Happy Birthday" to our sweet baby boy. We laughed as he took his fist and Ninja-chopped his smash cake, and then we opened gifts on the living room floor. When it was time for everyone to leave, we sent them home with leftover sugar cookies as treats.

I look back at these pictures now, and I can see the sadness in my eyes. While I remember Ridley's sweet smile and the laughter as I helped him blow out his birthday candle, my memories also hold the raw emotions that escaped from within me. I remember wondering if there was something wrong with me, and I've spent the last year trying to discover an answer. Hours have been spent perusing articles about women and anxiety. Long conversations have been had with family and friends, all who tell me that I put too much pressure on myself. When doctors ask me at my annual check-up what they can do for me today, I wonder if pills can cure the never-ending struggle of perfectionism.

If I could make a wish, I'd wish that I had not let the cupcake incident ruin my evening. I wish I had spent more time with my son on his actual birthday rather than cleaning and baking. I wish I had made the party about simply celebrating him and the light he is in our lives, rather than trying to recreate a Pinterest-perfect occasion that I would share later with my friends.

I can't go back, can I? He turns one only once, and that moment has passed. It's the bittersweet truth that I now face.

But, I can learn from my mistakes.

I must.

I *will*.

Melting down over life events not happening as I had planned seems to be an underlying theme that keeps rearing its nasty head, especially during moments that are supposed to be celebrated like my son's birthday party. I get so worked up over everything being perfect, and when it's not, I lose it. Do you do this too?

It seems to me that women are desperately chasing perfection, and when we don't capture it, we lose control over our emotions. Perfection is passion, an ideal that makes us feel so strongly about the matters of our hearts that we act in ways that make us later feel shame and unworthiness, like we will never quite measure up. Passion doesn't always lead to positive results. How can we pursue perfection without becoming undone?

A perfectionistic woman is someone who strives ambitiously, sets high standards for herself, and makes very critical self-evaluations. If perfectionism had a nametag, it would read, "Hello, I'm Christen." Could your name be written on the nametag too? As I've talked with friends, I've discovered that many goal-oriented women who like to plan battle perfectionism. It doesn't matter if we are planning a birthday party, who we will marry, or working toward our dream job; women want to achieve perfection because we want the best for ourselves, our people, and our futures. We know that there is only one life to live (no, not the soap opera!), and we want to make it the best. But, when a perfectionist's expectations are unmet, we experience breakdowns, blame ourselves (or others), and belittle. The pendulum of passion swings back and forth in a perfectionist's soul. Will this always be our label? Is there another way—a better way—to live?

Susan and I meet at a local bakery just before Lent. Neither of us are fond of coffee (the caffeine makes our already jittery nerves more jittery), so we both order hot chocolate with cream on this cold day. Susan leads us toward the back of the room, behind the open-air fireplace, to seats by the window. We sit next to each other and hang our purses and winter coats on the arms of our chairs, and as we wait for the cocoa to be cool enough to sip, she asks me about my family and work. I smile and share the silly, how Ridley follows his big sisters around wherever they go, but I know that this question-and-answer session is only a lead-in, that she is testing the waters, trying to determine what I need to talk about most today.

I've known who Susan was since high school, she's the mother of a girl close to me in age. Susan is a well-known hostess in our town, and I've been inside her beautiful home as she has hosted wedding and baby showers for different members of our church. Susan always seems to have a smile on her face, and I can find her sitting on the fifth pew most every Sunday. But today, Susan and I are going deeper than the polite smiles we offer one another as she entertains in her home or greets me at the door of the church. She has been a recommended resource for me, someone who has been trained to counsel other women. We've been meeting on occasion for a few months now, and she knows my struggle with perfection. Today, Susan's purpose is not to entertain me but to connect with me.

The chocolate inside our cups is no longer scalding hot. Susan takes a sip. I do the same. She smiles and holds her cup in one hand as she turns in her seat to face me better.

"When my kids were little, I remember how much I wanted to be a good mother to them. But, I also remember how exhausted I was. My husband was working overtime so I could be at home with them. I always felt guilty for needing a break, because having a husband, children, and a beautiful home was what I always dreamed of for my life. My family is my greatest ministry, and I wanted the time I spent with them to count. They are my people, my place, and my purpose."

Listening to her, I nod my head. She takes a breath and continues. "I admire you."

"What for?" I ask. She was the one I admired . . . what could she *possibly* admire in me?

"For how you raise your kids, the work you are doing in ministry, what you hope to achieve in the future. I could never do everything that you do so well."

I can't accept her compliment and find myself lowering my eyes. Blinking, I command the tears to stay at bay and not wash down my face. The room has grown terribly warm. I feel the need to confess. "Susan, I . . ." taking a moment, I search for the words I want to say next.

Susan finishes my sentence for me. "You put too much on yourself, don't you."

There it was. Out in the open, no longer shoved in my closet, it's an admission of truth. Me, a girl who attempts to create a life labeled with perfection, feels pressure instead of pleasure. I don't like who I've become, and Susan sees it in my eyes, my body language, and my stories. Am I capable of receiving joy?

I look up, and see nothing but kindness in her eyes. Clearing my throat, I respond, "Yes, yes, I do."

My friend Ashley once told me that people need to see God with skin on. I write this down in my journal during Holy Week. *What does that look like, exactly?*

God is perfect.

I am not.

Trying to obtain perfection has only left me feeling not good enough. It has commanded me to do more, be more, have more. When I am unable to achieve the unattainable goals I set for myself, my inner critic gives voice to everything that I'm doing wrong. This isn't what God with skin on is supposed to look like, is it?

In Hebrew, there are two words translated "perfect" or "perfection": *tamam* and *calal*. Tamam represents wholeness, while calal represents completeness and beauty.[1] Psalm 18:30 NIV uses tamam by saying, "As for God, his way is perfect: the LORD's word is flawless; he shields all who take refuge in him." Calal is often used to describe Zion, perfect in beauty. Zion is a place—Jerusalem—the city of God's presence. Here, the idea of perfection is not to be a perfectionist, but to acknowledge that God is perfect and has designed a perfect place to be His children's home. While Jerusalem is currently home to the Jewish people, it is also a place of great hope for all of God's people. Zion is where Christians believe Jesus will return for His second coming, to redeem us from our imperfections. While living amid our current Zion (our state of imperfection), we can have hope for a future Zion, a new Zion, a place of beauty without blemish.

God is not calling us home by way of perfectionism. No, He invites us to take refuge in His perfect presence. God is perfect so we don't have to be. He gave us His Son, Jesus, who is "such a high priest who truly meets our need—one who is holy, blameless, pure, set apart from sinners, exalted above the heavens," so that we may live flawed but forgiven. As we receive and show hospitality to others, we love as Christ loved us. And maybe, just maybe, more people will begin to see God with skin on.

Robert Hotchkins, a theologian at the University of Chicago, states, "Christians ought to be celebrating constantly. We ought to be preoccupied with parties, banquets, feasts, and merriment. We ought to give ourselves over to veritable orgies of joy because we have been liberated from the fear of life and the fear of death. We ought to attract people to the church quite literally by the fun there is in being a Christian."[2] Celebrations occur throughout the Old and New Testaments of the Bible. In Exodus, Scripture shares three annual feasts that all Jews celebrated—Feast of Unleavened Bread, Feast of Harvest, and Feast of Ingathering, and the Gospels of the New Testament share how Jesus performed His first miracle at a wedding. In Acts we read of the early disciples breaking bread together in their homes while eating with glad and sincere hearts. Celebrations occur when babies are born, as men become kings, and after God's people repent. God calls His people to celebrate not just for pleasure but for purpose. He invites us into His presence in different forms of celebrations with the purpose to taste, see, declare, and remember His goodness.[3] Celebrations are about connection, not perfection.

Parties serve as a way to connect people to God and each other, giving us an opportunity to come together and celebrate. The definition of connection is "a relationship in which a person, thing, or idea is linked or associated with something else."[4] In Genesis 1, God said, "Let us make man in our image, in our likeness." Our bodies and our souls are bound to God, the Son, and the Holy Spirit. Like links on a chain, the Trinity designed us in their image for connection. We were made for relationship with God and, as Hotchkins says, "to attract people to the church quite literally by the fun there is in being a Christian."

Wholeness is a process and salvation is a gift. John writes in Revelation 19:9 that an angel of the Lord said, "Blessed are those who are invited to the wedding supper of the Lamb!" At the end of my life, I want to attend this supper. Don't you? Accepting the gift Christ gave us today, the work He is doing in our lives will be complete when we join the invited people at His wedding reception. United and unblemished, we are connected with Him in peace forevermore. Heaven is our home, our place of belonging, where we will spend eternity with the people we spent a lifetime celebrating.

But in the meantime, why don't we have some fun?

Chapter 2:

THE ART OF ENTERTAINING

Beauty is in the cracks, the smudge, and the imperfect line. In an age of machine-made products, human touch is more valuable than ever. As with people, minor flaws can make objects more appealing. There is elegance in imperfection.

~ Dr. Samantha Boardman

STANDING IN THE BARE LIVING room of our first home, I began to dream about entertaining. The house that we had purchased was built in the 1930s, nestled in the historic district of Montgomery, Alabama, and from the street it reminded me of a gingerbread home with its red brick and classic Tudor trim. Our front door was a true gem, made of thick wood with a small window just below the arc. Walking inside our home, the living room was on the left, anchored with an ornate fireplace mantel, and the dining room on the right, with a door that led to an alley kitchen and sitting room. The tall ceilings and transom windows above the doors made the room feel spacious, and I envisioned myself preparing hors d'oeuvres in the kitchen with Raleigh uncorking the wine. Friends that we had yet to meet are greeted at our door, and we spend hours sitting at our farmhouse table, laughing throughout dinner, then make our way to the couch and chairs in the living room for dessert.

Raleigh interrupts my trance. "Babe, you ready to unload?" Taking one last look around the bare room, I smile back at him, ready to make this house our home.

Over the next few hours, our family helps us paint the living room and place dishes in cabinets, towels in bathrooms, and sheets on beds. Progress is made in each room, and by the end of the day, we all eat our first meal in the house together. Grimy but grateful, we share pizza from a local spot within walking distance of our home, and with each bite, we comment on what Raleigh and I are going to like most about this home. While I agree that we will enjoy the short commute and the space, I still drift back into my hospitality dream, anticipating the day when we can entertain with more than take-out pizza.

Mary Alice became my very first Montgomery friend, and we met at Raleigh's company cookout just after we moved to town. Short and smiling, she wore a jersey dress and Tory Burch flats, and she liked to use her hands as she talked. Her husband had recently joined Raleigh's architecture firm too, and we quickly bonded over our love for Auburn football. She liked to laugh, and we became the best of friends, fast. We'd ride to Bible study together, meet up at the coffee shop, and take walks around our historic neighborhood, talking until our feet couldn't walk any longer. She helped me decide if I should wear a long emerald green dress or a short cocktail dress to the fanciest wedding I'd ever been invited to (she voted the emerald green and she was right, it was the best choice!). Mary Alice was always gracious, inviting us to her family's lake house where we'd ride on ski boats during the day, eat peach cobbler with vanilla ice cream for dessert, and stay up late into the evening playing silly games. After each visit, I'd hug her neck, so thankful to have made a friend as wonderful as she was.

Mary Alice and I soon became friends with Katie, a friend of a friend from high school. Katie glowed even before she was pregnant, with her long golden hair and beautiful features. Even though she was gorgeous, she didn't make a fuss about herself and often sported work-out shorts and a ponytail, which made me want to be her friend even more. Katie convinced me to train with her for a triathlon, and it was while exercising that I truly got to know her personality; she was wise and perceptive but extremely easy-going and calm. Katie didn't make me feel like I had to try to be her friend; I just was her friend.

The six of us began to rotate house parties with a small group of friends that we'd all connected with in town, and we usually went pot-luck as we entertained. Mary Alice had fabulous taste, and her home felt just like her, elegant but warm, with a twist of whimsy and fun. The girls would hang out in her kitchen as the guys grilled steaks outside, and then we'd all eat together in her dining room. She served blue cheese spread to go on top of our steaks, and White Russians with dessert. Whenever we were invited to Mary Alice's, she always had a way of celebrating us with sophistication, grace, and humor.

While Katie was more reserved in a group setting, her husband never met a stranger, which always made for fun stories at their dinner table. He'd tell us of his adventures from growing up fifth in a family with nine kids, making Katie (who grew up an only child) just roll her eyes and smile. They fascinated me and were a true case of opposites attracting. They often cooked us tacos with peppers and onions, and we'd go old-school with warm cookies and ice cream after dinner. The six of us would sit on their back porch and dream about jobs and travels and what life would be like with kids one day.

Being a newlywed, the most experience I had with entertaining involved a karaoke machine with my college sorority sisters and bringing an appetizer to a football tailgate. Before we got married, Raleigh and I would cook together in my apartment, and we'd eat dinner side by side on TV trays or at my kitchen bar. I'd never really had a house of my own or hosted an adult party complete with a menu and matching silverware. Now, with cabinets filled with china and serving bowls, I was ready to learn how to prepare our house for entertaining. Flipping open cookbooks and etiquette books, I began to dog-ear pages of recipes I wanted to try, table settings I wished to recreate, and clever ways to invite. Ina Garten, the owner of Barefoot Contessa, writes in her cookbook *Family Style* that for every party she gives, she makes a timetable. This timetable is a real schedule that she uses to help plan her meals. While planning, she says to consider the tone of the party. Is it fancy or casual? Is it a sit-down dinner or a buffet with plates in your lap? How much time (and oven space) do I have? What do my guests like to eat, and what do I like to make? Once she has all of this figured out, she makes her schedule by working backward. Ina starts with what time the guests will arrive and what time she wants to serve the food and then looks at her recipe cook times to decide the order in which to prepare the food.[5]

When it was my turn to host our group, I noted Ina's advice and laid out my schedule. My dinner party wasn't fancy, but I did want it to feel like more than a casual get-together with friends. I set the table without a tablecloth the night before but at each seat had a placemat with a green and white quatrefoil design. In the center of the table, I placed bright pink flowers in a low vase so we could see one another while talking, and several votive candles were dispersed around the flowers. Each guest had a matching green cloth napkin, but I kept the napkins in the kitchen, along with the silverware and plates, so our friends could serve themselves the main course of shrimp and grits before sitting.

I chose shrimp and grits as a nod to Katie's home on the Gulf Coast, and as a promise that we would all one day take a beach trip together and eat the most delicious shrimp and grits ever at Great Southern in Seaside. The shrimp needed to be peeled first and had to go in the skillet last, so in between the shrimp I made the cheese grits and cut up bacon for extra flavor in the sauce and to be crumbled on top of the meal. Since the shrimp and grits were decadent, I served a fresh arugula salad with thin slices of Parmesan cheese shaved on top and tossed it in a light lemony dressing just before we plated our food.

When our friends arrived, the house smelled of bacon, and Raleigh had Coldplay jamming on the playlist. The party I had dreamed about was finally here! With drinks in hand, we all stood in the kitchen and talked about our upcoming trip to Nashville for New Year's as I stirred the cheese grits on the stove. Soon, it was time to eat. As we sat at the table, I noticed how the light from the candles bounced off of each person's smiling face. I couldn't have been happier, and I squeezed Raleigh's hand while we ate. It was my first time cooking shrimp and grits, and they weren't perfect but they were good enough for the guys to eat two helpings.

After dinner, I brought a cheesecake to the buffet that sits just behind our dining room table. Since cheesecake is best served cold, I made this the night before and then set out tiny ramekins just before the party that were filled with different toppings: raspberries, chocolate sauce, crumbled up Reese's, homemade whipped cream, and toasted pecans. Everyone fixed a plate, and we talked about everything and nothing, each of us with an opinion as unique as our slices of cheesecake.

This moment and these people stand out to me as a rare find, something that others spend a lifetime searching for. I'd never had friendships quite like these before, and might not ever again. Now, several years and miles apart, I think of this night as wholly good.

The hostesses who are the happiest in life understand that the art of entertaining is not about *what* they are hosting but *how* they host. Celebrations, whether they be special occasions, a surprise party, or a spontaneous cookout on a Saturday night, are about spending time with the people you love. While there are certain rules that are time-less, tried, and true for entertaining, there are other moments that require "planned spontaneity," a go-with-the-flow kind of attitude. In *New Manners for New Times*, Letitia Baldrige (a world-famous expert on manners who served as chief of staff for Jacqueline Kennedy in the White House) says that hostesses who understand how to apply social graces to spontaneous events are better prepared to deal with stressful situations and, in return, are able to enjoy the party they are hosting.[6] A favorite quote that I found by Emily Post relates to this idea of entertaining being an art. "The attributes of a great lady may still be found in the rule of four S's: Sincerity, Simplicity, Sympathy, and Serenity." When thinking upon the four S's, I've come to this conclusion about each of the four, which I firmly believe we can apply not only to entertaining but also to how we move and interact with others on a daily basis:

A hostess who is sincere looks directly into the eyes of her guests, making each feel like the most important person in the room. There are no false pretenses or any efforts for self-promotion, just true engagement and interest in the life of another human being. Not only are we sincere during the conversation, but true sincerity follows up afterward, checking in on the guest weeks after the party. Sincerity is not selfish.

There is beauty in simplicity. Simplicity is the statement piece of a party, and the byproduct of a life well lived. The basic rules of achieving simplicity are, well, simple: identify the essential, eliminate the rest. As a hostess, we can ask ourselves, "How can I simplify the decorations, the food preparation, the mailing of invitations - but not eliminate the beauty?" Simplicity is sophistication and very, very intentional.

Sympathy is often a result of empathy. If we are sincere as hostesses, our guests will often disclose something difficult that they are struggling with because they feel safe and connected as friends. Sometimes, these announcements can catch us by surprise; other times it's an ongoing conversation. Either way, our role as their friend is to listen and encourage. Usually, sympathy is a much better posture than offering them our advice. (Also, asking if they want more coffee and dessert never hurts!)

Serenity might be the last attribute listed, but it's one of the most important. A hostess who is unhappy over the unplanned and uncomfortable moments of party planning sets the mood for the whole party. Serenity is a unified state of the mind, heart, and soul. Even if disaster strikes, serenity is a deliberate action of calming ourselves from within so that we don't make or break a party.

If entertaining is art, then it is an expression of our own skill and imagination produced in a way to be appreciated by others. There is beauty to be found in the party, from flowers to linens, to mismatched serving platters filled with delicacies and conversations that stretch well into the evening. To entertain in a matter of sincerity, simplicity, sympathy, and serenity is to entertain beautifully. How lovely is that?

Just as a party has the characteristic of beauty, so do we as women. Beauty, by nature, has the characteristics of wholeness, balance, and radiance.[7] The beauty of a woman is found not just in her appearance but also in the hidden places of her heart, in her gentle and quiet spirit (1 Peter 3:3–4). To exude beauty, we begin by looking within. If a heart struggle of a woman is perfectionism, this is an indicator of our longing for wholeness, balance, and radiance in our lives. We desperately want beauty, but rather than viewing ourselves as whole, we see unworthiness. If change begins within, how do we transform our hearts to see ourselves as art?

Jesus says that the kingdom of heaven is like a merchant looking for fine pearls. When he found one of great value, he went away and sold everything he had and bought it (Matthew 13:45 NIV). Pearls are formed inside oysters, mussels, and clams as a way for the shell to protect itself from an irritant such as a parasite or grain of sand. When the irritant comes inside the shell, a fluid called "nacre" is used to coat it until a mother of pearl is formed. In order for us to attain beauty, we have to first protect our hearts from the imperfections that irritate us. We need nacre, layers upon layers of spiritual truth, as reminders that we are more precious than jewels, fearfully and wonderfully made.

Pearls are a work of art, of such great value that merchants would sell all of their possessions just to have them. Isn't it interesting how an irritant formed something so beautiful? If Christ is our pearl, perfect in beauty, and His Father has prepared a perfect place for us, we become the merchant, selling everything so we can follow Him. Christ, in His perfection, is what will make our hearts balanced, whole, and radiant. To release ourselves of disappointment, we find beauty through Christ, who covers our imperfections with love, grace, and mercy.

We will always have imperfections. We can't ever be perfect. But, we can still walk in beauty for the rest of our days, celebrating our people and how we were made. The Greek word for beauty is *kalos,* which means "good that inspires or motivates others to embrace what is lovely."[8] Let us see beauty in ourselves so that we can show *kalos* to those we share life with.

The home is a hostess's sanctuary. While many parties are memorable in locations other than the home, there is something special about sharing your sacred place with others. When we invite people into our homes, we are showing them our personality through our actions, our home's appearance, and our attitude. The struggle for every hostess is perfection. We want to present the best version of ourselves to our guests so we plan, prepare, and perform in ways that we think will make people like us more and enjoy being at our party.

While perfection is the goal of so many hostesses, it is actually a turn-off for their guests. Whenever you attend a party in someone else's home that is perfectly planned, do you walk away a bit envious? Do you wonder how she could afford her furniture, when she had the time to craft the party decorations, and where she found the outfit she wore?

The antidote to perfection is when we can see beauty in the imperfect and we present not only ourselves but our homes in an artful way. Let the toys stay stacked in the corner of your living room. It's okay to have a few dishes piled in the sink when your guests arrive. Instead of focusing on the flaws of your home and all the things you wish to fix, accept any compliments that come your way. Don't be your own worst critic. Give yourself grace. If beauty is in the eye of the beholder, believe that you and your home are, in fact, beautiful.

If a party is truly about connection and not perfection, we will radiate beauty while entertaining instead of being distracted by all the fluff. We worry less and go with the flow more. We sit at tables on back porches or perch on kitchen counters with plates piled high with food and glasses brimming with beverage, and we enjoy doing life with the people we love. We have better conversations, laugh more, and don't want to leave. We open not only our homes but ourselves, giving and blessing and receiving so much joy in return.

Beauty is the art of entertaining.

Chapter 3:

A CALL FOR COMMUNITY

A guest never forgets the host who had treated him kindly.

~ Homer

AS I TURN ONTO THE street, I notice the house before my phone tells me I've reached my destination. Even though this is the first time I've been invited into Susan's home, I can tell by the cars parked on the street that the white house with black shutters is the party house. Home for the weekend, I park my car, grab my purse and the gift wrapped in ivory paper, and open my door. Before I get out of the car, I take one last look in the mirror, making sure my lip gloss is on straight. I smile back at my reflection; a "go get 'em" smile in an effort to calm my nerves. Reaching the steps, I walk up one, two, three, and stop just outside the door painted yellow. It's decorated with the letter M for the bride's soon-to-be last name, and there are fresh hydrangeas, blue as the sky, in pots all around the entrance. The front door isn't intimidating; it's inviting. Tossing my hair, I reach for the doorbell, but the door swings open, and I'm face-to-face with Susan, smiling so big that I wonder if she's ever seen a frown.

"C'mon in!" she says.

"Thank you!" I reply.

She introduces herself and directs me toward the living room. We walk past the dining room, where more hydrangeas fill vases in the center of the table, with food flanking the flowers on polished silver platters. Two pound cakes tempt me on the outer rim of the table, one sour cream and the other chocolate, and bowls full of whipped cream, fruit, and chocolate sauce are ready to be ladled onto crystal plates. Mimosas in tall glasses line the corner table, along with a water dispenser filled with lemons and limes. I'm told coffee is in the kitchen, and Susan takes my gift before she leaves me to mingle.

My friend is dressed in white, already posing for pictures with her fiancé's grandmother, and I notice some girls from high school huddled together by the glass windows. Some women have already settled onto the couches, and family members are crowded around the groom's sister and her new baby. The guests soon begin to fill their plates, and I follow the line around the circular table, wanting to taste a sample of all the cakes, chicken salad, and cheese straws. I join my friends at seats by the window to watch as the bride begins to open her gifts. She blushes, not used to being the center of attention, and while everyone "oohs" and "ahhs" over her gifts, Susan discreetly walks around the room and asks if anyone would like more coffee. Certain that her guests are comfortable, she then finds a seat and enjoys commenting about cookware and china along with the rest of the women.

While sitting, I notice the story of her home. She's raised a family in this house, and by the gently worn look of the rugs, I imagine her children padding across this room, barefoot during the summer months home from school or in plaid pajamas on Christmas morning.

The room is painted a calm shade of cream, and her furniture is the distressed look, created before vintage became popular. Two bucket chairs sit in the corner by the piano, and a little table sits between them with a lamp and pictures of her daughters in silver frames. Her couch is a blend of rose and cream, giving the room a soft, feminine flair, and the pictures on the wall are elegant with hand-drawn birds and leaves, but they don't make me feel like I'm in a museum. In her guest bath, Susan showcases a collection of monogrammed and hand embroidered white tea towels, all stacked in neat rows on top of each other, along with a cross and her wedding invitation requesting the honor of her guests' presence almost thirty years ago. In her kitchen, pictures of her family cover her refrigerator door, taken on ski trips, at the beach, and a silly one of her with a Mexican sombrero on what looks to be her birthday.

Her daughter is one of the bride's close friends, and this is her love language, celebrating a girl who has slept-over too many times to count over the years. Once the gifts have been opened, she wraps the bride up in her arms, giving her a mama bear hug in front of everyone, saying how happy she is for this girl.

With a few crumbs and fruit left on my plate, another hostess says, "Let me take that from you," with a smile and adds it to the others stacked in her hands. We thank her and rise from our seats while smoothing our skirts and commenting about the errands we need to run after the party. On my way out, I make my way toward the bride, who is gathered in a group with her mother, Susan, and her daughter. Her cheeks are flushed from all the excitement of the morning, and she is laughing and smiling at a joke her friend has just made about their mothers. These four look like they've shared more memories than not, and I'm pleased that they open their circle for me to join them. The bride takes my hand and tells the women stories about being roommates in college. Susan listens and asks questions before excusing herself to bid the remainder of the guests farewell. Giving my friend one last hug, I thank her for inviting me, and I tell the hostesses good-bye as I leave. Walking back toward my car, a grateful grin slides across my face, and I drive away from the white house with a yellow door, glad that I came.

I've always wanted to be a hostess, but it has not come naturally to me. I've felt "less than" most of my life and grew up as the shy girl in the corner, which is why I still get nervous before social events today. Even though I grew up with a timid heart, I've admired many hostesses over the years. I've tried to emulate them in my own actions, hoping that with a bright smile and polite conversation, I could one day be the type of woman who had no fear as she opened not only her home but her life to others. My soul is drawn to entertaining and party planning because it is the very thing that scares me to death but also gives me the most joy when done well. Days like today are good for me, a reminder that celebrating friends is worth any pre-party jitters I might feel before I attend.

Women are designed for connection, community, and celebration. It's why we go to the bathroom together, have roommates in college, and plan parties. Brené Brown writes that women need connection because our greatest fear is disconnection, the fear that something we've done or failed to do, something about who we are or where we come from, has made us unlovable and unworthy of connection.[9] Not feeling like you belong, I think, is a common worry of women like you and me. We are timid to invite because of the fear of disconnection. Instead of living in community, we make our homes in silos, hiding behind our smiles, guarding our hearts, and hoping that nobody gets too close and discovers that we are a fake. But we are seen and invited to connect with one another. Women need friendship like a flower plant needs water. While water cycles from the sky to the ground and back up to the sky through condensation, my pastor once explained that fear is a cycle that begins with worry, then travels to anxiety, and settles on fear, which keeps us from God and our purpose. Instead of producing beautiful flowers like water, the fear cycle causes us to be dry and desolate. If God designed us for connection to Him and others, don't you believe our enemy will threaten us with the fear of disconnection? The best tool that we can have to fight the fear of unworthiness is to live actively in community with like-minded friends. Friendships help us feel understood, accepted, and loved. A friend is someone who completely accepts us as who we are and loves us at all times. True friends are like family, sisters who stick with us during the hard times and celebrate with us during the good times. Engaging in meaningful friendships might not always feel natural, but it's a necessity that we just can't live without.

"I'm not the hostess type."

Three of us are standing at Mary Alice's kitchen counter in Montgomery, munching on hummus and veggies, discussing the wedding shower I'd just attended, when Katie makes this statement.

"What do you mean, you aren't the hostess type?" Mary Alice shoots back at Katie, hands on her hips.

"You know . . . I'm not the type to prepare a party like *that*," Katie gestures toward me, "and I don't really have the time or energy to always decorate like you do," she says as she looks around Mary Alice's festive fall kitchen. "I just don't think it is how God has called me to serve."

If a hostess is someone who receives others, are we not all hostesses of some sort?

Wouldn't we consider teachers to be hostesses of their classroom, receiving children with love and teaching them how to walk in a line, listen, and raise their hands to speak?

Or, how about the women who greet us at the front desk when we sign in to see a doctor? Don't their smiles help calm our nerves or make our stomachs flip-flop in dread?

Could we not define volunteers who open doors for us on Sunday morning as hostesses as well? Being the first people we see at church, these volunteers have the ability to make us feel welcomed.

While yes, a hostess is someone who invites you into her home or someone who shows you to your seat, a hostess is not limited to just this definition. A hostess is a woman who makes an effort to extend hospitality to others, whether at work, at home, or in a social setting. For many of us, we believe because our homes are not pretty enough, our personalities are not jovial enough, or our cooking and decorating skills are not professional enough, we are not the hostess type. Our fear of failure stops us from ever trying. But, when we can view how we interact with people in our everyday lives through the lens of connection, not perfection, we begin to see that we can *all* be the hostess type.

Attending my friend's wedding shower at Susan's home, I experienced sincere hospitality. From the front door to the fine china, Susan lavished her guests with beauty and love. It's so easy to walk away from a party like that and feel like every party from now on just needs to be hosted by Susan because clearly, she is better at being a hostess than we are. But let's not allow comparison to cause disconnection. It's not worth it, not really, and I'm sure Susan would agree. Because women like Susan don't host parties with the purpose to make you and I feel less than. Susan is a hostess because she understands how hosting is good for her soul. One of the many benefits of practicing hospitality is happiness. Who doesn't want to feel happy?! When we make the effort to host social events, we are happier people than those who do not.[10] Hospitality brings happiness because it is about being nice to other people, and in return people are nice back to you. Isn't it interesting how celebrating someone else's special occasion can in return make us feel special too?

Hospitality and hosting extend beyond the surface of happiness; it is also a way for us to give God glory. The word *hallelujah* is spoken often in Scripture as a shout of joy, praise, or gratitude. What if we took on the posture of not just a hostess, but a hallelujah hostess?

A hallelujah hostess practices hospitality from the fundamentals of Scripture. She not only celebrates her friends, but she also loves strangers. She gives gifts to those who will never be able to repay her.

She offers her time, her home, and her money to help people who are gospel workers.[11] She is not just entertaining on a surface level but also extending grace to connect on the soul level. While she serves, she lifts her hands and her voice to declare "Hallelujah!" to God, recognizing that her service is to Him, not her own vanity.

Hallelujah hostesses approach every occasion as an opportunity to show Christ's love to others. It's not always grand celebrations. Often it's just in her smile or the way she says hello. Hallelujah hostesses can be found in classrooms, at doctor's offices, and at church, receiving others with a warm welcome and gentle word. To be a hallelujah hostess, we are sharing with others the gifts and talents that God has so graciously given us. We bake, sing, listen, paint, write, organize, play, dance, clean, and love others the way God has created us for connection. Only when we begin to expand our thoughts on hospitality and its purpose do we begin to see how many opportunities we have to serve hallelujah-style.

Have you ever wondered why women entertain more than men?

Think about it: how many invitations do you have on your refrigerator right now for parties you are invited to attend? Graduation parties, engagement showers, weddings, baby showers, birthday parties, house-warming parties—the list could go on and on. Invitations come in all shapes, colors, and sizes. Some invitations are simply sent as an e-vite, while others are written in hand calligraphy. Sure, men do this too, but usually a woman is behind the planning of most men's parties. (Can I get an amen?!) In fact, research shows that men connect more by doing things, while women connect by talking. (I guess that's why guys would much rather be found fishing than wearing a penguin suit!)

Dennis Rainey of FamilyLife says that while men usually speak about 10,000-20,000 words a day, women speak 30,000-50,000 words per day, sometimes up to 125,000![12] Many women have the gift of gab, and what better way to catch up with friends than over cake and ice cream?

In the book of Luke, we are told that after Mary found out she was pregnant with Jesus, she hurried to the home of Elizabeth, her relative. Elizabeth and her husband Zechariah lived in the hill country of Judea, and they too were expecting a child. But for five months, Elizabeth had been living in seclusion, and Zechariah was unable to speak because he doubted Gabriel's message of his wife becoming pregnant. Upon Mary's arrival, Elizabeth was overcome in joy as she exclaimed, "Blessed is she who has believed that what the Lord has said to her will be accomplished!" I'm sure Elizabeth was so excited to finally have a visitor and someone to talk to!!! Mary stayed with her relatives for three months and during this time, Elizabeth took on the posture of a hallelujah hostess. The women continued to give praise to God, rejoicing in the blessings of His hand, and remembering how He rescued those in need. During their time together, the two women helped one another in love. Can't you see Elizabeth leaving crackers at Mary's door if she had morning sickness during her early months of pregnancy? Or, Mary assisting Elizabeth as she nested and prepared a nursery? I can picture these friends walking through the hill country, breathing in the fresh air, and placing their hands gently on their stomachs, praising God for the beauty He was creating within them. What a beautiful portrait of women celebrating, connecting, and living in community!

So, I know you still might not believe that you fit the qualifications of a hostess. You might love the story of Mary and Elizabeth but be thinking in your head, "She stayed for *three months*? I can barely last three days with guests in my home!" Trust me; I'm in that club too! Because I struggle with perfection, I would have been such a people pleaser if I were in Elizabeth's shoes, wanting everything to be in place for Mary's arrival. But after a couple of days (oh, let's face it . . . a couple of hours!), my smile would grow weary and my heart for entertaining would be reduced to longing for Chinese take-out and ice cream. How can we be hallelujah hostesses when all we want after a party is our pajamas and a nap?

You and I were made to be hallelujah hostesses, but making the transformation begins with understanding how we were designed. Yes, we were each crafted in God's image, but that doesn't mean we all have the exact same personality. Some of us are heart people, others are head people, and another portion of us are gut people. Depending on what type of person you are, you will react according to your emotions, intellect, or instincts.[13]

While our personalities guide our behavioral patterns, they also tie into how we practice hospitality. Did you ever watch the sitcom *The Office*? If so, you've got to remember the Party Planning Committee comprised originally of Angela, Phyllis, and Pam (oh, and Meredith!). The Party Planning Committee hosted parties in the Dunder Mifflin paper company's conference room and loved to celebrate birthdays and holidays. The PPC didn't always agree on how to host the party because each of the members had her own unique personality, which caused some pretty funny moments. Pam, a heart person, was a doer, the one who could stay calm and fix any pre-party disaster, but she also struggled with what people thought of her, which caused anxiety. Angela was clearly a gut person, bossy and controlling, but deep down wanted the party to be amazing. Phyllis, a head person, was a strategist who figured out how to replace Angela as the Party Planning Chair even though she preferred the corner instead of the spotlight. Each of these characters had both positive and negative behaviors. Can you relate to one of their personality types?

It's not always comfortable to be under the glaring light of our imperfections, but when we are, we can honestly admit that the struggle is real when it comes to connecting with others. Instead of feeling shame about the negative parts of ourselves, we are invited to see God in us. Every person has a layer of goodness in their personality. C.S. Lewis writes that badness is only spoiled goodness, and there must be something good first before it can be spoiled.[14] Embedded in each one of us is a quality of God that has the capacity to outweigh our flaws as we interact with others. We are His children, and we are continually being transformed to be more and more like Him every single day. Hallelujah hostesses aren't a one-size-fits-all commodity; they are women who live their lives either by their gut, heart, or head while showcasing God's goodness throughout their day. Taking on the posture of a hallelujah hostess is a small but significant act of worship, a declaration that we believe more in the something good within us than the sin that challenges us daily.

A woman who illuminates the room directs her light toward the One worth celebrating, not herself. This is the way of Mary and Elizabeth. *This is the way of you and me.*

Together, we can begin to take notice of both the light and darkness within us, and choose to walk in the light.

Chapter 4:

A TIME TO PLAN AND A TIME TO PARTY

I know that there is nothing better for people than to be happy and to do good while they live. That each of them may eat and drink, and find satisfaction in all their toil—this is the gift of God.

~ Ecclesiastes 3:12–13 NIV

LIFE, LIKE AN EVENT, GOES through cycles.

In the book of Ecclesiastes, Solomon poignantly writes that "There is a time for everything, and a season for every activity the heavens" (Ecclesiastes 3:1 NIV). As Solomon writes this book during his later years in life, he describes how there is a time for us to experience both happy and hard moments, but there is never a time labeled "perfect." Not once does Solomon say, "There is a time for everything in your life to go perfectly according to your plans." Instead of perfection, God promises us hope. Paul writes in Romans that we receive hope while we suffer, and perseverance develops our character. Our happiest moments are usually eclipsed with heartache, but "hope does not put us to shame, because God's love has been poured out into our hearts through the Holy Spirit, who has been given to us." (Romans 5:5 NIV).

I've come to believe that even if our circumstances change, depending on the season of life that we are in, we typically cycle through seven emotions: excitement, anxiety, frustration, confidence, relief, satisfaction, and exhaustion. These seven emotions vary in degree, but all have the ability to build us up or break us down. Hope is crucial as we rotate through these emotions because it is our anchor, the steadfast, unchanging, never-ending truth that while there is a time for every activity *under* heaven, there is also the promise *of* heaven. In heaven, we will be free from anxiety, frustration, and exhaustion, and we will find relief from our days of chasing perfection.

But, until that day comes, we are given the Holy Spirit, our counselor, the one who groans for us when we have no words, our help in time of need.

Swoosh.

The sound of the pencil slashing through my to-do list brings a triumphant grin to my otherwise tense face. The Relay for Life event that I'd been planning for almost a year was the next day. The phone hadn't stopped ringing, which only led to me adding hastily written items to my list, but today I was knocking them out, one punch at a time. Boxes were piled in the corner of my office, waiting to be loaded up and taken to the event site. A box of Thin Mint Girl Scout cookies lay half eaten on my desk. With adrenaline running through my veins, I kept moving, working, and slashing lead lines through scribbles.

Being an event planner, I often feel like a magician. I juggle balls in the air, delicately throwing and catching them with systematic grace. Hat tricks are also in my repertoire, I can pull a white rabbit out of dark holes, making my volunteers cheer in glee. The grand finale of my show is the ability to overcome an obstacle so big and scary that even I am filled with wonder. With my event only hours away, I look around my office, seriously wondering if I've already joined a three-ring circus. It's maddening, the work. The pressure of wanting to pull off a perfect event and please all the people who are involved causes me to lie awake at night, adding notes to the list that I've left next to me on the nightstand. Even though events go through planning stage cycles, it's like I'm constantly turning wheels on a bike, pushing myself to climb up an incline. With the peak in sight, it's now all about mind over matter. If I think I can pull it off, I know I can (but, one more Thin Mint might give me some motivation).

My favorite part of planning an event is the beginning, when the notebook has yet to be filled and the date is still months away on my planner. In the beginning, my mind is free to dream, doodle, and design the perfect event, and I have plenty of time to plan. Excited, I start a new secret folder on Pinterest and feel like a sleuth uncovering treasure with every adorable decoration and food pin that I place inside that folder. The fun begins as I pick out color palettes, create the graphics, and order the promotional items. The event still seems like it is mine to plan because I have yet to release it to the world. It's in these initial planning moments that I truly believe that anything is possible. I will reach my fundraising goal, recruit enough volunteers, and plan an amazing event that sells lots and lots of tickets.

Once the event is scheduled, the event cycle shifts to the initial planning stages. Sponsors are secured, volunteer task meetings are scheduled, and sign-ups begin. People ask me questions, lots of them, and I answer them with confidence. Most of them, anyway. The ones I don't have an answer to, I write down in a notebook, promising that I will come up with a solution. That's the thing about being an event planner: you never let on that you don't know. You don't let them see the anxiety that causes your heart to beat fast inside your chest. Only a small handful of faithful volunteers or staff gets a glimpse of what's on the other side of the event planning curtain. Everyone else just sees the image of success, the magician that has the show all figured out.

After the planning comes promotion. I put on two coats of mascara and a long sleeve blouse for the television interviews and am careful not to wear a necklace that will jingle next to the microphone. I laugh it up with radio hosts who do a mean Elvis impersonation, and I send press releases to local magazines, websites, and newspapers. Our billboard ads rotate on the busy highways, yard signs are stuck in our neighbor's yard, and flyers are distributed to every family restaurant within our district, urging people to buy their tickets, save the date, and join the fun.

It gets real once the event goes live. More meetings happen, and we evaluate what we need to do to reach our goals. Some volunteers kick it into overdrive, while others apologize and drop out. Still others begin to stress out and send me e-mails with subjects written in all caps that scream "URGENT, OPEN NOW!" My to-do list exponentially increases, and I log major overtime hours as I try to keep calm and carry on.

And that's when *it* happens. The unexpected rolls in and punches me in the gut. It happens with Every. Single. Event. Not kidding. Anything can be the unexpected and catch me off-guard—the weather, sickness, lost luggage, wardrobe malfunction, leaks in the location bathrooms, a vendor not showing up or sending me the wrong item—it doesn't matter what it is, exactly. What matters is how much it catches me off-guard. For a moment, everything seems lost. The unexpected messes with my plans and grips my throat so tightly that I wonder if I'll ever be able to breathe again.

After the unexpected drama, I'm frustrated and wonder if I am chasing wind. So often, I've found myself like Solomon in Ecclesiastes, wondering if everything is meaningless. What's the point in planning if those things unplanned wreck everything I've worked so hard to put together?

There's no way to plan for the unexpected except to know that it will happen. When events happen that are not on my to-do list, my only hope is to trust that God has a plan and He promises that trials will develop character. (Oh, do I wish this would be easier!)

Once the initial shock of the unexpected settles, I have a choice: either quit or find Tim Gunn inside my head telling me to "Make it work." The unexpected is not the right time to quit. Quitting only leads to temporary relief and causes others to pick up the slack while I'm crying in the corner. By embracing the unexpected, I'm challenged to hope when life feels hopeless.

Having gone through all these stages of the event planning cycle, it's truly a relief to finally have the finish line in sight. Grabbing my keys, I turn off my computer, pleased with the work that I've accomplished not only today, but over the past year. Tomorrow, all the hard work will finally pay off.

As my alarm wakes me the next morning, I open my eyes and immediately know that today is The Day. Eating breakfast, I mentally run through the order of The Day in my head before I brush my teeth and change into my set-up clothes. I pause and flip through my Bible until I reach Galatians. Scanning the passages, I find the one I need for today. It's highlighted with a blue pen, Galatians 6:9–10 NIV, "Let us not become weary in doing good, for at the proper time we will reap a harvest if we do not give up. Therefore, as we have opportunity, let us do good to all people, especially to those who belong to the family of believers." *Yes.*

With confidence, I arrive on site, ready for set-up. Throughout the day, I direct volunteers on where to hang banners, set up tables, organize games, and do a sound check on stage. We take t-shirts out of boxes, fill balloons with helium, and unpack food. The work is tiring, but I don't grow weary. As the day slips into evening, I steal a moment to change in the bathroom before the attendees arrive. Fixing my hair, I see my reflection in the mirror. I'm sweaty and desperately need more deodorant, but I see a girl who had a dream and has worked tirelessly to make the dream become real. The girl looking back at me in the mirror is beautiful, even with bags under her eyes. I put my makeup and hair brushes away, grab my phone and nametag, and I leave the stillness of the bathroom stall.

It's go time.

Greeting guests, I flash smiles and hug necks. A buzzing sensation is in the air as people check in, gain their bearings, and begin to peruse the product tables. Volunteers are in place, the sound is on, and selfies are already being taken. Ready or not, the event is happening. We've done the work, and now it's time to put the plan into motion. Behind the scenes are countless volunteers following instructions and preparing for what's next on the agenda. When an event runs smoothly, I am able to watch the attendees enjoy the experience we've created for them. There's nothing more rewarding than seeing all the hard work pay off.

During the event, I feel myself buzzing from all the stimulation, people, and chocolate that I had consumed over the last twenty-four hours. I'm high on adrenaline and pedaling on overdrive. The Relay begins with cancer survivors taking the first lap during opening ceremonies. Standing by the stage, I watch my dad's best friend reach over to hold his wife's hand as she took her very first walk around the track as a cancer survivor. With tears streaming down their faces, these brave men, women, and children circle a dusty track lap after lap. I finally understood the purpose of all my months of planning. These fundraising events celebrate life, honor loved ones, and give people hope for their futures. There's nothing more satisfying than seeing how all the hard work has helped someone else.

Then, it comes to an end. As the night ends and the next day begins, the teams take one final victory lap around the track before they begin to pack up their tents and head home. All of the months of planning are over, and all that's left are decorations to be torn down, food to be packed up, and leftover programs to throw away. My committee helps with break-down, and before long the field is empty once again. We say good-bye to one another, and I am the last one to pull out of the parking lot. Taking a final look at the field, I shake my head in disbelief. *Three hundred and sixty-five days of planning, and our event is finished. What am I to do now?*

In the weeks to follow, I go through the post-event motions of discussing wrap-up meeting evaluations, writing thank you notes, and putting things away. Even though my calendar still has everyday items on it, I am in post-event shock. This is when the exhaustion sets in, and I know that while there is a time to plan and to party, there is also a time to rest. Without rest, burnout will set in, which is never good. Rest invites me to celebrate and remember so that I may continue to press forward.

Looking at my planner, I pick up my pencil, but not to make another list. Instead, I carefully pencil in a day to take off later in the week. Maybe Raleigh and I will travel to the beach for the day, or I might just stay in town and get a pedicure. It doesn't matter what I do to rest, as long as I take time to do it.

The parties we experience in our lives are events that shape us into who we become:

- a time to say good-bye to old friends and a time to make new friends,
- a time to mourn the loss of a loved one and a time to celebrate the birth of a new baby,
- a time to throw grand events, and a time to enjoy the slow pace of the simple,

- a time to invite and a time to be invited,
- a time to say yes and a time to say no,
- a time to be a hostess and a time to help,
- a time to bake birthday cakes and a time to order a cake from the bakery.

If there is a time for both happy and hard moments throughout our lifetime, couldn't this mean that there is a point for all of these festivities?

A cancer survivor whom I love wears a purple t-shirt that says, "There's no such thing as too many candles. More birthdays mean more celebrations. More cake, more candles, more presents, more wishes, more music, more games, more joy." Parties *do* have a purpose; they aren't just for plastic kicks and giggles. Celebrations bring joy into life, and joy makes us strong. [15] Solomon is right. There is nothing better for us than to be happy and do good while we live. For us to eat and drink and find satisfaction in what we do – this is a gift of God. When we can release all the tension of preparation, only then we will experience the true joy of celebration. God has made our lives like a cycle so even if we are challenged with a new event, we are still promised hope. He has made everything beautiful in its time but like a cancer patient, we can't always see the beauty until we've walked through the brokenness. Our seasons of suffering develop perseverance within us, changing us into survivors. Survivors understand the beauty of celebration, the joy of blowing out one more birthday candle each year.

Are you a survivor who has seen the beauty of your sufferings or are you just trying to survive your to-do list today?

Take heart and remember that as a believer in Christ, you've been given the Holy Spirit. If you are feeling the pressure of perfection and people pleasing with your to-do list, think of the Spirit as your counselor. Take a seat on the counselor's couch, and tell Him all of your anxieties, frustrations, and fear. The Spirit can help you survive the pressures of today by gently encouraging you to release your plans. Even if you don't know what to say, He will work for you, in you, and through you so that you may see the beauty on the other side of surviving.

Just as parties go through a cycle, so do our lives. We all have a beginning season of life where we dream about our future weddings, children, jobs, and homes. Then there is the middle, when we are preparing for the big event just on the horizon. Yet there are some days that look a lot like the week of the event, and we are stressed out and tired. Once the newness of a life event wears away, it's easy to slide into post-celebration burnout, when we need rest and feel a little lost without a big event to plan. While we go through the different cycles of life, remember that God has set eternity in the human heart, and He makes everything beautiful in its time. His perfect love will not fail us, so let us put our hope in Him. This is the gift we were made to receive.

Part Two:
Celebrations

Chapter 5:

WEDDINGS

{BEING SURE OF WHAT WE HOPE FOR AND
CERTAIN OF WHAT WE DO NOT SEE}

*The church is the bride of Christ. The kingdom will be the eternal
celebration of the wedding of Christ and the church. We will enjoy
rapturous celebration as the bride of Christ in the eternal kingdom.*

~ Paul Enns

THE GLOW THAT RADIATES FROM a bride in love is breathtakingly
beautiful. Promise extends from her groom's gaze at the end of the
aisle, beckoning her to come, now. With every step she takes toward
him, the way he looks at her is confirmation that he's ready to be her
husband, the man her father has agreed will watch over her, protect her,
and love her. Here, two people grow from girl to woman, boy to man.
Long-awaited hope is fulfilled. The joy of this momentous occasion
dances in the air after the church bells have collided in their merriment. As the couple takes each other's hands, they don't know what
to expect next, but they solemnly swear anyway to love one another
for as long as they both shall live.

The wedding reception is just as beautiful as the bride. Every detail had been carefully crafted, from the floral arrangements to the white tents and the twinkling lights that were strung back and forth across the dance floor. Just like all the girls who had gone before her, this was her perfect day.

Later, as the couple left the reception to friends waving sparklers, the bride's parents gave her one last hug and kiss before the newlyweds hopped into the old-timey car and drove away. That drive was more than the end of a beautiful night; it signified the beginning of life together.

Sometime soon, the realities of two people living together will collide with newlywed bliss. It's inevitable. Our perfect facades begin to crack, and we are firsthand witnesses to one another's faults, fears, and failures. The future we hoped for begins to form, sometimes just as we planned, but more often not. It's in these moments that we must remember that marriage is a lot like faith. Faith gives us the confidence to commit our lives to one another, to say yes as we jump wildly into the wilderness.

Jesus performed His first miracle at a wedding. His mother was in attendance, helping out the event planner behind the scenes. When the wine ran out, Mary knew that Jesus could fix the problem. I imagine when she came to Him, she looked around the room and then bent down to where He was sitting, lowering her voice to be discreet as she said, "They have no more wine." He looks at her, asking, "Dear woman, why do you involve me?" Can't you just see Mary give her son a look that said wordlessly, "I know what you can do. Help me with this one, okay?" The wedding feast was not yet finished, and Mary wanted to save the family from social embarrassment. (In Jewish custom, some families were actually *sued* for not providing enough food and drink at a wedding!)[16] But, Jesus was not to be swayed just because His mother asked Him for a favor. He responds with the word "woman" instead of "mother" to give their relationship some distance and as a reminder to Mary that He was not just her son, but Christ. Mary is very careful not to tell Jesus what to do, but it seems clear that she hopes He will do something. She walks away, back to the preparation tent, understanding that He will do what He chooses to do, but as she passes by some servants, she tells them to "do whatever he tells you" (John 2:5 NIV).

Jesus knew what was coming, and He knew His time had not yet come. He made a choice to help anyway, but He didn't perform this miracle with bells and whistles or in an effort to please His mother. He simply had the servants fill six stone jars with water. I can imagine them working quickly, trying to stay unobtrusive and unnoticed but also probably murmuring that this guy was crazy to one another under their breath. This water was from the well and used for cleansing, not drinking. It was *gross*. Once the jars were filled to the brim, He told them to draw the water and take it to the master of the banquet. The servants obeyed, even though they had not tasted the drink. The banquet master was the event planner of this party, the one responsible for the details of the celebration. I'm sure he was about to burst from worry, not knowing how in the world they ran out of wine, so when these servants brought him more out of nowhere, he knew that this was a miracle.

Jesus wasn't just a guest at a fancy feast. He made Himself known as the Son of God that day so three years later people would understand that His mission was to redeem us from our distresses so that the wine of joy would flow fully. [17] This miracle was performed not to draw attention to Himself but to make us aware that we can give Him glory in the unexpected, unplanned moments of life.

Have you ever been like the master of the banquet and had something unexpected happen, causing you to panic? As women, we have these perfect ideas in our heads of what our lives are supposed to look like. We've been planning for years what our husbands will do for work, where we will live, how many kids we will have, what our house will look like. Not often do we throw the unexpected into our plans. I have a friend who is in her thirties and single. She has dreamed of her husband for over a decade but still hasn't found him yet. We meet for lunch, and she tells me about how others are constantly trying to set her up with their single friends. It's easy to see the angst in her eyes as she questions what her future holds, but then she smiles and says, "Well, at least I have Jesus."

Jesus redeems the unplanned events of our lives. While some of us are struggling to understand why we still have to invite a plus-one to a wedding and others of us are struggling to survive the first years of our marriages, empty nests, or the loss of a spouse, we all have circumstances that are unpredictable.

Unplanned events occur at parties, but they also happen in the midst of our everyday living.

Honeymoon babies

Renovation nightmares

Divorce. Death. Disease.

Prodigal children

Job relocations

Financial struggles

We are all battling something, no matter how perfect we look on the outside. Dissatisfaction leaks into my marriage when unplanned events wreck my ideas of what I thought my marriage would be. With each unplanned event, my marriage takes another hit. How many times can we take a punch before we fall?

What I didn't understand as a newlywed, and what I'm only beginning to grasp now, is that marriages survive when spouses stop putting so much expectation on one another and more expectation on Christ. I've spent years expecting my husband to provide for our family, making him feel so much pressure in his job and his role as the male of the household. While he has an excellent job and has taken care of my many needs, his best has always fallen short because of my false expectations of him. He has provided for my basic needs, but his provision does not cover my wants. Because I tend to look toward the future, I always want *more*.

We will only be satisfied when we believe that Christ will provide abundantly more than anything we could ever ask or imagine. He teaches us to want more of Him. When Paul scribed that "love conquers all," he says that when perfection comes, the imperfect disappears. The Greek word for perfection in this passage means "completeness."

As a girl, one of my all-time favorite movies is *Jerry McGuire.* (C'mon, you know you love it too!) We love this movie because it is about two people falling in love, with Jerry saying, "You complete me," and Dorothy responding with "You had me at hello." We melt for romance because part of our plans for our lives is falling in love and living happily ever after. But, marriage is hard. We are not always patient or kind. We envy. We are rude and easily angered. And when we reach a point where we see that the person we married will not always live up to the standard we set so high because we are all imperfect, we find ourselves smack dab in the center of conflict.

My husband does not complete me, nor do I complete him. Jesus completes us. Jesus steps into our marriage and sacrifices Himself for our imperfections so that we might love one another perfectly. And one day He will come again and take us as His bride to His kingdom in heaven, where we will *finally* live happily ever after.

As the bride and groom exchange their vows to one another, Raleigh takes my hand. He is quite dapper-looking in his tailored navy suit, and the skirt of my mint chiffon dress drapes over the edge of my chair. I look at him, and as he laces his fingers through mine, an un-spoken gesture marks that we still believe the oath that we took to be true. We've been married long enough to understand the complexity of loving one another for richer or poorer, in sickness and in health. We've cried, and we've celebrated. We are in this thing together, even when it is tough.

Marriage *is* a lot like faith: being sure of what we hope for and certain of what we do not see. When I married Raleigh, I had hopes, dreams, and expectations for our future together. I built our lives around these things, for better and for worse. These ideas have caused breakthroughs and breakdowns in our relationships with ourselves, each other, and God. I'm continually reminded that the only thing I know for certain to be true is that God has a plan for my life and our life together.

Because we are not perfect, a better hope is introduced, by which we draw near to God. Maybe this is why Jesus first performed a miracle at a wedding. The wine ran out, yes, but His love overflowed the barrels with the promise of life everlasting. Jesus is "God with us" and a reminder that love conquers all. He is with us during the height and the depth, loving us through the complexities of life. Jesus takes away our pain and our struggle, and He celebrates our love and our laughter. He is with us, perfect and full of promise, reminding us that we are His bride and He is our groom. His love will never run out, the wine barrels will never go dry.

The Spirit and the bride say, "Come." Let anyone who hears this say, "Come." Let anyone who is thirsty come. Let anyone who desires drink freely from the water of life.

~ Revelation 22:17

If the promise that Jesus offers us is true, then why do we keep letting the unexpected circumstances of life get the best of us? Jesus filled the wine so the guests at the wedding could continue to celebrate. He brings joy through our sorrow, and He makes all things work together for the good of those who love Him. For us to fully live a life of love, we must understand that love is not a gift but something that comes out of us when the Spirit is inside of us. God is love, and we model His love for us by loving others. John says, "Whoever lives in love lives in

God, and God in them. This is how love is made complete among us so that we will have confidence on the day of judgment: In this world we are like Jesus." (1 John 4:16b–17 NIV).

At the wedding reception, Raleigh and I find a table to sit at with friends, and then we head to the bar. The bride has chosen a sunset margarita as the cocktail drink, complete with an orange slice and striped straw, and her guests are scattered in clusters around the back lawn of the mansion, holding their tangerine drinks as the sky sets in its red-yellow glory, with shades of peach, rose, and lavender mingling amid the clouds. Her reception is outdoors, and she has two white tents with long rows of tables and chairs flanking the aquamarine pool. The dance floor is on the far side of the pool, with twinkling lights crisscrossing above. Before we begin to eat, we catch up with friends on the back steps of the mansion. We swap stories about jobs and motherhood, our homes and acquaintances, and for a moment, I forget about the expectations I had put on my husband and myself. We are bubbly, like the champagne that is uncorked before the bride and groom cut the cake, and I want this moment to last. As we join the buffet line, we eat with our eyes first, placing bright strawberries and creamy brie on our plates, along with mini crab cakes, grilled veggies, focaccia flatbread, and sliced tenderloin. With plates piled high, we continue our conversation at the table, just as the bride and groom grace the dance floor as husband and wife. We watch as their eyes sparkle, and he gives her a gentle twirl. She glides effortlessly back into his arms. It's dusk now, and the candles on our table, nestled under an arrangement of peach peonies, blush roses, and fresh white hydrangeas, begin to glow. We sit and laugh too loud at stories from our friend who served as a bridesmaid, and I could sit there all night, soaking up the time and wishing we could all see each other more often.

At weddings, it's funny how people either tell you everything or tell you nothing at all. It's like we know that we will see each other for only a little while, so we decide with the help of the atmosphere if we really want to be honest about the hard stuff or keep it stuffed inside. Tonight was one of those nights where the fancy facade came down and we let each other in.

I split a piece of wedding cake with my friend as she tells me about being single again after her split from her husband. She looks good, but the darkness in her eyes gives away her pain. Another friend is out for the first time after having her daughter, and she drags us onto the dance floor. We get our dance on, shimmying like we are back in college (all we needed was the band to play "Hey-Ya" to really shake it like a Polaroid picture)! After dancing with the girls, I turn and put one hand on my hip and flirt with my husband with the other as I beckon him to come join me. He stands and begins to dance toward our group. Together, we spin round and round, singing and dancing until my hair begins to stick to the back of my neck. The band plays all the classics: "Sweet Home Alabama," "Brown Eyed Girl," and even does a Prince tribute of "Purple Rain." Before the final dance, they play "Shout," and we get a little lower and a little softer, then a little higher and a little louder. We are jumping, waving our hands above our heads, singing in unison, "Hey-Hey-A-Hey, Hey-A-A-Hey!" Looking around, I see old and young, married and single, all jumping along with us. We are a tribe, connected for a moment of celebrating, and we don't really care about the unexpected, unplanned, and unrealistic expectations that have weighed us down. All we want is to be free.

Isaiah 35:10 says that when the redeemed enter Zion, we will be singing with everlasting joy crowned on our heads. Gladness and joy will overtake us, making sorrow and sighing flee away. Perhaps the joy we feel at wedding receptions is a glimpse of what it will be like when we enter the gates of heaven. We will be so full of praise as we worship our God face-to-face, like a bride who has long waited for her groom. On this day, we will finally be home free.

Chapter 6:

MOTHER'S DAY

{ACCEPTING HOSPITALITY}

I have found the paradox, that if you love until it hurts,
there can be no more hurt, only more love.

~ Mother Teresa

"HOLD ME, MAMA."

It's late, and my toddler-girl can't sleep. The glow of the computer screen illuminates the room as she stands at my door, and I notice how her hair is already a tangled mess from tossing and turning. In her hand, she's holding her Kirby bear and my yellow baby blanket. Her princess pajamas are almost too small, but they are her favorite, and I let her wear them anyway. My hands stop moving over the keyboard as she approaches, and I get up and reach out to scoop her up in my arms. We rock and sing her song, with her legs wrapped around my waist and her head resting gently on my shoulder. Her skin smells of the lavender nighttime cream I rubbed on her after bath time, and her hair is still slightly damp. She slows her breath and pats my back as I rub hers. It's just us, daughter and mother, swaying to the night song until her eyelids grow so heavy they begin to shut. Pulling her in tight, I hold her and this moment, already aware that this will not last forever.

My entrance into motherhood did not happen as I had planned.

When the ultrasound technician called us into her room, I prepared myself to see a baby that looked like a little peanut. As she squirts the cold goo on my abdomen and begins to rub her wand over my belly, I see on the screen a tiny baby. Then, I look closer and notice that I see *another* baby. "Is that what I think it is?" I ask in disbelief.

Smiling back at me, the technician replied, "You are having TWINS!"

With eyes wide, I whip my head toward my husband. We look at each other, knowing in this moment that our lives will never be the same. Without hesitation, he and I begin to laugh, cry, and point at the screen in disbelief. Twins!

Raleigh and I were in shock at the news, but as we left the doctor's office, we began to prepare ourselves for being parents of twins. During my pregnancy, I did my best to follow my doctor's rules. Gone were the deli turkey sandwiches and the Diet Cokes. Even though I spent half the day with my head in the toilet, I still went on walks, trying to breathe in the fresh aroma of the jasmine that crept up the tree trunks at the corner of my block. We bought books on raising twins, read reviews of the best double strollers, and received great reports at every check-up. But, with three months left in my pregnancy, I went into pre-term labor. The pain in my abdomen felt like a knife stabbing my insides, and I called my doctor at four a.m. telling him that something was terribly wrong. He advised me to take a warm bath and time the length in between the pain. Shaking, I drew the tub with warm water and gingerly climbed in. The lights were still off, and in the moonlight I could see the rise of my belly just above the water's rim. The twisting inside of my stomach became so severe that I suddenly knew that this would be my last time I would see my pregnant belly.

"Raleigh?" I croak into the darkness.

He rushes into the bathroom. "I'm here." His hair is still a mess from being woken in the middle of the night. I can tell by his response that he, too, is worried.

I reach out my hand, and as he helps me out of the tub, I quietly whisper, "We need to go to the hospital."

Once inside the hospital's automatic doors, we are directed to the triage room upstairs. The nurse on call is wearing hot pink scrubs and comes to my side to ask the standard run-down of questions. I can still smell the bacon in the corridor, and as she hovers over me, I realize that we had interrupted her breakfast. Stripped into nothing but a hospital gown, I give her a trembling smile as she glides her wand over my belly. Seven months ago, that magic wand had shown two babies growing inside of me. What was I about to see now?

"Can you hear their heartbeats?" I ask, not wanting an answer I wasn't ready to face.

To my relief, the sound of one heartbeat, and then another, filled the tiny room. After the ultrasound, the nurse checks me and confirms that I am fully dilated and the babies will need to be delivered *now*. Words start to spill out of my mouth, "But my water hasn't even broke.

What do you mean it's time to go? It's too early. Are the babies going to be okay?"

"Mrs. Price, you need to stay calm. Lie down and let us wheel you to the examining room. Your husband can join you soon," Hot Pink says as she, along with another nurse, lifts me from the stationary bed onto a wheeled gurney.

As we zip through the hallway, I become totally disoriented with where I am. All of a sudden the doors open into a very large, brightly lit room. Goose bumps begin to pop up on my arms as I am greeted with a cool rush of air. I hoped the frozen temperature disguised the fear that made my body tremble.

Once the spinal tap was injected into my back, my body slowly became numb, but my mind raced with uncertainty. *Who are all of these people? What are the nurses talking about? Why is there a plastic box in the corner? Where is my husband? Why is this happening to me and my babies?*

The activity around me made my head spin so I closed my eyes, trying to remain calm. *Trust in the LORD with all your heart* became the mantra running on repeat in my mind as I was prepped for surgery. Suddenly, I felt a hand squeeze my own. I opened my eyes to see my husband dressed in scrubs standing above me. I felt some tugging on the other side of the sheet draped over my stomach, and as I kept my eyes on him, he gave me the play-by-play of the delivery. I waited for the squelching cry of newborn babies, but the only sound I heard in the room was the voice of my husband, who told me that Adeline was born first and Maralee second. I still can't see anything and only later do I learn that they were lifeless and so black and blue that he wasn't even sure if they were alive. As our doctor finished stitching me up after the surgery, I heard the wheels of the incubators roll out of the exam room doors, and I was left without babies in my belly or in my arms. Raleigh tried to calm me, but all I wanted was to know where my babies were taken. As my brain tried to process what had just happened, I slipped away from the bright light of the exam room and into a deep, dark sleep.

Once I woke up in my recovery room, our neonatologist explained to Raleigh and me that the girls weighed two pounds each and were extremely premature. After giving us this news he gravely warned us, "Your girls are doing well, but not great."

Raleigh and I shared a secret glance; both lingering on his final words. After hearing this news, I was wheeled down the hall to see the twins for the first time in the Neonatal Intensive Care Unit (NICU). They were the smallest babies I had ever seen. Their faces were completely covered up with masks, and they had huge tubes going down their throats. But they were alive, and they were beautiful. Wheeling closer to Adeline, I noticed how small her arms and legs were. It seemed like each space on her frame was covered with wires. Her chest had four attachments to monitor her breathing, and there was a long black line running through her belly button. A little band was wrapped around her ankle that had another wire running through it. An IV was stuck in her right arm so the nurse could draw blood through a little tube. Her small body was curled up, and her legs were in a frog-like position bent out from the knees.

After they were born, we still had no explanation for what caused their pre-term delivery. While I wanted to believe that this was all part of God's plan, I struggled with believing that He would allow our babies to suffer. As I watched our girls breathe through a ventilator in the NICU, the only thought that came to my mind was that this was all my fault. Wasn't it my responsibility as their mother to protect them?

Day after day, I'd come home from the NICU and walk upstairs to their empty nursery. Two cribs sat unused under windows draped in pink and white linen. Tags had yet to be ripped from their newborn clothes. The diapers next to the changing table remained stacked high. In the quiet, the only sound was me rocking in the nursery chair with arms tucked instead of full. Raleigh would find me there, but I would shrug off his embrace. I didn't deserve it.

My body had failed to do what it was designed to do. As I slipped back into pre-pregnancy shorts to drive to the hospital, I didn't delight in my changed figure. Instead, I wished for my belly with my babies still inside. Giving birth is supposed to be a time of celebration, but all I could feel was grief. Adeline had fluid around her heart. Maralee's scalp was shaped like a cone, and she had a staph infection. Their bodies resembled push-pins from all the IVs. Unsure of my job or how to provide for them, I'd sit in a chair next to their incubators and watch the nurses check monitors, change tubes, and give the girls medicine. They were the ones taking care of my babies, not me.

Having premature babies opened me up to the realization that life is precious. I always knew that babies were a gift, but not until I actually became a mother did I understand how precious that gift truly is. Our premature children had a fifty-fifty shot at making it, and each day felt like it could be our last.

On Mother's Day, Raleigh gave me black and white pictures of the girls' hands and feet. My engagement ring is slipped around their delicate wrists, and his band rests gently beside their arms. Looking closely, I see tiny pricks all on the bottom of their feet. Both happy and sad tears spill out of me.

Do I rejoice or ask why?

One infection could end their lives. While their bubble homes offered them protection, I still lacked peace. Desperate, I wanted to take charge of their little lives, assure them safety from sickness. But, whether they would survive the NICU or not wasn't up to me.

I was not in control.

This became my first lesson in mothering.

My second lesson?

Pray.

A month passed, and I still had not held Adeline or Maralee in my arms. Weak from worry, I fell to my knees in the room off the kitchen. Facing the French doors of our back patio, I began to groan. Unable to speak, my tears formed a pool on my hardwood floor. Raleigh was at work, and neither of our moms were in town. It was just me and God. My weeping turned into wailing, and when I was finally able to speak, I began to loudly beg, "God, *please* let me keep my babies."

This went on for what seemed like hours. When I didn't know what to pray, the Holy Spirit took over and prayed with words I could not express. I gave God everything, and when I couldn't go on any longer, I sunk into our blue chair, exhausted but encouraged. I was not in control and for the first time since the twins were born early, I accepted that this was part of God's perfect plan. I felt peace with our circumstance. I had sought God, and He answered me by delivering me from my fears (Psalm 34:4–5). Gone was my shame, and I could finally see light through the darkness.

With every heartache, God gives us hope. Hope comes in the most mysterious of ways and settles inside our souls as a promise yet to be fulfilled. When Hope comes knocking on our doors, we eagerly invite her to come in and make herself at home. She's gentle and calm like an anchor in the middle of our unpredictable storm. Instead of running around in a constant state of anxiety and fear, we begin to wait in anxious expectation for hope to bring joy through our pain. Like the morning sun, she assures us that tomorrow will come.

A life of faith is more promising than a life filled with fear. Hope didn't give me the outcome of our babies' survival, but it did usher in a desire to dwell in God's presence. I learned over the summer that this word *dwell* meant to lodge, reside. Even though our girls were lodged in the hospital, I had hope that this was their temporary home. Our nurses became our extended family, and I began to understand that we all played a part in Adeline and Maralee's road to recovery. So, I kept asking God to let my babies come home. This was the desire of my heart, and I didn't feel shame as I gave God this request.

Hope shows me that true hospitality is about entering into God's presence by inviting Him into my life. God gives me the Holy Spirit, who becomes my ever-present companion, confidant, and courageous leader. Whenever I would experience shame, the Spirit stitched me back up. Sanctified, I am saved.

If hope is holy, I was in heaven on the day that Adeline and Maralee were finally placed in my arms. As I kissed their red skin and held them close, I finally felt the rite of passage into motherhood. Inside my soul, the Spirit dons a party hat and makes a robust commotion with party blowers. With Maralee nestled against me and Adeline in Raleigh's embrace, I lock eyes with him, finally at peace. Rocking our babies in hospital chairs, we hold onto hope and wait for the day we will welcome them home.

It's the hard moments in life that make us grateful for the happy moments. St. Augustine writes, "How does it come then that from the bitterness of life we can pluck fruit so sweet as in mourning and weeping and sighing and the utterance of our woe?"[18] Might our sufferings be a way for God to draw us into His hospitable embrace? Trauma can lead us to triumph, thankfulness, and trust. Our worst fears can be the best things that ever happen to us, because it is an opportunity to receive the abundant love of Jesus. Our sufferings give way to spiritual growth, teaching us to lean not on our own understanding, but to ask God to help us persevere through our pain.

We groan the more we are grown.

Suffering chisels away at our character, until all that is left is us and God. Do we trust that He is the Sculptor who will create a work of art out of our marble slabs? If man is created in God's image, will He not create something good out of the grotesque? Did He not allow the hammer and the nails to penetrate the flesh of His one Son, so that we will suffer only temporarily?

God does not allow anything to enter our lives that isn't able to glorify Him. By drawing us into deeper intimacy with Him, He reveals His glory in unfathomable ways. It is just as the psalmist writes: "Those who sow in tears shall reap with joyful shouting."[19] We don't expect joy to come from our sorrows, but it comes out of us like a geyser, bursting its water from the deep hole of darkness and shimmering in the noonday sun. Knowing that joy will come after the tears gives us hope and helps us push through the pain. We rejoice in the hope of the glory of God.[20]

There are moments in life when we will be on the receiving end of hospitality. Instead of giving out hugs, we need to be held in the embrace of the people who love us most. When we are going through dark times, we may push people away because they don't know what it's like to go through our particular circumstance. Sitting in our hospital rooms, it's easy to ask God why He has not shown us mercy or compassion and why everyone else around us gets to avoid the type of pain we are enduring. We can grow bitter instead of getting better. Or, we can view our painful times in a hospital as a way to receive hospitality from others.

Throughout the twins' 86 days in the NICU, I experienced love and compassion from people like I never had before. The nurses became our family, holding me as our girls received emergency care. On a particularly hard day, my mother wrapped me in her arms like an infant on my living room couch and then tucked me into bed as she had so many times as a child. Her womb had become a tomb for two of my siblings, and she understood the unspoken pain of motherhood. In Hebrew, the word *yada* means "to know," which means a deep emotional experience, a bonding between two people when one truly feels the emotions of the other. A mother is bonded to her child, feeling every pain, every heartache, and every emotion imaginable. Just as a mother holds her child, God helps cradle our pain.

Generosity is hospitality. When people we love are going through a difficult time, we must become generous with our time, resources, and gifts. Generosity might look like sitting in the waiting room with a stale cup of coffee as your mother receives her chemotherapy. Or, it could be baking muffins for your neighbor who is recently widowed. Generosity looks like giving someone your frequent flyer miles or contributing to a GoFundMe account. Generosity is setting up a Take Them A Meal schedule or sending a card to cheer up your friend. Generosity is offering ourselves to others the way Christ offered Himself for us. We can show hospitality to those we love by mourning while they mourn. We might not have any control over the outcome of the situation, but we can serve by holding our loved ones in our arms.

But let us not forget about rejoicing.

Just as we mourn, we too must celebrate the happy that comes from the hard. If joy comes from within, we need not hide our elation when we hear good news! Rejoicing is the time for us to use the praise hand emojis, eat cake, and be the "yay" girls. Buy balloons. Use lots of exclamation marks when you share with Facebook friends. Do the happy dance. Hug deeply.

After their three month stay in the NICU, the twins were released from the hospital on my twenty-sixth birthday. Our tiny, two pound babies had grown to weigh four pounds each, and we rejoiced in knowing that while they still had so much growing ahead of them, they had grown strong and big enough to come home. In our front yard, I stuck a welcome home sign in the ground, and our neighbors stopped and cheered as we pulled into the drive. Raleigh and I unsnapped the twins from their car seats and posed with them in front of our wooden front door. Inside, we introduced the babies to our dogs, and then we carried them upstairs to the nursery. I sat in the pink rocking chair, the same chair that I had rocked in for eighty-six days, only now I was holding my daughters. When we came back down the stairs, my mother had placed a birthday cake with twenty-six candles on our dining room table. The glow of the candles danced on the faces of my children, and after the birthday song, I had no wishes left to make. Instead, I lifted up my thanks.

Proverbs 14:13 says, "Even in laughter the heart may ache, and rejoicing may end in grief." I realize that we don't always get the result we were hoping for from our sufferings, but none of our suffering is ever in vain. Suffering always serves a purpose, and it is not up to us to decide the ending to our stories. God's ways are higher than our ways, and His thoughts higher than our thoughts. Trusting in His plans begins when we let go of ours. Trust leads us on a path free from fear. We can laugh without fear of our futures, knowing that in all things God works for the good of those who love Him.

Hospitality received is quite possibly the best medicine for a sick heart. Be the one who gives hope. Rejoice, weep, and pray with your people. Give yourself permission not to have it all together and to receive the embrace of others. Love *will* carry you through the pain.

Chapter 7:

FATHER'S DAY

Barbecue sauce is like a beautiful woman.
If it's too sweet, it's bound to be hiding something.

~ Lyle Lovett

I NEVER THOUGHT I'D MOVE back in with my parents.

But on Raleigh's third Father's Day, the twins and I say good-bye to him and travel the two hours south to my parents' house in Dothan. I was to start work the next day at our church as the Children's Ministry Director, while Raleigh would continue to travel back and forth from Montgomery as he set up his office in Dothan. I drove off as he waved from the front door, a for-sale sign in the yard. When I finally pulled up to my parents' house, they were standing in the driveway, the same one I'd driven into a thousand and one times, waiting to help me unload.

Mom was in good spirits as she showed me what she'd done to my old room. She added a desk by the window and cleaned out the dresser drawers for me to put my folded clothes in. The bathroom had new towels piled in the corner, and she'd taken all of her stored Christmas items out from the shelves. Inside my closet were tubs full of pictures, memories of cheerleading, soccer, and dances with Raleigh that I had snapped in high school. I put my pillow on my bed and rolled my suitcase into an open spot to unpack. On the other side of the house, the twins moved into my brother's old bedroom next door to my parents' room. He had a king-size bed with no rails, so we stuffed pillows around the borders before they went to sleep. The twins didn't say anything about the giant deer heads mounted on the walls. Mom promised to make it a little more girly during our stay.

After settling in, we sat outside on the back porch, watching the girls play in the yard. Dad already had the grill fired up, slow cooking a Boston butt, and the aroma could be detected halfway down the block.

My parents had a system as they grilled our dinner in the evenings. They'd prep and prepare the meat early in the day. Dad had a whole cabinet just for spices, and his favorite gift was homemade barbecue sauce that we found on our travels. He also made his own sauce that was a throwback to the vinegar-based version found at the original *Dreamland Barbecue* restaurant in Birmingham. Mom usually stayed out of his way while he was prepping the meat, but sometimes he called her in to help. I usually found her rolling her eyes at him, telling him to lay off the spice. "Oh, Connie, live a little," I'd hear him say with a smile.

Once the meat was prepared, he'd determine what time the grill would need to be ready. Over the years, he'd used a gas grill, charcoal grill, a Big Green Egg, and a cheap little Weber grill. He always went back to a charcoal grill, and he stacked hickory chips in the fire to give the meat extra flavor.

When the fire was ready, he would do a little jig as he got the meat out of the refrigerator and laid it on the warm flame. Depending on the type of meat he was cooking, he would determine if it needed to sit directly on the fire to get crisp grill marks or needed to slowly burn in the corner. He often wrapped his food in tinfoil, preventing them from getting too crispy early in the cooking process. As daylight would fade to dusk, he'd give my mom the go-ahead to get the rest of the meal ready to eat. Our go-to sides were baked beans, homemade cole slaw, and sweet potatoes loaded with butter and cinnamon sugar. We always had to remind Mom to take the bread out of the oven before it burned. She assembled everything on our kitchen bar as Dad brought in the meat. No different than dogs, we'd be drooling, ready to fill our plates and devour the deliciousness that lay before us. My grandfather blessed the food, and then Mom would tell us to help ourselves. We'd fix our plates and sit together in the dining room with dad at the head of the table, and after we could eat no more, we'd finish our meal and collapse on the couches in the living room.

Tonight, on my first night back in town, we ate the food my parents had lovingly prepared for us. We raised our glasses to celebrate my dad, but to also celebrate this new beginning for our family.

Arriving home, I was both comforted and hesitant of the familiar. Dothan was my hometown, and my parent's house held more than rooms with beds. Their home was etched with the stories of my past—our past—and the memories that bond and break a family. How could we start new while surrounded by so much of the past?

Because my dad is such a great cook, he'd often receive gifts on Father's Day that had something to do with grilling. As children, my brother Courts and I would give him tacky aprons that'd have cheap plastic words like "BBQ King" ironed on the front. I remember how he'd hold up the apron and make a show of wearing it as he prepared our food over the grill. Barbecuing is his love language, the gift that was passed down from his father to him and him to us. Cooking over a flame is what brings him such joy . . . but it also revealed much of his pain. Because barbecuing is a process, he'd have time to reflect while preparing our food. Sometimes Dad would think with a red plastic cup in his hand. Over the years, I've watched my hero slowly sink into his own private hell as he remembers the moments that he just can't forget. While we all struggle with pain, it has always troubled me to watch my dad grieve. He is my protector, the parent who provided strength when I felt weak. Dad had all the answers to my questions, and he taught me how to believe in myself. Growing up, I'd try to fix and change him, but these efforts were never fully received, which usually amounted to me casting blame and judging. Church became my legalistic understanding of right from wrong and my faith kept me out of trouble, but it was never something of an intimate nature. Instead, Jesus became a definition of perfection, and my job was to try to live up to His example. I labeled myself as The Responsible One, all while having a quiet anger toward my parents.[21]

As a young woman, I still did not understand the reasons why Dad struggled with darkness, and I began to rebuke his advice. In high school, my role models became girls just a few years older than me. I watched how they flipped their Bibles open and had certain passages underlined. Trying to fit in, I bought the same kind of clothes that they wore and asked my hairstylist to cut my hair in a similar fashion. They'd invite me over to dinner, and I'd see how their dad would smile at their mom. I wasn't exposed to their dark tendencies, which led me to a false comparison of their home life versus mine.

Surrounded by friends who seemed to have it all, I piled responsibility after responsibility onto my plate in an effort to prove just how good I was compared to everyone else. During college, I organized homecoming pep rallies, sorority recruitment week, and showed new students around campus. I hid my shame by pretending that I had no skeletons from my past. But, as I'd walk back to my dorm from studying, I'd feel the weight of my lies as heavy as the books I was carrying in my backpack.

Whenever I'd come home for a weekend visit from college, I just wanted everyone to be normal. Sometimes, we were. Other times, we weren't. On these occasions, I'd drive away from my parents' house, pushing my foot hard against the pedal as my knuckles turned white from my grip on the wheel, going farther and farther away from the messy pain of my family.

Living under my parents' roof again, I was afraid of who I'd become once I'd been immersed in their lifestyle. As I settled back into their home, I didn't love my parents well or treat their hospitality with respect. Their presence brought back the temperament of my youth, and I couldn't stop the rush of words and tears that streamed out of me.

Feeling the need to escape, I met Ashley for dinner. She's one of the only people I've ever felt like I could talk to about my parents. After the waiter placed our chips and dip on the table, she asked me how I was doing.

Glancing over at her, I noticed her wearing the aqua necklace I had given her recently as a birthday present. Her eyes locked with mine, and

I couldn't mask my pain behind false perfection tonight. "Not well," I responded in anguish. The heaviness of my pent-up frustrations was overwhelming. She spent most of the night listening to me. Finally, when I finished, she gave it to me straight.

"How can you forgive them?"

Her words struck a nerve that went back to my youth. As much as I tried to distance myself from my parents, wishing they were different, my family will always be connected to my story. They aren't perfect, but neither am I.

Ashley gently reminded me of this, pointing out how much they had grown spiritually since the twins were born. While Mom held me in her arms physically, my dad had held me up emotionally. Because they had experienced multiple miscarriages, my parents understood how vulnerable I was to darkness. Dad didn't want me to fall prey to pits of insecurity, and he once again became a source of strength and security in my life. When the twins were in the hospital, Mom and Dad rededicated their lives to the Lord. They recognized their imperfections and began living by Romans 8:1-2, "So now there is no condemnation for those who belong to Christ Jesus. And because you belong to him, the power of the life-giving Spirit has freed you from the power of sin that leads to death." They had changed, so why couldn't I?

The circumstances that we experience in our childhoods don't define who we are, but they certainly set a foundation for how we interpret good and evil, right from wrong. From these experiences, we can grow up either rebelling or becoming self-righteous.[22] Rebelling against the practices of our parents, we set out to create a different life for ourselves. Sometimes this looks like moving across the country, getting a tattoo, or dressing and decorating our home in an opposite fashion. Yet, our parents' influence never truly vanishes; it's inscribed in our souls and bursts out of us when we least expect it to.

Millennial women have been told our entire lives that we can be anything we want to be. In the movie *The Intern*, Anne Hathaway's character Jules remarks, "I mean, like, we were the generation of 'you go, girl.' We had Oprah."[23] Because we have set such high expectations for ourselves, we are labeled "the good girls" and unintentionally view our generation as more superior than our parents'. But our self-righteousness comes off as preachy, hypocritical, and smug, which doesn't leave much room for reason and compromise.

Christ taught us this lesson through the parable of the lost son. A father had two sons, and the youngest ran away with all the money his father had given him and hastily spent it, reckless and wild. This son went from feasting to famine and ultimately found himself eating with the pigs. Muddy and miserable, he eventually came to his senses and said, "I will set out and go back to my father and say to him: Father, I have sinned against heaven and against you" (Luke 15:18 NIV). (There's nothing like sitting in manure to make you realize how much your life stinks, is there?) So, he returned home, hoping his father would hire him.

On the other hand, his older brother stayed by his father's side, working the fields and being the "good son." When his brother returned home without his money, the older son became angry as he watched his father run to his younger son and welcome his brother with open arms. But his father said, "My son, you are always with me, and everything I have is yours. But we had to celebrate and be glad, because this brother of yours was dead and is alive again; he was lost and is found" (Luke 15:31-32 NIV).

While the oldest son was self-righteous, the younger son rebelled. Both sons sinned, but only the younger son repented. Jesus says earlier in this chapter that "there will be more rejoicing in heaven over one sinner who repents than over ninety-nine righteous persons who do not need to repent" (Luke 15:7 NIV). Repentance covers rebellion and righteousness, leading us to rejoicing.

I'm not sure which camp you fall in—the rebellious or the righteous. Either way, your sin can destroy your relationships. But, repentance can repair the damage done. When we confess our misguided ways, we are connecting with Christ, whose perfection covers our imperfection. In their book, *Finding Your Way Back to God,* Dave Ferguson and John Ferguson describe our actions by stating, "Each of us spends our lives on a journey toward God. Yet often our most deeply felt longings—for meaning, for love, for significance—end up leading us *away* from, instead of *toward*, our Creator and the person he made us to be."[24] The ties of family are shared throughout Scripture with stories of both rebellion and righteousness. While our longings lead us away, we come back to God by forgiveness.

My favorite part of this story is after the father has greeted his lost son and he says, "Quick, let's have a feast and celebrate" (Luke 15:23 NIV). The father was so overcome with joy by being reconnected with his son that he wanted to throw a party immediately! Celebration is what makes life sweet, like cake with white frosting, and it's the only thing that can cut through the salty tears of sorrow. Just like the father in the parable, God has offered us forgiveness through His Son so that we may feast in our forever home. He too is waiting to celebrate and be glad as we find our way back home.

Studies show that 74% of young women say they feel pressure to be perfect.[25] Perfection has been described as a combination of characteristics valued by our peer culture: intelligence, thin and fit physical appearance, and social poise.[26] This pressure of perfection stems from a place deep inside us that we don't like to admit is there, but it is. This place is the mindset of wanting to be the best: the smartest, the prettiest, and the friendliest. But striving for a perfection that does not exist makes women feel that they will never be completely competent. Inadequacy mingles with imperfection, shaking us up and breaking us down.

Brené Brown, the author of *The Gifts of Imperfection*, says, "Owning our story can be hard but not nearly as difficult as spending our lives running from it. Embracing our vulnerabilities is risky but not nearly as dangerous as giving up on love and belonging and joy—the experiences that make us the most vulnerable. Only when we are brave enough to explore the darkness will we discover the infinite power of our light."[27]

Embracing our vulnerability begins by admitting our imperfections. My works made me no better than my parents' actions because I did it to elevate my perception to others. I needed forgiveness just as much as my parents did. But, I couldn't save myself from my self-promoting tendencies. Paul says in Romans 3:22–24 that there is no difference, for all have sinned and fall short of the glory of God, and are justified freely by His grace through the redemption that came by Christ Jesus. We are made right with God when we accept our imperfections and the imperfections of others. This doesn't mean that we'll never be disappointed again, but it does mean that we can give each other grace, a gift that none of us deserve but all need.

"Did we give you a good childhood?"

I'm in the car with Mom and Dad, years after I moved back into their home. We're traveling the interstate once again to New Orleans, and as we cross state lines, my mother hesitantly asks this of me.

I pause, wanting to choose the right words to say. From behind, I see my dad's hands wrapped securely around the steering wheel. My mother, without thought, reaches over to rub his shoulders. Before me are two people who have loved and lost, were dead and now alive. My parents gave me life, celebrated and comforted me. They needed affirmation, not accusation.

Taking a deep breath, I tell my mom, "Y'all have taught me what it means to love. Nothing else really matters."

Neither one of them responds, but I see my dad smile in the rearview mirror.

Moving home, I and my parents become family again. I often join them in the kitchen to prepare the barbecue, and we cut up as Mom tries to tame the spice added to the meat. I've learned that the reason bourbon tastes so good in a barbecue sauce is because aged corn whiskeys have a sweet vanilla flavor that balances out the tang found in the sauce. The secret to making a great bourbon barbecue sauce is to reduce the bourbon. This process rids the bourbon of its overbearing alcohol taste, leaving the sauce with the perfect blend of salty and sweet.

We all have a little bit of whiskey in us that needs to be reduced by God's amazing grace. Until we can see that the only way to rid ourselves of our impurities is by forgiveness, we will never experience true celebration of a life dependent upon the light of Christ.

Perhaps coming home wasn't so bad after all.

Chapter 8:

HOMECOMING

{HOW TO GET OVER THE FEAR OF MISSING OUT}

*What should young people do with their lives today? Many
things, obviously.
But the most daring thing is to create stable communities in which
the terrible disease of loneliness can be cured.*

~ Kurt Vonnegut, *Palm Sunday: An Autobiographical Collage*

THERE IS A STORY BEHIND every woman's smile. Some stories are
happy, which makes it easy to smile, while other smiles hide the hard,
the unspoken, the deep. When people look at us, they first notice our
smiles (or lack thereof). Smiles build and break, invite and turn away.
We smile with our eyes first, lighting up our faces. Smiles give way
to laughter, sometimes in the most surprising of moments. They are
contagious, and a nonverbal cure for a frown. Smiles tell a woman's
story, an indicator of where she has been, what emotions she is experiencing in the present, and who she is becoming.

The story behind my smile is most often summed up in six simple
words: *I want people to like me.*

"What do you want for your birthday this year?"

We are at the pool, Raleigh and I, sitting in lounge chairs by the deep end. Not much had changed since I was a kid. The tennis courts still are to my right, past the shallow end and the dressing rooms, and the pool house sits next to it at the far end of the pool. As children, we would order ice cream inside, charging it to our parents' accounts, and play red light/green light with the lifeguards whenever the pool would close for a brief summer rain. Back then, our parents would drop my best friend Susanne and me off at the clubhouse for tennis lessons in the morning, and then we'd stay afterward, ordering club sandwiches and curly fries with a Shirley Temple to drink. We'd sit in the corner of the room in the rounded booth overlooking the golf course, laughing and making jokes with all our friends. It was our first taste of freedom, those lazy summer days when we'd have nothing to do but be silly and have fun. We didn't know then how safe our little lives were or what it meant to say good-bye. The only plans we made were deciding after we swam if we would get a Mickey Mouse ice cream bar or a Firecracker.

But now, on my birthday, I look around like a detective in my oversized Hollywood knock-off sunglasses before I answer.

"I want to move back to Montgomery."

Tears begin to prick my eyes, hidden behind my shades. It doesn't matter if I cry. Nobody knows me here anymore. Since our move to Dothan a few weeks ago, everything is different. Susanne still lives in Birmingham. Now, whenever I went out, I'd run into the parents of all my childhood friends and have to ask them how those friends were doing. Did they enjoy whatever city they were living in? How were their babies? While I was happy for my friends and the lives they were building elsewhere, a twinge of sadness always followed those conversations. Why couldn't we all be home again? Some of my old friends were back in town, and we'd connected a few times since my return, but between my starting a new job and going back to Montgomery on the weekends to be with Raleigh, there really wasn't that much time for anything else.

When Raleigh and I first began thinking about moving home to Dothan, we didn't anticipate the tension found living in transition. I think back to our initial conversation on our Montgomery back porch as we spoke about our dreams and desires for our lives. So many of the things we wanted were wrapped up in a deep sense of craving stability. We wanted to finally feel at home, settle down, and plant our roots in the place where we grew up. We were tired of the temporary taste that the other cities left in our mouth. Dothan was home, and it was what our souls craved.

But, the back-and-forth lifestyle we were living wasn't solid. I confess this to Raleigh while watching kids jump off the diving board. I didn't know just how much I'd miss our first house and the friendships we'd made in Montgomery. I thought moving home to Dothan would be seamless, and I'd fit right back in with all my old friends. Why did a place that I knew so well seem so different?

Harvard psychology professor Daniel Gilbert has spent years studying why some people are happy and others are not. He says that the key to human happiness can be summed up in one word: *social*. He says,

"We are by far the most social species on Earth. Even ants have nothing on us. If I wanted to predict your happiness, and I could know only one thing about you, I wouldn't want to know your gender, religion, health, or income. I'd want to know about your social network—about your friends and family and the strength of your bonds with them."[28] Moving home, I saw people being social all around me.

Being on staff at our church, I had slowly begun piecing together the friend circles in Dothan. Many of my old high school friends were now friends with girls I had never met before. One of these girls, Amy, had brought a poppy seed chicken casserole to my parents' house recently. She was close to me in age, and standing by her side was her daughter, just a year behind my twins. We stood on my parents' front porch for half an hour, and I learned that she'd lived in Dothan for seven years, is a stay-at-home mom, and her daughter's favorite princess was Ariel. Amy was talkative but not overbearing, friendly but not fake.

I immediately wanted to be her friend.

After Amy left, I asked her to be my friend on Facebook, and I saw through her pictures that she was friends with several other girls I recognized. They smiled in pictures together from girls' nights and their children's birthday parties. Sitting alone in my childhood bedroom, I felt the pull of wanting to belong. I tried to push it away, but it bubbled out of me anyway. The room was silent, but the pictures that I scrolled through on my screen told tales of inside jokes, recipe swapping, and group texts.

Just weeks earlier, my feed looked similar to hers. My life had been full with friendship, but even on the weekends that I traveled back to Montgomery, I could already feel the distance. My texts with the

Montgomery girls had become less frequent, and we'd have to plan playdates or dinners based around the days I was in town. Whenever they'd post pictures of things they'd done together during the week, I'd like and comment, "Miss y'all!" but the image of them together without me stayed ingrained in my mind long after I turned off my phone. Montgomery was no longer my home, and living in transition left me with a crippling FOMO: *Fear of Missing Out.*

Having FOMO was causing me to feel both disconnected and lonely. I didn't have a problem meeting people, but I wasn't taking that next step to invite them into my everyday living. Blinking through tears at the pool, I could hear my husband assuring me that one day, real soon, I was going to feel like everything was normal again. I shrugged, finding it hard to believe him. Living in this state of imbalance had left me unsure of the decisions we had made. I didn't embrace the hard, and my hope had begun to waver. As Raleigh comforted me, he said, "You know, this girl Amy chose to bring you a meal. She didn't have to do that, but she did. If she's got a little girl, why don't you try and schedule something with her?"

His advice brightens my outlook. The following day, I invited her to a play date at the local park. She met me, and soon our girls were running around the playground, pretending to be princesses chasing adventure. Even though our conversation stopped and began with every request for a juice box to be opened or for a pull-up to be changed, Amy and I shared life with one another. She told me about the cute shop where she bought her shorts and how her daughter's room is about to explode with toys. I ask her if she's been to any of the cooking classes that a restaurant new to town offers. We talk about nothing and everything, and by the time our girls have sweaty hair and stains on their shirts, we've become friends.

Packing up our things as we were about to leave, I shyly said, "I don't want to seem like I'm trying too hard or anything like that, but I've just really missed having friends to do stuff like this with." Amy smiled and said she understood. I believed her. As we buckled screaming kids into car seats, we promise to do it again soon. Driving away from the park, a peace that I hadn't felt in months rose and settled inside me.

I'd made a friend.

Do you ever wonder if people really like you? I do, all the time. Even the most social people question their own self-worth and neediness. Anxiety is a constant companion, causing us to have a critical spirit about ourselves. While FOMO stands for a "fear of missing out," the root of this social disease is fear. Fear causes us to be afraid of being rejected, which hinders us from making friends. So, instead of being rejected, we find ourselves alone. We can be alone only for so long.

I've read that over 86 percent of young people feel the pressure to succeed in their relationships, finances, and jobs by the time they are thirty. We've begun to believe that we must have our lives all together before we let others in. This is so messed up. The whole point of friend-ships is to share the different stages of life together!

After my play date with Amy, I realized that I was worried about missing out because I wasn't letting anyone new in. All of my relation-ships had been surface since I'd moved back to Dothan, and I had a false assumption that making friends would be as quick as making a no-bake cheesecake. I wasn't putting in the time, so I wasn't seeing the results.

Friendships are a lot like dating; they are something that takes time. If someone looks like they'd be fun to hang out with, we've got to take the first step to initiate the conversation. While we might not go on "dates" with our friends, we do have to plan times to get together, whether it is for coffee, a play date, or a girl's weekend away. The more time we spend with others, the more comfortable we get with the relationship. Inside jokes happen only when we let people in. Outfits can't be swapped if we don't know that the other's favorite color is blue and she looks great in an A-line dress. Group texts happen only if you say yes to showing up.

Because I already had friends in Montgomery with whom I had gone through the dating stages, I wasn't ready to put myself back out there. I wanted what I had, but I needed to move on if I was ever to feel like I belonged. I couldn't let fear keep me from starting over.

If we allow fear to hold us hostage, we will always feel threatened by its grip. Instead of cowering to fear, might we find courage to stand up to it? Fear will never allow us to experience the true joys of living in love. Fear punishes us and pushes us in a corner, telling you and me that we are alone.

But, we aren't.

God hears our soft cries against our pillows as we sit lonely in our rooms. He hears our hearts break when we are turned away. He hears the sadness in our voices as we talk to friends of the past, wishing we didn't now live so far away.

First John 4:7 says, "Dear friends, let us continue to love one another, for love comes from God." God showed His love by sending us His one and only Son that we might live through Him. Believing this, we can live in the confidence of knowing that we are loved.

There is no fear in love. We are never missing out. Even though we can't see Him, God lives in us, and His love is made complete in us. Whenever we experience loneliness, the Spirit is ready and willing to be our friend.

People are people. We all experience FOMO, but it's because we are so desperate to be part of one another's lives. We don't want to miss out; we want to have friends and do fun things together. But, sometimes we let our own insecurities or selfishness get in the way of truly connecting with one another. We don't call someone after we promise to get together, or maybe we don't invite someone to join our group because they are a little awkward. (But let's face it, we are all a *little* awkward!) We are messed up, but we were made to love. When we can get past our FOMO, we can become more proactive when it comes to friendships.[29]

If loneliness is a disease, we must cure it with a good dose of community.

It is scientifically proven that being around friends is sometimes better than medicine.[30] Friends of the good sort build us up and are by our sides when we break down. We get people like this in our lives by spending time with them and sharing our struggles with one another.

Every good friend that I have has come out of having authentic conversations over time. Even if I immediately fall in love with someone's disposition, it takes continual effort to really call them a close friend.

While social media is a great tool for connecting people, it is still just a starter kit for friendship. We can use it to find old friends and meet new people in interest groups, but we must still engage in personal conversation.

For years, I followed the blog of a girl named Kayse. We had so much in common and struck up a friendly banter by leaving comments on one another's websites. But, that was as far as that relationship went ... until I met her in person at a blogging conference. Spending a few days together, we were able to form a much deeper relationship than we ever would have if we just stayed online friends. I know now what her laugh sounds like and what she carries in her purse while traveling (lavender oil). Meeting her in person gave us the opportunity to continue our friendship online, but in a much more meaningful way.

There are other people I am friends with online that might have been my friends during a past period of my life like college or during my early working years. Some friends have traveled the world, others have adopted, and some have had a lot of success in their careers. I see their fancy new homes; elaborate birthday parties, and glamorous vacations. Sometimes, when I look at these people's feeds, it's easy to wonder if they made better life choices than I have. It's easy to let comparison steal my contentment.

Instead of wasting my time comparing myself to others, I needed to find out what was meaningful to me, which was feeling included. I like to be invited to social events and lunch and weekends away.

Friendships that happen face-to-face also battle the comparison trap, but when we can stop looking to the right and left and fix our eyes on what is directly in front of us, we can stop feeling so envious and begin to be thankful for the crazy beautiful lives that we've been given.

Let's use our phones to actually *call* the people who matter most in our lives. When we say "let's get together for dinner," we need to schedule a time on our digital calendars right that very second and make sure to set a reminder so we don't accidentally overbook ourselves. Our phones are a tool meant for connection, not comparison.

Community can be real, both in person and online, but the only way we will feel like we belong in it is by love. God did not just create love as an emotion; He literally IS love. Perfect love begins and ends when we can extend the love He has shown us into our relationships with others. It really doesn't matter what other people are doing and posting to their feeds. Let us celebrate our friends' successes instead of living in comparative solitude! And, if someone's feed just keeps pulling you down? Maybe unfollow them for a while or take a social media sabbatical. My life isn't perfect, but neither is my friend's, even with 7,000 followers on Instagram. God did not give us a spirit of comparison; He gave us a spirit of love.

Love is not afraid of fear. God tells us over 365 times in the Bible to have no fear. That's literally a whole year's worth of Scripture, just on this one particular subject. God knows that this is something we constantly battle, but we must not let our fears get in the way of extending fellowship to one another. Our primary reasons for existence are to love God and to love others. Loving others begins by hating what is evil—things like comparison, fear, and loneliness—and clinging to what is good.

To live unafraid of rejection, we are free to invite people to be our friends. Some will say yes, while others say no. If we are trying to extend love to others, let us not take it personally if they choose not to be our friends. When we overanalyze a negative response, this just spirals us into the comparison trap, and we are stuck with a critical spirit of ourselves and bitterness toward the other person. Instead, let us cling to what is good and to the people who have said yes to being our friends.

People are desperate for real friendship in our communities. My friendship with Amy might have begun over poppy seed chicken casserole, but it has grown into so much more because we were both willing to make the effort to spend time together. I can tell Amy about my fears because I know she will love me in spite of them.

Just as friendships take time, so does our spiritual formation. Yes, you and I need to love like Jesus, but it takes spiritual maturity to actually understand what that looks and feels like. Reverend Bob Mulholland says that spiritual formation is the process of being shaped and formed in the image of Christ for the sake of others. Moving to a new city and having to make friends has been part of my spiritual formation so I can better love others and get over my FOMO.

We can recognize a true friend by how they love, and we can be a true friend by how we reciprocate that love. Let us hold onto these people, in real life and online. If the great call on our lives is to love as Christ loved us, might we do this, one poppy seed chicken casserole at a time?

Chapter 9:

BABY SHOWERS

{FINDING PEACE THROUGH STORE-
BOUGHT STRAWBERRY CUPCAKES}

*You can't buy happiness, but you can buy cupcakes. And that's
kind of the same thing.*

~ Anonymous

I AM IN A CUPCAKE WAR.

Standing in the kitchen, covered in confectioner's sugar, I had been
defeated by my strawberry cupcakes. It's ten o'clock on a Wednesday
night, and I've lost all hope at winning this battle. I'd volunteered to
bring cupcakes to the baby shower I was hosting, but my recipe had
turned into one big blob of pink mess.

The first mistake I made was using two different kinds of boxed
strawberry cake mix. Even though I scooped them to the same measure-
ment, one batch of cupcakes rose higher than the other and ended up
with browned edges. Once they cooled, I tried to cover up the edges
with my homemade strawberry icing. It's a delicious cream cheese based
icing with real strawberries pureed in it, and my secret ingredient is a

dab of Crisco to help form beautiful blush peaks. However, I couldn't find my correct size pastry tip, so I used a different pastry tip for piping on the icing. I wrestled with the bag, trying to recreate the Georgetown Cupcake signature swirl, which resembles a soft round cloud with a peak in the center, but instead my swirl looked as though it had been done with a Cheese Whiz can. Wiping my forehead, I tried one more time to fix this cupcake catastrophe by assembling little cupcake toppers of baby bottles, safety pins, and booties that I had purchased at Michael's. Stepping back to examine my handiwork, my cupcakes looked cheap instead of cute.

These cupcakes just would not do.

Why did I think baking *anything* was a good idea while most of my cooking utensils were still in boxes? I had been at work all day and was feeling stretched as a mom with toddlers. The cupcakes were a nightmare, and I couldn't stop wondering what people would say about them at the shower.

I had wanted to bake these cupcakes because they were a sweet reminder of our twins' first birthday party. I was in my cake-baking prime when the girls turned one, and I had made strawberry and lemon cupcakes to match our pink and yellow party in the park theme. I'd also made their smash cakes and decorated them with coordinating pink and yellow fondant and flowers.

Raleigh's grandmother had always made her grandchildren's birthday cakes when they were younger and had taken several advanced baking classes to learn different piping techniques. Over the years, she taught me a few of her tricks, and I'd made several birthday cakes and cupcakes for family and friends. One of her best secrets was to bake the cakes the day before and then put them in the refrigerator. The cold cakes made the icing stick instead of melt and caused less bits of crumble to get in the icing. Another trick was to buy butter-flavored extract and clear vanilla extract to add to buttercream icing. The butter extract gave the icing richness, and the clear vanilla kept the white icing bright. Once I began baking, I'd share with her tips I found on making homemade fondant with simple ingredients like marshmallows and confectioner's sugar, and she'd show me how to make chocolate icing for a seven-layer chocolate cake. It had been fun being creative in the kitchen and making memories with Raleigh's grandmother, but now I was out of practice. These cupcakes were not pretty enough to serve at a party.

Insecure, I allow the frustration of failure to mess with my head, causing me to spiral into doubt, which steals my confidence. I hear a soft whisper that *I* am like these cupcakes . . . not good enough. Instead of letting good enough be good enough, I want to be, have, and give the best of myself to every aspect of my life. That's why I thought I could make these cupcakes, and now that's why I'm being overly critical of myself.

Good enough can't be good enough when there is always someone or something better. This lie keeps circling inside my head like a vulture, popping up when I'm at church, when I look at myself in the mirror, after my kids have a meltdown, when I'm out with friends, and even when I'm alone with my husband. The more I believe in this lie, the less I believe in myself.

I've taken personality type tests over the years and have determined that I fall into the category of a Type-A personality, which basically means I have an action-emotion complex that motivates me to want to be perfect and to hate making mistakes. But, what makes me a unique Type A is that I disguise my Type-A-ness behind being nice instead of bossy, quiet instead of loud. But my Type-A tendencies course through my veins, urging me to produce, achieve, and organize. Are you a Type-A person too? (If you are Type B, praise Jesus!) When taking an Enneagram test, my result labels me as something similar: A Type One Principled Reformer/The Good Person. My basic fear is of being bad, defective, and corrupt. The Type One person has a hard time accepting imperfections—other people's and, above all, their own.

Good girls like you and me want perfection, not good enough.

Plato once wrote that the mind has two sides: the rational side and the emotional side. He labeled the emotions to be like wild horses and the ration to be the charioteer steering. Plato discovered that emotion and ration have to work together as a team.[31]

Science has proven that the female brain is genetically more complex than the male brain because the amygdala (which controls emotions) is fatter in women than in men. Like a beautiful, rigorously trained ballerina, we are hard-wired to be flexible. Our brains are so sensitive to external inputs that their physical wiring depends upon the culture in which they find themselves.[32] If we never feel good enough, our brains begin to shape and stretch around this lie, making it feel like the truth. The words *emotion* and *motivation* share the same Latin root, *movere*, which means "to move." How can we move our minds from thinking harmful thoughts into more positive ones?

The struggle for every Type-A perfectionist is to have peace with what we produce. Because of our fear of being bad or producing bad things, we pile so much stress on ourselves to be good and make good things that we become anxious, have negative self-talk, and lose joy. Anne Lamott notes, "Perfectionism is the voice of the oppressor, the enemy of the people. It will keep you cramped and insane your whole life."[33]

Like a tightly knit ball, the strings of anxiety tangle our insides. Questions race around the tracks of our minds, sidetracking us into believing the worst possible outcome for our current situation. Suddenly, alternative story lines replace fact, and fictitious characters come to life to ruin us. Burnt cupcakes with Cheese Whiz icing become the talk of the shower, and I imagine girls standing in corners of the room mocking me. As I walk past, they whisper, "Who does she think she is, Martha Stewart?" and then they laugh. My cheeks burn bright as I duck my head and pretend that I didn't hear their cruel words. Why did I ever believe I could make something that people would admire?

These thoughts have to stop.

Anxiety attacks. It makes us fret about everything, even the simple things like strawberry cupcakes. When we experience an attack, we spiral into a state of panic, causing more harm than good. We know that it is unhealthy, but it has become our imaginary friend, following us wherever we go. Because anxiety is our constant companion, everyday tasks like baking become a source of anger and perfectionism, making us uptight and overly critical. The crazy thing about anxiety is it is self-destructive. When the unplanned happens and we feel out of control, we let the tangled web of anxious thoughts trip us up, which allows Satan room to walk right into our minds, whispering to us words of inadequacy. And it is then, when we are sobbing on the floor, that we lose peace with ourselves and feel like we just aren't good enough.

The struggle is real when it comes to anxiety. The Anxiety and Depression Association of America states that from the time a girl reaches puberty until about the age of 50, she is twice as likely to have an anxiety disorder than a man.[34] The difference between anxiety and depression is anxiety is linked more to the future, while depression is linked to the past. Depression is the past superimposed on the present, and anxiety is the future superimposed on the present.[35] Anxiety disorders also occur earlier in women than in men, most likely because women's brains have more trouble processing serotonin, which regulates mood and emotion.

Because women suffer anxiety at different levels, often the form of treatment for mild anxiety is counseling, and for more severe anxiety, antidepressant medication. Currently one in four women in America is on some form of antidepressant.[36] Women taking antidepressants are often battling their own insecurities or going through a difficult life stage. Between working, raising kids, and trying to get everything done around the house, the juggling act becomes exhausting, and women reach out to their doctors for help. The medications are fast-acting and serve a purpose for the cases where women are correctly diagnosed. But, the medicine doesn't always make women feel happy; women still struggle with feeling guilty or worthless because they had to take medicine to try and make themselves feel better.

Anxiety and depression braid together the mind, body, and soul. There are some preventive measures we can try, such as exercising, journaling, and meditation, to avoid falling into depression, though they may not always be successful.

Have you ever felt like you needed something more than medicine and physical activity to stop believing the lies of unworthiness? I do. Whenever I feel the strings of anxiety tighten my insides, I try to lean on truth instead of my feelings. A passage that I return to often is when Paul writes to the Philippians:

> *Do not be anxious about anything, but in every situation, by prayer and petition, with thanksgiving, present your requests to God. And the peace of God, which transcends all understanding, will guard your hearts and your minds in Christ Jesus.*
>
> ~ Philippians 4:6-7 NIV

In the King James Version, the words "do not be anxious about anything" are written as "be careful for nothing," which means that no one—not even Type-A perfectionists—should allow worry and anxiety to steal our joy. The key to changing your anxious thoughts is to stop letting perfection have such a tight grip on your mind. Nothing—not cupcakes, test scores, body image, family, careers, finances—should make you fret. This is the complete opposite of the way the world has taught you to think, but you must train your mind to *think differently.*

Going back to the idea of our minds being like a ballerina, we have to exercise our minds to think on good things. Daily, we are to listen to the voice of our Instructor, choosing to be students that show up to class, willing to learn the art of beauty and discipline. In ballet, a classic term is *adagio*, which is when a dancer completes a succession of slow and graceful movements that may be simple or complex. For our minds to be like ballerinas, we are to become less anxious one step at a time by thinking on things in our life that are noble, right, pure, lovely, and admirable. These thoughts will range from simple to complex, but the more we think on these things, the more we are full of grace.

When I watch ballerinas practice their movements, so often they perform in front of a mirror so they can see what they look like and correct what is not proper form. The mirror is a tool to help them achieve success. As a woman, we look into the mirror to apply makeup, fix our hair, and brush our teeth. The mirror can easily become our enemy, and the lies of perfectionism can make us see a horribly grotesque person standing before us. But, the mirror was made as an aide, something to be of use to us. What if the mirror actually helped us overcome anxiety and perfectionism and we used it to see ourselves as Christ sees us? He created us with beauty, grace, and to be lovely, just like a ballerina who twirls and glides across the dance floor.

In an effort to decrease perfectionism and increase positive thoughts, I've begun writing in my Jubilee journal. The name of the journal originated from a year described in the Old Testament called "The Year of Jubilee" which means "liberty." This was a special anniversary year for the Israelites, one that happened once every fifty years, where everyone returned to their homeland and slaves were freed. The Jubilee was a crucial celebration in the Old Testament because no one would dare celebrate the Jubilee unless they had a deep trust in God's ability to provide for their needs. After I write the date, I scribe a key verse for the day and write down what is happy and what is hard. At the bottom, I have a table with one side labeled *confession* and the other side labeled *celebration*. Under the word *confession*, I write out all the things that are not excellent or praiseworthy. After months of journaling, so many of my confessions begin with, "God, please forgive me for . . ." and then I list the ways I've harmed myself and others: my short temper, anger, unrealistic expectations, vanity, guilt—the list keeps going. My scribbles of confession in blue, green, and purple ink bring me freedom and take my mind to a place of restoration and freedom. After confession, I then move to celebrating. I write "Connection, not perfection" and believe that God can restore me to the joy of His salvation (Psalm 51:12). Celebration becomes my liberty bell, ringing its merriment and setting my thoughts on statements that bring me peace.

Returning to Philippians 4, Paul writes for us to not be anxious about anything, but before that statement he tells us to rejoice. "Rejoice in the Lord always. I will say it again: Rejoice!" (Philippians 4:4 NIV). The Greek word for *rejoice* in this text means to boast. Paul is telling us to boast in the Lord under all kinds of circumstances, including the circumstances that make us worry. How can we boast in God while feeling anxious?

We pray.

Anxiety and prayer are two great opposing forces in the life of a Christian.[37] While anxiety is self-centered, prayer is a submissive act of worship. The very definition of prayer is "a solemn request for help or expression of thanks addressed to God." Prayer is the glue between God and us, sticking our hearts to His. When we pray, we move our minds away from ourselves as we give God our problems. In *The Case for Character*, Drayton Nabers comments, "We need help beyond ourselves to adhere to God's principles, because our sinful natures are strong and the temptations of the world are great. Our own strength is inadequate, so we must look to the strength of God."[38] Boasting and rejoicing in what good things God has done in our lives will shift our minds from anxiety to a state of thankfulness. Prayer is an action that shows God that we trust in Him. We can never truly celebrate and be "careful for nothing" until we trust God and confess our harmful thought patterns.

After Paul instructs us to pray, he says "and the peace of God, which transcends all understanding, will guard your hearts and your minds in Christ Jesus." Isn't it interesting how he begins this verse with the word *and*? Linda Dillow remarks, *"The Living Bible* suggests that the word *and* at the beginning of the verse means 'if you do this.' If we make the choice to pray instead of worry, we will personally experience God's peace."[39] Peace *is* possible, even if our minds are constantly battling perfectionism. Divine peace is what makes you and me whole, one with God. Paul says in Philippians 3:12, "I don't mean to say that I have already achieved these things or that I have already reached perfection. But I press on to possess that perfection for which Christ Jesus first possessed me." Paul believed that the true secret to being content lies not on perfectionism, but by following the teachings of Jesus, so that we will be filled with His peace instead of anxiety.

If a simple task like making homemade cupcakes causes us more anxiety than happiness, we need to make a change. The next day, I woke up and called a local bakery to order two dozen strawberry cupcakes.

To my relief, they said the cupcakes would be ready at five. I had spent a whole evening worrying about something that was easily fixed by making a phone call.

When it comes to parties, we all need to be mindful of just how much we can do ourselves. Sure, I had a fabulous recipe for strawberry cupcakes, but I was too rushed to make them look as appealing as they tasted. The cupcakes were a Pinterest Fail, and the added pressure of perfection didn't help my confidence either. I should have saved time and stress by placing an order for the cupcakes when I agreed to bring them to the shower instead of trying to make them myself. This strawberry cupcake fiasco taught me to worry less, pray more, and buy a store-bought cupcake!

Arriving at the baby shower with boxed cupcakes in hand, I arranged the cupcakes on a white tiered cake stand on the dining room buffet. They were quite a lovely centerpiece, these miniature cakes with not one but *two* layers of icing adorned with pink pearl sprinkles that shined like jewels under the chandelier lights. As the guests began to fix their food, I noticed a pink cupcake on almost every plate. They were delicious, beautiful, and store-bought, but it didn't make my contribution to the party any less. The mother-to-be said that these were her favorite, and she took a box to go.

After the shower, I came home to a house still filled with two dozen cupcakes. They certainly weren't the prettiest looking cupcakes, but I split one with my girls, and we all agreed that they still tasted good. I threw away the burned cupcakes and rummaged through my to-go containers until I found some small pastel cake boxes. I added four cupcakes to each box, sealed it with a sticker, and wrote "Homemade

Strawberry Cupcakes" on the package. The next day, we delivered our batches of cupcakes to family and friends and shared laughs about my cupcake war. Everyone who received our cupcakes were thankful for their sweet treat and not the least bit upset that they looked like a four-year-old had made them. Gifting our friends with this treat brought me such joy after unnecessary turmoil.

Another version of Philippians 4:6 that I love simply states, "Don't worry about anything; instead pray about everything. Tell God what you need, and thank him for all he has done." Let's stop getting so worked up over things and trust that God will provide for us, even on matters as simple as store-bought or homemade cupcakes.

Now, go eat a cupcake!

Chapter 10:

SURPRISE PARTIES

{WHEN THE UNPLANNED BRINGS LAUGHTER}

Plan . . . to be surprised.

~ Steve Carell, *Dan in Real Life*

THE FIRST SURPRISE PARTY I ever attended was for my dad in our own backyard. When he turned forty, mom invited all their friends and our family over for a luau celebration. She had ordered decorations from the party supply store in town, and our suburban-Alabama home turned into an Alvin's Island version of Hawaii. Tall coconut trees, spray-painted and cut out of Styrofoam, were propped on either side of our gazebo. Water lilies with candles floated in our pool, and a platter of shrimp and oysters from our famed seafood restaurant, Hunt's, lined the bar.

My brother and I, dressed in leis and bright fluorescent sunglasses, stood by the back gate and acted as greeters to our guests. Mom was rushing around the house in her Hawaiian shirt with my grandmother at her heels, telling everyone to hush because Jim was about to arrive. Waiting in the backyard, we saw him pull his old Bronco into the drive with his best buddy in the passenger seat. We barreled toward him, yelling, "Surprise!" After throwing ourselves into his arms, his friends clapped and hollered, "Happy Birthday, Jimbo!" Not long after that, he was thrown into the swimming pool, and we spent the night eating and laughing and staying up past our bedtime. To my childish eyes, my dad was the celebrity, a man who was known, accepted, and loved by his family and friends. When he wrapped me up in his arms, I felt like I, too, was special.

Here's the thing with surprises: because they are unplanned, we can find ourselves broken or bemused. Some surprises, like my dad's fortieth birthday party, are sweet memories, but other surprises leave us standing still and speechless.

Planners don't know how to handle surprises well. To be perfectly honest, we don't always like surprises. Surprises are not dates circled on our calendars, events that we have been preparing for. People who plan like order, itineraries, and daily schedules. Planners are on a mission to *do something* with their lives. We own monogrammed planners, calendars filled with color-coded events, and days divided into time blocks with sections in our notebooks labeled for each of our children. We tailor our planners with pages for All-the-Things-We-Do—vacations, blogging, grocery shopping, fitness and food plans, expenses, and gifts. Planners like stickers, washi tape, and have favorite pens. We set our alarms to Eastern Time to get up early so we can pre-order our planners for the following year. Sometimes, we even have *more than one* planner just so we can stay super on top of things. We like to prepare our days so we can feel at peace.

When we planners are caught off-guard, we're like a kid learning to ice skate, trying to hold on to the rail as our feet fail us on the slippery ice. Falling fast, the unexpected leaves us unbalanced, uncertain, and unraveled. Shocked and sore from impact, we find ourselves yet again shivering on a cold floor, wondering, "How, with all my plans, did I not see this coming?"

Moving home, I was not prepared for the amount of anxiety I experienced. Because I was feeling more anxious than usual, I hesitantly scheduled an appointment with my doctor. I didn't want to have a problem, but I no longer could deny that our move left me feeling darkness. His nurse called me back from the waiting room, and we headed toward the scales. We soon verified that I was still a few pounds heavier than my pre-baby weight (thank you very much), which she noted on my charts. From there we went to an examination room. I was chatty, making small talk about the weather and work, trying to give her the impression that I was *fine*, just there for a routine check-up. But then she sat at her computer and began to ask questions.

"Is there anything specific you'd like to talk to the doctor about today?"

I squirmed in my blue plastic chair and ran my sweaty palms across my skirt. I chose my lemon skirt with black trim from Anthropologie, hoping that it would make me look happier than I felt.

"Well . . . I, um, I've been feeling really tired lately," I said.

"I bet," she responds. "Having small children and going back to work is no easy task."

"True." I smiled but then continued, "But I just don't feel like myself, you know?" Tears began to build behind my mascara'd eyes. "I think I'd like to talk to the doctor a little more about anxiety and depression."

She nodded her head in understanding and quickly made a note on the computer. It was officially documented now, my silent fears suddenly on record as a possible fact. I might have something wrong with me, and now we would be having this conversation for years to come. After the nurse left the room to get the doctor, I felt like the child on the ice rink floor, just wishing she could skate effortlessly instead of falling once more.

My doctor walked in and sat across from me. I noticed his plaid shirt underneath his doctor's coat as he began to rattle off facts from my charts. He cleared his throat then and began to talk about depression and anxiety. He asked me to describe how I was feeling. I explained how I've just hit a wall. I was crying all the time and unhappy. I'm not who I thought I'd be and I'd just started a new job and wondered if I would ever live up to the expectations and goals that I had set for myself.

"I hate feeling this way. I have a wonderful life. I love my family. I have a great job, nice clothes, and a supportive network of people who care about me. I work at a *church*. I know God is bigger than this. Why am I so unhappy?"

I took a shaky breath and wiped the corner of my eyes with a tissue. My doctor looked at me. He didn't condone my feelings. Nor did he immediately write me a prescription for Xanax. Instead, he told me a lot of women and men feel like this and that he'd like to run some blood work to see if anything showed up abnormal.

It's natural that planners don't like surprises and experience anxiety attacks since the root of anxiety is to not know what is going to happen in the future. Because we are unable to process the unplanned and unexpected, we allow our minds to project the worst, and sometimes we need medicine or counseling to help us feel stable. But, what if surprises were a way to help us with our anxiety and turned out to be something unexpectedly beautiful, part of God's plan to make us whole?

"I want to talk to you about the subject of plans . . . life plans and how we all make them. But if we're really honest with ourselves, most of our plans don't work out as we'd hoped. So instead of asking our young people, 'What are your plans? What do you plan to *do* with your life?' maybe we should tell them this: Plan . . . to be surprised."[40]

After my doctor's appointment, I retreat to Scripture, thirsty for replenishment. Light . . . it's what I needed and hoped to feel. Had I not read time and time again that the divine presence of God is *with* me, and has a plan *for* me? If this is true, why has He not shown it to me?

When God was making Abraham the father of all the nations, He first approached Abraham in a vision, then a smoking firepot and a blazing torch, and also appeared in some form of His glory. Then, in Genesis 18, God, along with two angels, comes to Abraham's tent, embodied as a man. It is early afternoon and when Abraham sees them, he hurries to greet the men and then bows to the ground, a gesture of Near Eastern hospitality. He offers them water to wash their feet, a place to rest under a tree, and something to eat. They accept his invitation, so Abraham hurries back inside his tent to his wife Sarah. "Quick," he said, "get three seahs of the finest flour and knead it and bake some bread" (Genesis 18:6 NIV).

A seah is an ancient Jewish measuring tool for dry ingredients. What is so interesting to me is that one seah of flour is 7.7 quarts,[41] or 30.8 cups of flour. For Sarah to bake bread with three seahs of flour meant that she was using 92 cups of flour!!! Also, because the bread was made with fine flour, it is suggested that it was formed into round, thin loaves of cake, baked on embers on a hot hearth stone, a true delicacy. How Sarah prepared this bread quickly, I'll never know!

While Sarah was preparing the bread, Abraham ran to the herd and selected a choice, tender calf. He asked a servant to prepare the meat, and he then brought his guests butter and fresh milk to complete the meal. The passage does not say much about what the guests were doing while Abraham and Sarah prepared the meal. Because the meat and the bread were both cooked over a fire, I imagine the bread being baked in batches, like pancakes or fried food, and possibly served while the meat continued to cook. I wonder if there was any conversation while the meal was assembled, or perhaps the guests continued to rest under the tree until they were called to the table.

Once the meal was ready, Abraham stood under a tree while the men ate. How interesting it is that he did not sit with them at the table as their host. Commentaries note that he did not join the men at the table because he was taking on the posture of a servant. Abraham sensed that these men were no ordinary men, so he humbled himself before them. Abraham, the father of nations, a man who had heard from God, took on the form of a hallelujah host, offering hospitality to God with food, shelter, and refreshment.

While eating, the men asked him, "Where is your wife Sarah?"

"There, in the tent," he said.

At the mention of her name, can't you see Sarah sit up a little straighter, fix her hair, smooth her apron, and wipe away any leftover fire soot from her face? Glancing at herself in the mirror, she saw the resemblance of a once-beautiful woman who now looked perspired and weary from unanswered prayer. Abraham already had a son with Sarah's maidservant Hagar. *"What could this man possibly want with me?"* she thought.

Then the LORD said, "I will surely return to you about this time next year, and Sarah your wife will have a son."

Through the thin walls, Sarah laughs to herself as she thought, *"An old woman like me? Get pregnant? With this old man of a husband?"* (Genesis 18:12, MSG). This was news to Sarah but not to Abraham. Earlier, God had told Abraham that He would bless Sarah and give him a son by her. Abraham, too, had laughed in disbelief (Genesis 17:15–17). Even though God appeared to both Abraham and Sarah *in the flesh*, they still could not believe that He was going to fill this desire.

As God sat on the other side of the tent, He sensed Sarah's unbelief and asked Abraham, "Why did Sarah laugh? . . . Is anything too hard for God? I'll be back about this time next year and Sarah will have a baby" (Genesis 18:13–14, MSG). This phrase "is anything too hard" can be translated as "too wondrous" and the Hebrew word used, *pala*, refers to God's miraculous works.[42]

The next year, Sarah gave birth to Isaac, a name which means "laughter." Looking down at her long-awaited son, Sarah exclaimed, "God has brought me laughter, and everyone who hears about this will laugh with me" (Genesis 21:6 NIV). After years of life not going according to her plans, Sarah experienced a divine surprise, one that left her with only joyful sounds of laughter. I imagine Isaac's birth made Sarah feel ten years younger, and brought her so much joy that she looked back over those years of disbelief with regret. God was with her, even when she didn't understand why her plans continued to fail. Now, she could see that all her anxiety wasn't worth it, because God had a plan for her life.

Women today remind me a lot of Sarah. Sometimes we have to see God's surprises before we believe that they will happen. We are so used to making plans and taking matters into our own hands that we deny the wonderful timing of God. It's a struggle for control, really, because we believe it is better to make things happen ourselves, instead of trusting that God will work all things together for the good of those who love Him. We live in a do-it-yourself world, but we can only DIY for so long before burnout sets in and breakdowns happen, depleting us of our joy. As planners, our hearts strive to perform for approval. But the Spirit gently whispers to our souls, "Stop trying so hard. I see you." Instead of always having to plan, God invites us to a party where He simply asks us to show up and be surprised by His grace. We are the guest of honor, the center of God's attention. Nothing is too hard for Him. Only after we experience the surprise, do we laugh in wonder.

God is the Perfect Party Planner, one who has planned an amazing story for your life. He hasn't invited you into a disorderly, unkempt life but into something holy and beautiful— as beautiful on the inside as the outside.[43] He uses the hard times, the unanswered prayers, and the way you feel out of control as a method to prune and refine you so that you may draw closer to Him. God wants you and me to recognize that we were made for connection, not to do life according to our own well-crafted schedule. Yes, His presence is with us, but do we lean on His help and direction? When we shift our posture from planner to partner, we are able to participate in humble, open-handed service and receive wonderful gifts from God. These gifts are not always perfectly wrapped presents, tied neatly with a bow. But they are delicately wrapped in grace, love, and mercy.

First Corinthians 14:33 states, "God is not a God of disorder but of peace." When we can strip away our performance and see Jesus for who He truly is, we can fully experience peace that only His joy can bring. Our plans, no matter how organized they may be, will never compare to God's perfect timing. He always outdoes us with His surprises. The only thing He asks of us is to accept His invitation. He's not trying to scare us, judge us, ridicule us; He wants to give us peace with our present circumstances, past mistakes, and future fears. Will we trust that God has a plan for our lives?

I think Abraham told Sarah to make so much bread because he knew that God would lavish them with gifts beyond what their hearts could imagine. It was his simple but profound way of recognizing that God is the great I AM, and we are made to serve and honor Him. Jesus reminds us of Sarah's actions when He shares the parables of the mustard seed and the yeast. He says, "The kingdom of heaven is like leaven that a woman took and hid in three measures of flour, til it was all leavened" (Matthew 13:33 ESV). The leaven in this passage refers to yeast, and Jesus explains that just as yeast grows in a batch of dough, so can the kingdom of heaven in our lives.[44] We are made beautiful on the inside, just as the outside, when we let go of our to-do list to be in Christ. We are broken and born again so that we may bake and rise. Christ is our Light, our coping mechanism when anxiety attacks, our hearts' way to wholeness and holiness. This is hospitality in its rawest form.

Since I approached my doctor about anxiety, I've learned that my body didn't need medication, but my lack of B-12 was causing me to be anemic and tired. Knowing that exhaustion has caused me to feel unsettled, I've made an effort to shift my attitude. Like Sarah, I've had to realize that my life is not going to look exactly how I imagined it would be, but God keeps showing me His presence in the middle of my most unpredictable circumstances. Knowing that I am not alone helps calm my anxious heart.

If we plan to be surprised, we start our days differently. We still make plans, but we recognize that unplanned events will happen, and that's okay. To prevent the potential breakdowns, we spend time in Jesus' presence, asking for peace. It's a slight but powerful action that guards us against anxiety attacks. Planning to be surprised, we let go of worry and approach our days with lighter hearts and laughter.

When Mom planned my dad's surprise party, I'm sure there were some unexpected events that could have easily rattled her. But when I think back on that day, my memories are of us swimming with my dad, dancing under string lights, and the buffet in our gazebo being filled with tropical fruits, smoked meats, and sticky desserts. Because she took time to plan a party for her husband, we all experienced a night of joy and celebration.

Let's invite surprises into our days and be women who are unafraid of what the future holds. May we see ourselves as God sees us—His chosen people—whom He finds great delight in celebrating. Only when we let go of our plans and accept God's peace are we made whole.

Chapter 11:

SMALL GROUP SOCIALS

{TURNING A RENTAL HOUSE INTO A HOME
WITH FOOD, FRIENDS, AND FEBREZE}

*Let him who is not in community beware of being alone. Into the
community you were called, the call was not meant for you alone; in the
community of the called you bear your cross, you struggle, you pray.*

~ Dietrich Bonhoeffer, *Life Together*

IT'S OCTOBER, WHICH MEANS ALL things pumpkin have taken over Pinterest.

Pumpkin spice caramel lattes, pumpkin brownies, pumpkin appliqued t-shirts, pumpkin decorating ideas, pumpkin costumes for dogs—there is a pumpkin idea for everyone! I'm in Pennsylvania for a blogging conference and can't help but admire the velvet pumpkins placed in the center of the check-in table. Outside, the air is already crisp like an apple, and the leaves dance with color on the other side of the hotel window.

Ready for fall, I'm dressed in my boots, tall socks, and a navy long-sleeved dress with an orange scarf slung around my neck. Inside, women with nametags are filling the historic hotel lobby, and the chatter makes me about to burst with excitement. All around me, people are gathering in groups, shaking hands hello, and checking out one another's Twitter handle. It's my first time traveling to this conference, and after months of adjusting to a new city, it feels good to be social with people I would never have met in my hometown.

Still new to the blogging community, I connect with girls from Mississippi, Birmingham, and Atlanta during the after-hour social, and we spend the whole weekend becoming friends. It was so easy to talk about our families, ministry goals, and blogging tips, and I don't want to blink because I'm having so much fun.

I had decided months earlier to attend this conference to learn more about writing as a craft, but the real lesson that I was taking away from the three-day retreat was that we were made for belonging. Isn't that so true and just like God? He has a way of connecting us to one another, starting a chain of impact one person at a time.

While the conference was focused on building online communities, the break-out session that stuck with me most was all about going local. The facilitator, Laura, shared with us how she had been blogging for a number of years while living in a city that also had a large college campus. She was surrounded by technology and millennials who thought outside the box, but she felt like her blog had become more about what she wanted instead of what God wanted for her life. Then, her husband was transferred to a rural farm community. As her family transitioned from city to country life, she shared that while she had hopes and dreams for her writing, she realized just how small she was when she moved to a town where Bingo was much more popular than blogs. As they adjusted to their new lives, she asked her husband, "How can we be a light to this city?"

For Laura, the answer was a community website that hosted information about local events, commerce meetings, and updates from the community school and civic groups. Laura used her gifts of writing not for her own name's sake but to connect her small town to one centralized site with useful information. Laura says that she decided to live where her feet, hands, and heart resided instead of trying to build a community of people that she might never get to meet face-to-face.

Sitting in my seat, I pulled my scarf tighter around my neck. Laura was speaking my language, and she renewed my hope that we had made the right choice to move. So often, people relocate to cities for work, schools, or entertainment. We moved home because we loved the people who call our city home. Even though the faces had changed, we still felt a pull inside of us to pour our lives back into the people who live in Dothan. After leaving Laura's session and also on the plane ride home, I wondered, "What does our community need that we have to offer?"

During the conference, Raleigh packed up the last of our personal items in Montgomery and moved us into a rental house in Dothan. The house sat on a corner lot in a wooded neighborhood just a few minutes away from my parents' house. The light over the back deck was on, and I clunked my suitcase full of clothes and books up a flight of stairs to enter through the laundry room door. Opening the door, I was greeted by our dog, Obi, who had been keeping Raleigh company in Montgomery the past five months. I bent down and pulled him in close, smiling as his tail wagged furiously back and forth.

A room that we will use as an office was located beside the laundry room, and a hallway to the left led me into our kitchen. It's dated with Formica countertops and flowered wallpaper, but our dishes had already been placed inside the cabinets. Walking through a doorway, I found our master bedroom and bath. Our pale blue bedding was so welcoming that I dropped my suitcase and sat on the edge of the bed, soaking in the reality that we finally had a home in Dothan. Without delay, two sets of feet came bursting through my door. Adeline and Maralee were in their princess pajamas, and their hair was still in pigtails. Shrieking with delight, they tackled me with their love, and we fell backward on the bed. Raleigh walked in and jumped on top of us, making the girls laugh even harder. Lying on our paisley duvet cover, I smelled the girls' skin, still baby soft, and Raleigh's Dial soap all intermingled with my wrinkly just-off-the-plane scent. Looking at my husband, I saw that his eyes shone bright.

We were a family again.

The next day, I found it shocking when he pulled into our driveway at five-thirty. We began to make a new routine in the Wood House, with me parking inside the garage and him, the side drive. After dinner, we loaded the girls into the buggy and walked the dogs down the road to feed the ducks in the pond. We laughed as Obi chased after the geese and watched as they flapped their wings and quacked at him for disturbing the peaceful water. It's on these walks that we let each other in on our days. As we looped around the pond and turn the buggy toward home, I said, "So, I've been thinking . . . "

"Uh-oh," Raleigh teased. I nudged him with my shoulder before I continued, "I've been thinking that now is a good time to start a small group."

Pausing, I glanced in his direction. He nodded, giving me courage to go on. "I know our house isn't much to boast about, but with you being home and all, this might be a way we can get to know some new people."

"Who do you want to invite?" he asked.

"Well," I paused as I passed Maralee her sippy cup, "there are a few moms I met during VBS. They have kids our age. And, we could ask some of your soccer buddies. You guys haven't gotten to hang out much since you've been back. Maybe some of the girls I work with too? I don't know, I'm sure we can come up with some names."

Glancing at him, I could see he agreed with me. A "yay!" bubbled out of me and the rest of the evening I daydreamed about our new group. The following day I typed out an e-mail to a handful of people from church. Pressing send, I silently prayed that God would send us just the right people for our group.

A week later, we tossed unopened boxes into closets and sprayed Febreze throughout the house. The girls kept dragging toys from the third bedroom that we've converted into a playroom down the stairs, forcing me to walk up and down more times than I could count. Raleigh turned on iTunes as I set out some finger food on my borrowed dining room table. I'd made pumpkin brownies and had spiced apple cider warming on the stove. Heavy 1980s drapes framed the table, and tan shag carpet was thick under our feet. I was moving at hyperactive speed, placing flowers in a vase beside the kitchen sink and lighting some candles on the fireplace mantle. I knew our guests would see the maroon and hunter green flowered wallpaper first, but I hoped these few personal touches would stand out against the dated décor. I wasn't sure who, exactly, was coming, but I placed an extra roll of toilet paper in the bathroom just in case.

Tonight, I'm dressed in my dark jeans, flats, and a Piko top. I decided at the last minute to add a statement necklace and run through some perfume. I can't stand it when a hostess douses herself in perfume and dresses fancier than all her guests. It's like she's saying, "Smell me! Look at me! Welcome to my home, but PLEASE DON'T TOUCH ANYTHING!" Or, something like that. Tonight, a little spritz covers up the perspiration that lines the underwire of my bra. Personally, I like to see a home just a tad bit messy. The toys stacked in the corner make me feel like I'm at home, and I'd much rather hang with a girl who dresses up just enough to let you know that it's a special occasion, but not over the top glitzy to the point where I look at her and immediately want to turn around and get back in my car because I'm underdressed.

Having people in your home for the first time is like playing matchmaker. When you invite people who might not know each other, it always helps to know a little bit of background about each of your guests so you can introduce them to others with a lead-in conversation starter. It's the hostess's mistletoe and a way to quickly rid the room of awkwardness. (Of course, a bottle of wine works wonders too!) Putting a drink of any kind, really, in someone's hands immediately helps us not cross our arms or nervously pull at our hair. Instead, we feel like adults, having adult conversation, holding a glass in one hand and using our other to tell stories.

I've found that there's always someone who has the party laugh. You know, the athletic guy with an even bigger belly laugh, or the friend you can hear talking from across the room, and there's always the tiny one with the falsetto that surprises you with her humor. The laugh comes out early sometimes to hide their nervousness, but if it's a good party, the single laugh turns into a chorus that can bring tears into your eyes.

I'm one of those people who can't eat and talk at the same time. Hard as I try, I can never swallow my food fast enough. If I'm hosting, I'm always the last to eat, but sometimes that works well because everyone else has already settled into their corners, and I don't feel like my guests are looking to me for direction. I always make Raleigh start the food line because everyone is trying their darnedest to be polite. He's my wingman at parties, especially like the one we are hosting tonight. As the doorbell rings, he makes the introductions first, and then I hug necks as I shoo them into the den. A little past six, we've got six couples and a few singles in our den. The kids grab the cookies off the table, and we hear them jumping up and down upstairs. Raleigh's a natural storyteller, and I've had a lot of practice rolling my eyes at his jokes, so we begin jesting about our retro home and the recent move. We know it's not beautiful, and this helps us not to be apologetic about our amenities.

So often I will visit a friend's home and the first thing she does is point out everything that she wants to change. I've done this plenty of times myself. It's not that we are embarrassed or ungrateful for our homes, but we want you to know that we know there are updates to be made, and one day we will get to them (we can even show you our *For the Home* Pinterest board). Somehow, praise Jesus, my thankfulness for having a home to entertain in outweighs any shame I would have normally felt. As I share how easy my pumpkin brownie recipe is and laugh with Raleigh about our home, I can't help but think that this is *exactly* what we can offer to our community. It's not much, but it's so much more than we ever knew we needed.

We've been meeting together now for four months. Some Wednesdays, we meet in the church, other times we come back to the Wood House or go out to eat. For most, this is their first small group to be part of, which makes me feel honored but also responsible for helping them grow spiritually, which can weigh heavy on my and Raleigh's hearts after meetings. We sit in a circle, and I love to see what kind of socks Jeff chooses to wear. He usually comes straight from work in his business suit, but he always has on fun socks. Tonight, they are navy with lime green polka dots. Sarah sits beside me and shares openly with the group; her transparency is admirable. Andi is across from me and always brings her Bible, journal, and planner with her to group. I've already decided she's in charge of birthdays and keeping up with prayer requests. Allison and Melissa, along with their husbands, complete the circle. Our conversation this night is on the topic of discipleship. Raleigh clears his throat and opens the evening by asking, "Why is discipleship so important to Jesus?"

Quickly, we find out who reads the book (mostly the teachers) and who shows up for discussion on Wednesday night (usually their husbands). The back-and-forth banter is like a ping pong match, and I never know who's going to have the winning thought that leaves us all speechless. Andi flips to a section she had underlined in the book and shares that as a teacher, she sees discipleship as a way to teach others to learn about Christ, how this is our call. Others nod their heads. Sarah's husband, still in his work clothes from servicing cars, is sitting in his chair with one leg crossed at the knee. I can tell he's thinking of his response. When the conversation lulls, he states, "Yeah, but we aren't all teachers. I don't feel like I can tell somebody about Jesus when I'm still learning about Him myself, you know?"

"What do you think?" He glances toward Raleigh and me. "Why would someone that I barely know listen to *me* talk about discipleship?"

We glance at one another, trying to decide who would speak first.

"They'd listen if you invited them here." I look him in the eyes before continuing. "I agree with Andi, discipleship is about teaching others to follow Christ. But . . . I think to answer your original question," I glance back at Raleigh, "discipleship was so important to Jesus because He was all about relationships. It's a lot easier to understand Scripture and how it transforms us individually when you can study it in community. I know it is for me, anyway."

I stop talking then, and we move on to the next question. Could they see the way my face blushed as I spoke, how I was speaking about them, to them? How they had come, expecting us to teach, when it is they who were teaching us?

We've decided to meet each week. At least once a month we have a social. Our favorite place for socials is a Mexican restaurant close to the church, and we always sit girls on one end of the table and guys on the other.

One time, the group surprised Raleigh and me with a gift. I unwrapped it at the table and found a distressed cross. It was unexpected but so very thoughtful, and I've placed it in our office as a sweet reminder that God heard my prayers. These socials are just as important, if not more important, to the vitality of our group because it's on these nights that we learn about the best brand of dry shampoo to purchase and other items of very important nature.

When we are in between studies or can just tell it's been a really hard week, we don't open our Bibles right away. Sometimes, we simply ask how we can pray for one another. Allison surprises me and speaks up first. Reaching toward her husband's hand, she openly confesses how they've had to change their lifestyle now that they've moved back to Dothan. Melissa begins to cry, and I notice Sarah dab her eyes on the other side of the room. We all get it, the struggle of provision and guilt, and let her talk. One by one, we go around the room. Some have exciting things to pray about, like a new job or pregnancy, while others are going through the unspoken struggles, like Allison. Even though we wrestle with different circumstances, it's apparent that we are one and the same. We all need God to hear our prayers.

The beauty of being with these people every week is I get to see all sides of their personalities. We let each other in, revealing secrets and sweet surprises. Our friendship isn't forced; it's forged together by showing up and sharing openly. To me, it's the best kind, and without our Wednesdays, I don't know what I would do.

A renovation might serve the Wood House well, but it wouldn't feel quite the same. Its bold floral wallpaper, heavy drapes, and shag carpet brought our small group together, and even if the interiors never change, I know that I have. Into the community I have been called, but the call was not for me alone.

Chapter 12:

CHRISTMAS

{HOW TO HAVE IT ALL}

This is the month, and this the happy morn
Wherein the son of Heaven's eternal King,
Of wedded maid and virgin mother born,
Our great redemption from above did bring;
For so the holy sages once did sing,
That he our deadly forfeit should release,
And with his Father work us a perpetual peace.

~ John Milton, "On the Morning of Christ's Nativity"

I'VE ALWAYS WONDERED HOW OTHER women seem to have it all together. I watch them with envy, balancing work and motherhood, family and friends, all while throwing Pinterest-perfect parties in their Pinterest-perfect homes. These women never seem to struggle with finding community, they just naturally *belong*. I'm sure they made friends the minute they moved to town and adapted to the pace of their work with ease. When they weren't working or planning birthday parties, they were having quiet time and training for a half marathon. These women were the quintessential Proverbs 31 woman, whose worth was far more than rubies. But the expectation they set leaves us always feeling like we don't quite measure up.

As women, our struggle to have it all usually begins with the state of our hearts. Ever since we were little girls, we've been dreaming of our perfect lives. We set out to make our dreams come true by chasing after what we *know* will make us happy—a good job, someone to love, a place to call home—and believe that if we are good enough and try hard enough and are pretty enough, then we will actually *be* enough. This is a classic good-girl story, but the part that always seems to be glossed over in the storybooks is the side-effects of striving. The story continually seems to say, "If you get what you want, you will be happy." But this really isn't true, is it? Even the women who seem to have it all always want more. I read a statistic recently that over 45.8% of people struggle with stress and time to relax. Our hearts are unsettled, pumping so fast and hard to keep up the pace that we miss out on joy.

I thought of this while I was in the kitchen, watching my girls play with the leaves that had fallen on our back porch. Adeline picked up a handful and dumped them into the play kitchen, causing Maralee to double over in shrieks of giggles. Back and forth they played in the afternoon sun as I sat at the small wooden table, organizing my calendar. With only a month left in the year, I had lists for presents to buy, work to do, and parties to attend. It was our first Christmas not having to travel home for the holidays, but it was also my first Christmas working in a church.

December became a blur as we prepared for the Children's Christmas Eve service. My team single-handedly put up two gigantic artificial

Christmas trees, which was like wrestling a lion, and then decorated the trees with bright fuchsia, lime green, and turquoise balls from Hobby Lobby. We turned our fellowship hall lobby into a winter wonderland with hundreds of paper snowflakes hanging at various heights from the ceiling. We covered the walls with white paper and the floors with fake snow, and we painted the window panes with frost. As the children walked through the winter wonderland, they passed through a forest of Dr. Seuss topsy-turvy trees that were light pink with glitter, and then they walked into the great hall where they could decorate their own Christmas cookies for Santa and drink hot cocoa. At the foot of the stage were over fifty brightly colored presents (with bows!) stacked on top of one another, and on the walls of the fellowship hall, we'd cut out and painted gigantic ornaments and hung them, along with six-foot-tall wreaths, to complete the Christmas ensemble. For more than a week, we'd stayed late going over the skit and the timing of the production with the band. Once Christmas Eve finally arrived, I was at the church by two-thirty, going over last-minute details before the program began at four. As families began to pour into the church, children would point their fingers up, begging to touch the snowflakes with wonder on their little faces. Others headed straight for the cookies and cocoa, and soon the table was littered with marshmallows and crumbs. The band walked onstage wearing Santa hats, and the room echoed the sounds of "Joy to the World." The skit went smoothly, and the real live baby Jesus slept during the entire performance. After the final song, families filed out of the fellowship hall to the parking lot to meet their relatives for dinner and an evening of opening presents. A few volunteers stayed, and we cleaned up the last of the marshmallows. After weeks of planning, the program was over in under an hour.

I slipped into the candlelight service in the sanctuary just in time to hear the soloist sing "O Holy Night." She stood in the middle of the stage, wearing a simple black jumpsuit, and the light shining down on her blonde curls made her look like an angel. Before she hit the peak of the song, she crooned about the weary world rejoicing because a new and glorious beginning was about to happen. Captivated, I felt the ancient words grab my heart, begging me to listen. The rhythm of my days was to plan, prepare, perform, produce, and then repeat. Now, at the end of a year of unrelenting change, I felt a tiny question begin to rise within me, asking, "Where's the joy?"

I didn't have an answer.

I knew my joy should have come from serving and teaching, but I felt only the weariness spoken of in this song. So much work went into the events, and suddenly they were over. It hurt, because I knew that I shouldn't have felt this way, but I couldn't deny this quiet confession. My heart swelled that night, as if it knew that the best gift I could receive this Christmas was accepting the fact that I could not continue trying to do it all.

That's how it is with Christmas, isn't it? We dash into the season with all the hope of a child sitting on Santa's lap, but by the end of it, we've allowed all the hustle and bustle to steal our focus, making us forget why we celebrate. Between the decorating and the presents and the full calendar, we spend so much time trying to make the most of the season that by Christmas Eve, we just want to put our feet up and say *adios* to all the merry and brightness. But, if we are parents, the fun is just beginning. Because the holidays are all about us wanting our kids to have the best memories of Christmas, we hide the Elf on the Shelf, eat the cookies left on Santa's plate, and plan when we are opening presents with both sides of the family and who we will eat with on Christmas Day. We stay up late, putting bicycles together and laying baby dolls in cribs, stacking presents on either side of the fireplace mantel so the next morning when the kids come tumbling down the stairs, they will each have their own pile to open. Once our children rip through the packages with their names on it in under five minutes, we look around our living rooms full of stuff and wrapping paper and realize that after over a month of planning, Christmas has come to an end. By this point, all we really want is a nap, but it's time to play with the new toys, and in an hour we've got to get dressed and head to Nana's for lunch.

Once again, our hearts silently ask but never speak out loud, "Where's the joy?"

If it's true that 45.8% of people struggle with stress and time to relax, I'm sure that percentage almost doubles during the holiday season. We are all either shopping for the perfect gift or are working at the store in which the perfect gift is to be found. We are the Doorbusters, Black Friday crazies, or Last-minute Laurens, but everywhere we go, we stand in line (except on Amazon Prime, praise the Lord!) just so we can buy one more thing to make one more person happy. Around and around we chase after the illusion of having it all, only to rack up debt, one small swipe at a time.

Having it all is a lie.[45]

Presents under the tree might make our kids happy, but it is so very temporary. If this is how we are going to spend Christmas after Christmas, chasing the storybook cliché of chestnuts roasting on an open fire, we miss the joy every single year. But, when we can stop and recognize the holiness of the night and put ourselves in the smelly manger surrounded by animals, we can see the work of God, not only in the story but also in our own lives. Because God draws us into His presence in the most unexpected and unconventional ways, we become silent in the night, waiting for the first cry of a child coming out of his mother's womb so that we might be delivered from discontent.

Mary did not have it all, but she did have it all.

I'm not sure where Jesus' crib bedding came from or what her friends bought from her registry or if she even had a baby shower, but Mary understood what was important in life and what wasn't worth worrying about. Mary had to let go of her ideal version of her life when she first found out she was pregnant. She had to remember that the whispers of the townspeople were lies as she walked with her head held high and a hint of a baby bump along the dusty Nazarene streets. Mary didn't have the dream wedding, and I'm sure she quickly found out who her true friends were after her pregnancy was made public. Instead of comparing her life to the other women, she celebrated.

While receiving guests who gazed on her newborn son, Mary was weary from labor but wore the look of a girl who knew that this moment would be forever marked by time. Luke tells us that as shepherds shouted and wise men brought gifts, she "treasured these things in her heart." Mary filled her soul by storing up the simple. She believed that, against all odds, she was worthy of the name "mother" to a little boy who was destined to deliver us.

God gives us babies to change hearts.

When Pharaoh was oppressing the Israelites and throwing every boy that was born into the Nile, Moses was born. He was delivered from death and grew up as the son of Pharaoh's daughter, only to one day lead the Israelites out of Egypt.

After Naomi's husband and sons died, she returned to Bethlehem as a bitter woman. But her daughter-in-law, Ruth, had hope, which caught the attention of her kinsman-redeemer, Boaz. Soon they married and had a child, Obed, who was the father of Jesse, the father of David. Naomi took the child, laid him in her lap, and cared for him, no longer bitter, but pleasant and at peace.

God ultimately delivered us with the birth of Jesus. He delivered us from discontent, depression, and disappointment by giving the world a child, a tiny, baby boy, who depended on his mother to care for and nurture him. He grew up and experienced what any man experiences—love, laughter, sadness, anger. Jesus was just like us, but he was different. Jesus consistently shocked the Jews with His actions, turning all of their laws and practices upside down. As He called men like Matthew to be His disciple, He'd dine with both tax collectors and "sinners." When asked why He would choose to live life among such vast scopes of people, He said, "It is not the healthy who need a doctor, but the sick. But go and learn what this means: 'I desire mercy, not sacrifice.' For I have not come to call the righteous, but sinners" (Matthew 9:12–13 NIV).

The ways of Jesus surprised the supposedly righteous Pharisees, making them question every expectation they had perceived of the Son of God. Jesus was a wrecking ball, tearing down the false teachings so that the prophecies would be fulfilled. His kingdom came from his birth in a manger, and He devastated us with His love when he chose to die for us thirty-three years later.

Yes, babies change us. Will we, too, be like Mary and treasure these things in our hearts?

To treasure means to remember. I want to remember these years of working and raising little ones not just as a time when I am always juggling and trying to have it all, but as a time where I can remember how tiny pieces of dried leaves stuck to Adeline and Maralee's pigtails as they played on the back porch before Daddy came home for dinner. I want to remember their sweet prayers to Jesus before bedtime and how what we wanted most this year for Christmas was to feel like we were finally home. I want us to remember what is important in this temporary life and what is not.

A word that is commonly used during the Christmas season is *believe*. Being a mother of little girls, I'm guilty of treating them to secular experiences like sitting on Santa's lap and singing about Rudolph the Red-nosed Reindeer, but we also talk a lot about Jesus and how His birth brought life to our world. They don't quite get it yet, and I chuckle as they confuse Santa's "ho, ho, ho's" with "Hosanna," but my hope is that with time and understanding, they will believe in so much more than a man who eats cookies after he kisses momma underneath the mistletoe. Not only do I want our girls to believe that God sent His Son to be born of the Virgin Mary, but I desperately want them to believe that because Jesus was born to deliver them, they are worthy and good enough to be called His sisters. They don't have to chase after contentment; it is there, ready for them to receive.

It's the simple things, like a soloist singing *O Holy Night* on a stage, that make me believe there is joy to receive even when we are weary. Galatians 6:9 reminds us of this, urging us not to grow weary in doing good, for at the proper time we will reap the harvest if we do not give up. This joy does not come from chasing the American Dream, filling our living room with gifts that last only for a season, or even from planning Christmas Eve programs. This joy comes from something greater than anything man can create. Without Christ, we are like trees on stands, stunning for a moment but soon withering away. But, when we receive Christ into our hearts, we are given hope. Perhaps we need to give up the things that aren't good for us so that we don't give up in doing good.

When we focus outwardly on trying to have everything that the world says we must have to be happy and fulfilled, we are only putting discontentment into our hearts. Discontentment drains us, and we find ourselves with our cups turned up, begging for just one more drop. One can never fully experience joy with a discontented heart. But, if our hearts are a well, it means that they can be a source of something original and bountiful and good. Instead of always running the race like the woman on the Target commercials training for her shopping spree, what if we put things into our lives that brought us hope?

Hope is our something more, and it's a promise we don't have to chase. If our heart is the center of our being, fueling our minds and storing up treasures, we must try to protect it so it can keep producing this life-giving freedom. Proverbs 4:23 encourages us to guard our heart above all else because it is the wellspring of life. Guarding our hearts begins when we can accept that having it all is an illusion. Those women that we compare ourselves to, the ones who seem to have it all? They are figments of our imagination. They leave us weary and worried that they've discovered some secret to contentment that we have not yet been given. But they haven't. The women who "have it all" are struggling too, but we don't see it the same way they do. We *all* need to give ourselves more grace for what we are doing instead of feeling not good enough.

If you struggle with contentment too, give grace to yourself for Christmas this year. Grace could look a lot like rest or gratefulness for what you do have. Grace might be about pausing to see the beauty of the holidays—the twinkling lights, snowflakes on the windowsill, or children sound asleep in their footed reindeer pajamas. In the book of Psalms, a common word seen before a passage of Scripture is the word *selah*, which means to pause. Christmas is meant to be selah time, giving us whitespace to believe in miracles and to celebrate that we *do* have it all—we have been given the gift of grace and the hope of heaven—and this is simply enough for our worn and weary souls.

Joy blossoms from grace, giving you and me energy to enjoy the season. Contentment is found when we allow thankfulness to pump from our heart into our veins and arteries. In the *Celebration of Discipline,* Richard Foster says this about joy: "If we fill our lives with simple good things and constantly thank God for them, we will be joyful, that is, full of joy." Thanking God is how Mary stayed content, and this is how we too can live full of joy. Daily, God gives us simple, good gifts, and when we can recognize the blessing, our hearts don't stray as quickly into the temptation that more is better. Instead, we pause and remember that the greatest gift of the world came as an infant so that we might have it all.

Chapter 13:

TEA PARTY

{FOR THE MOM WHO NEEDS A CUP OF GRACE}

Manners are a sensitive awareness of the feelings of others. If you have that awareness, you have good manners, no matter what fork you use.

~ Emily Post

6:00 A.M. – INSTEAD OF getting out of bed, I hit *snooze* on my alarm for fifteen more minutes. My sheets are soft and my bed is deliciously warm. The twins are still silent in their room just down the hall. Staying in bed for a little bit longer won't hurt, will it?

6:15 a.m. – The guitar strums for me to get up, but I feel like I've been super-glued to my bed. Inside my head, I hear the words, *"Get up, get up, get up,"* but my body wills itself to stay under the sheets. I hit *snooze* just one more time.

6:45 a.m. – Adeline busts through the door with her hair knotted like a bird's nest on top of her head, asking for juice and an episode of Mickey. Looking at the clock, I realize what time it is and break from my morning slumber to finally get up and get going. Slipping my feet into my slippers, I reach for my glasses on the nightstand only to knock over books that I'd left too close to the corner. Suddenly, I realize that not only do I need to tinkle, but we are already running behind schedule for the day. Throwing myself out of the bed, I pad down the hallway to pour Lucky Charms into bowls. Maralee is awake now and asks for her yellow blanket as she sits at the bar. Now it's 7:00, and I'm fully aware that today is Tea Party Day at school, and we are running late.

Tea Party is a highlight of our preschool program, and the girls have been talking about it all week. It's a time for the kids to not only learn about the letter "T" but also to show their parents how they've learned to use their manners. We've had it circled on our calendar for months now, and last night we picked out their tea party outfits. Adeline chose a pink linen dress, while Maralee preferred the baby blue, and as accessories they begged to wear their flower sun hats, princess shoes, and plastic pearl necklaces. Oh, and they each picked out a purse. (How can we not have a purse?!) With Raleigh being away on a business trip, I went to bed confident that I could get the girls ready by myself the next morning. But now, after ignoring my alarm, I'm throwing my hair into a ponytail and applying mascara with one hand as I pull jeans over my legs with the other. I look like a hot mess, so not ready to have tea.

After breakfast, I scoot the girls into their bathroom to brush their teeth and comb their hair. No matter how hard I try, I can't get the tangles out of Adeline's wild mane. She throws a sassy remark my way, screaming as I pull down with the brush. Maralee is beside her sister, refusing to brush her teeth. My heart picks up its pace, so I give them their first warning: "Girls, I need you to work with me."

We finish up in the bathroom and head to the second round of our morning routine of getting dressed. There is no time to make up beds after I throw their fancy dresses over their heads. One twin immediately whines and stomps her foot, telling me her tag is itchy, while the other begins to sob that her shoes hurt. The clock in their bedroom says 7:55, and I know that if we don't leave in the next five minutes, we will miss the party. Instead of being sympathetic to their problems, I become a drill sergeant, clapping my hands to get them to focus on me and not their first world problems. They look at me in confusion with their big blue eyes, but I press forward, telling them we must hurry if we want to make it to the party.

My first order of business is to cut the itchy tag out of the dress. Once I calm that child down, I firmly tell the other to wear another pair of shoes. She protests. I raise my voice, trying to be an authority figure, but as I hear myself speak, I cringe at my tone. After all, it wasn't their fault that we were running late. If only I had gotten up after my first alarm, we would have at least had enough time to fix these problems without so much drama. But the snoozing has thrown us all into a state of hysteria, and our hormones are raging against one another. Pointing my arm toward the door, I say, "Let's go. NOW."

Why can I plan events for three hundred people but can't get the three of us dressed and out the door before eight in the morning? Angry words toward my children are not my pleasure. As much as I try to hold my tongue, I continue to battle the inevitable breakdown that comes from running late. Knowing I shouldn't blame them, I do it anyway, and I feel incredibly guilty afterward.

We careen into the parking lot just when the party begins at 8:30. The shoes on one twin are still uncomfortable, and it is then that I realize I forgot to bring them an extra pair to change into after the party. Fail again. She's crying, so *not* in the tea party mood either, and we stop in the midway just to catch our breath for a moment. I kneel and wipe away the tears that stain her sweet face, recognizing that she wasn't just upset about her shoes. She wanted today to be perfect, just like me, and our tardiness was causing all of us to miss the whole point of the tea party—treating one another with respect. I offer my apology and a huge hug, and then we walk into the building, late but together.

Inside, the four-year-old hall has huge banners hanging from the ceilings—like one would find in a castle—with hand-painted teapots and the letter T. The outside of each classroom is set up like a child's tea party with stuffed animals sitting at tables with tea cups. It is fantastically over the top and special. Inside, the children's tables are set with a yellow laminated place mat, white paper doilies, and flowers at the center. We were the last ones to arrive, of course, but I find a place in the corner and send the girls to their seats.

For the party, their precious teacher leads all the children in a rhyme at the front of the classroom about their manners, and then they sing "I'm a Little Teapot." It is at this time that I realize I forgot my camera and my iPhone, so I just watch instead of document this sweet moment. My girls give me a smile and thumbs up. I'm relieved that they are enjoying themselves and have forgotten our getting-ready debacle. After the songs, the boys take the girls by the hand and pull their seats out for them to sit at the table. Once the children are all in their seats, they eat bright strawberries, sweet sugar cookies, and tiny pinwheel sandwiches from their plates. I kneel beside my girls, and they ask me if I am proud. Pulling them in close, I whisper in their ears, "Always."

Time: it seems as if there is never enough of it. We set alarms, pick out clothes, plan ahead, but we can't predict the days that time won't be on our side. Waking up late, we feel like the racehorse that got a bad start out of the gate, and now we are chasing dust, trying to catch up.

Whether we are moms rushing our children to school or professionals on a deadline, we all have our moments when we feel like the rabbit in *Alice in Wonderland*, yelling, "I'm late, I'm late, I'm late for a very important date. No time to say hello, good-bye, I'm late, I'm late, I'm late!" Running behind schedule not only causes us to miss out on important events but also causes us to feel internally frustrated or makes others be frustrated with us.

If the root of manners is to have a sensitive awareness to those around us, we can once again apply Emily Post's etiquette rule of four S's (sincerity, simplicity, sympathy, and serenity) to our daily living. Our goal is to not only be sincere hostesses at social events but also at home with our families. When we wake up on time, we can have more meaningful talks with our family members before our school and work days begin. We can be sincere during the conversation and stay calm instead of rushed with our words.

What is essential for us to spend our time on each day, and what needs to be eliminated? Studies show that there are seven different types of people who run late, but most people fall into the top three categories: The Deadliner, The Producer, and The Absent-Minded

Professor. The Deadliner likes the thrill of rushing and often waits until the last minute to begin a project. The Producer crams just one more thing into her schedule, always trying to make the most of her time. Finally, The Absent-Minded Professor is easily distracted, whether it is from attention deficit disorder or flakiness.[46]

As someone who identifies with The Producer, I tend to jam pack my day with just one more thing to complete, which in turn causes me to rush. If I instead choose simplicity, I would focus on one thing—my statement piece—instead of many things. In return, living simply will help me fill my time with the people and projects that matter most, leaving me more fulfilled and happy with my work and home life.

Sympathy and compassion are rooted in biblical hospitality and were direct influences of Jesus' ministry. As Jesus headed to Jerusalem to attend a feast, He stopped at the Pool of Bethesda, where the blind, lame, and paralyzed gathered. Jesus met a man who had been lying near the pool for thirty-eight years, hoping for healing but not receiving it because no one would help him into the pool. Theologians remark that the man did not know who Jesus was and was so focused on getting into the pool to be healed that he had no faith. But Jesus healed him anyway, telling him to "Stand up! Pick up your mat, and walk" (John 5:8).

While we need to be like Jesus and show sympathy toward those incapable of helping themselves, we also need to ask ourselves a very important question: Do we want to get well? "People who are chronically late are often wrestling with anxiety, distraction, ambivalence, or other internal psychological states," says Pauline Wallin, Ph.D., a psychologist in Camp Hill, Pennsylvania.[47] Before we can show sympathy to others, we've got to get to a place where our hearts and minds are well. If we can grow closer to Christ during our own times of ailment, we can better understand and encourage our family while they endure difficulties.

Celebration is a spiritual discipline that comes after we have learned to practice serenity through prayer, meditation, and fasting. When we have clear minds and peace instead of anxiousness within, we are able to exude the sophistication of simplicity, add comfort instead of commotion in times of sympathy, and speak evil of no one. Serenity is about being in a place where we can give God our anxious thoughts and believe that He will make all things work together for the good of those who love Him. Serenity is a unified state of the mind, heart, and soul. To become more serene, we can take a deep breath before we feel an outburst bubble within us. We can walk away from the problem to cool down. Serenity is a deliberate action that begins within but affects those around us significantly.

You know what always makes me feel better on the days that I mess up? Knowing that I'm not the only one who ever makes a mistake. I'm not the only mama who needs fifteen more minutes of sleep, applies her mascara in the car at the red light, and forgets her kid's extra pair of shoes to slip on after the tea party. I'm a mama who needs grace, and I bet you are too.

We try so hard to do this thing called motherhood perfectly, but daily we fail. Sometimes we fail big, and other times we fail small, but you know what saves us each and every time?

Grace.

Mamas need grace, each and every day. Grace comes in the form of hugs, "I'm sorry," and "let's start over." Kindness stemming from grace covers a multitude of mess-ups and is a true reflection of the heart. Words associated with grace are gifts, favor, benefit, blessing, gratitude, and thankfulness. To love and be loved, grace has to be part of our family's vocabulary.

Receiving grace is another reminder for me to let go of perfectionism and be found perfect in Christ. Jesus understands my struggles with tardiness and temper, and He too gives me grace, favor, benefit. Mostly, He gives me rest, which I so desperately need. Motherhood is a constant movement of getting our children from one place to another on time, dressed, and happy.

While grateful for the busyness, we need time to rest physically, emotionally, and mentally so that we can be moms who break down from exhaustion less. Grace is something that God desires for us to have so that we will not live in the darkness of our failures. Grace is why God gave us Jesus, so that through Him, we are forgiven, loved, and can move on with our days with no more guilt.

Not having mommy guilt changes things, doesn't it? Motherhood is full of seasons, and each one is filled with special occasions. There will come a time when my house no longer has little girls looking forward to their school tea party. Instead, they will be girls getting ready for first dates, graduation, and marriage. I want to hope that as my girls grow and experience different life events, we can celebrate these events with our imperfections covered in grace and gratitude. Joy, not guilt, is what Jesus desires for us to have in our hearts. I'd much rather be a mom who is imperfect, but covered in grace, so that she can experience joy, don't you?

Grace is a lot like manners. The Greek word for *grace*, "charis," references people who use words with gracefulness and elegance, such as when Paul encourages us to not use foul words or abusive language, instead "let everything you say be good and helpful, so that your words will be an encouragement to those who hear them" (Ephesians 4:29).

The best way to stop an outburst before it happens is similar to our efforts to stop being so tardy: we've got to set non-negotiable boundaries. Again in Colossians Paul writes, "Let your speech always be gracious, seasoned with salt, so that you may know how you ought to answer each person" (Colossians 4:6 ESV). To show kindness instead of anger, a good idea is to come up with a list of choices/responses that we can refer to before the time of event. For example, if running late causes me to yell at my children, I could instead choose to use humor or let my children know that I am angry.[48] Instead of making a rational choice in the moment, I have my non-negotiable choices ready to reference during heated moments.

Women who truly amaze me have the gift of being gracious with their words as well as using their words to influence others. To be able to control our outbursts, we can teach those around us—our children, our coworkers, our friends, or family—how to be charming and add wit to a conversation. Salt not only stings an open wound but also adds flavor to the food it is poured onto.

Being on time and kind with our words is both a social courtesy and an indicator of women who have overcome anxiety from within. Self-control and setting boundaries will take practice, much like learning to use our manners. When we apply these steps to our daily routines, we are no longer the flustered rabbit, but women with elegance and poise.

Being late to the tea party taught my girls and me something that we'll never forget: kindness far outweighs timeliness. I can't guarantee that we will never be late again, but I have made an effort to be gentler with my words, especially on our most-rushed mornings. We've made some small changes to our schedule, but we've made some big changes to the disposition of our hearts. We respect each other more with our words and our actions, and we continue to give grace, one cup at a time.

To have good manners is the mark of a woman who cares deeply about her people, a way to show them just how much they matter to us. While etiquette is a set of behavior rules you can memorize like a map, manners are much more, since they are an expression from the heart on how to treat others.[49] Let us show good manners to others by applying the four S's, becoming women who are sensitive to the needs of those around us, and giving ourselves grace on the days that just aren't going our way.

Who's ready for some tea?

Chapter 14:

FUNERALS

Even the darkest night will end and the sun will rise.

~ Les Misérables

OUR MONTGOMERY HOUSE HAS BEEN on the market for a year, and I'm beginning to think that we will live in the Wood House forever. All winter, I've been wrestling with questions unanswered. I've paced the floors of this old house, leaving imprints on the carpet. Raleigh and I stay up past midnight, and the questions become a battleground as we aim and fire and then hold up apologetic white flags. We switch realtors, re-stage furniture, and paint the walls a neutral beige. Henry from small group suggests we bury a St. Joseph statue in our backyard. I type that into a search engine and find one that can be delivered to my door for $1.99. Another friend encourages me to pray for the future owner of our home. I'm at the point where I'm beginning to lose hope, leaving me again with more questions than answers.

Why doesn't anyone want to buy our house?

When will we get to move and where will we move to?

Why are you, GOD, not making this happen?

My question to God lingers a bit longer than the rest. This move to Dothan was a desire He had planted in our hearts. Wasn't it? I don't even know anymore. If He wanted us to move home, why has every step been so difficult? Nothing has happened as I had planned, and I keep finding myself unearthed from my ideas of what life was supposed to look like. More questions come. Was this a punishment? Have we disobeyed? Where do we go from here?

I drop to my knees on a Saturday morning and begin to wail. I'm angry by this point, and with no one in the house except for me and my dog, I yell at God, "THIS. IS. NOT. FAIR!!!!" It wasn't supposed to be like this, and I couldn't handle not knowing when the end would come. I wanted our house to sell—yesterday—so we could move somewhere, anywhere else, just so I didn't have to stare at the Pepto-Bismol floral wallpaper any longer. Didn't God get it?

At the end of myself, I rock back on my legs so I can steady my breath. Breathing in, I'm reminded of the passage of Scripture that I can't seem to get out of my head. It's from Romans, when Paul reminds us that suffering produces perseverance; perseverance, character; and character, hope. Before this, he retells how God promised Abraham that he would be the father of all nations, but Abraham had to wait until he was a hundred years old to see that promise fulfilled by the birth of his son Isaac. Against all hope, Abraham in hope believed. Paul goes on to write, "He did not waver through unbelief regarding the promise of God, but was strengthened in his faith and gave glory to God, being fully persuaded that God had power to do what he had promised" (Romans 4:20–21 NIV). Through his waiting, Abraham's faith grew stronger. Yes, he had to suffer, but he persevered, believing that the promise God gave him would come by faith and by grace.

Perhaps God is asking me to wait. Is He asking you to wait too?

Something shifts after my argument with God. It's subtle, and I don't even notice it until a few weeks later. I still have questions, but like Abraham, I begin to believe again in the sound promise that hope brings. Our move had not happened as I expected it to, but the waiting season began to draw me into a quiet communion with God. I'd return to the same spot in the house where I'd argued with Him weeks earlier and kneel on a bench. In the corner, I kept a stack of books on prayer, and some days I would read those prayers aloud. Other times, I'd sit there in silence. On the wall above the bench, I placed a cork board. With brightly colored tacks, I stuck pictures of happy family times, ripped pages from magazines, and quotes as a reminder to dwell on the good and simple.

Waiting changes our outlook from being women who are anxious to the point of bitterness to women who are anxious with expectation. I didn't know when and I didn't know how, but I knew in my heart that someday we would finally feel at home. But it didn't do me any good to wait until that day to have a positive outlook. It took changing my posture to change my heart.

As Americans, we live in a rushed state of mind. Our economy is run like a fast-food restaurant, and our model of hospitality is like a drive-through window where we can order, wait for only a few minutes, and receive our processed food in a brown paper bag, only to be devoured in the car before we reach our destination. We are efficient and want to feed our hunger immediately. Not just our hunger for food, but our insatiable hunger to receive what we deserve. A ring. A promotion. A new house. A kid. Another kid. A bigger house to fit all of our kids . . . you get my point? Quantity is placed over higher value than quality because we don't want to waste any time—we want what we want *now*.

Who wants to wait? No one. We want to eat quickly and leave so we can go on to the next big event, task, or step in our masterfully crafted plan for our lives. We want to be in control. We don't take well to change so when lines get backed up, toys break, or the person preparing our food leaves the pickles on our burgers, we like to tell the manager that the service is simply unacceptable. We are consumers, and this fast-food economy feels like home to us.

Is this how we were intended to live?

No, I don't think so.

Abraham did not live his life with a fast-food mentality, and every time he tried to rush God's plans, they backfired. Telling Pharaoh that his wife was his sister led to serious disease and Abraham getting kicked out of Egypt. When Sarah's womb remained bare and she gave Abraham her maidservant Hagar to bear him a child, this caused such a mess between the two women that Hagar and her son Ishmael were sent away, distressing Abraham greatly. Abraham didn't always make wise choices while he waited, but he did listen to a voice of promise, urging him to be patient so that he might receive his reward.

Unlike our fast-food hospitality mentality, the story that God has written is all about us having faith that what He promised to us is true. Faith isn't always fast; it invites us to sit, be still, and wait for the promise to be fulfilled. Faith is trusting that God is perfect and has a perfect plan for each of us. But often, He calls us to wait so that plan can be revealed. God knows the desires of our hearts because He is the one that plants them inside us from the beginning. Waiting is a sifting process, one that shows us what is pure and impure, selfish or submissive. Waiting prepares us to receive the gift. When we finally open it, we can in turn give God glory. Faith isn't something we have; it's something we've been given. We can practice our faith by trusting in God's plans instead of our own and by viewing the wait as refining our souls to receive His goodness.

Jesus did not practice hospitality with efficiency or predictability. He did not treat His disciples as an assembly line, rushing through His time with them. Instead, He washed His disciples' feet, taking a moment with each man to show His love for him. We read about how Jesus told parables like "When someone invites you to a wedding feast, do not take the place of honor, for a person more distinguished than you may have been invited. Take the lowest place, so that when your host comes, he will say to you, 'Friend, move up to a better place.' For everyone who exalts himself will be humbled, and he who humbles himself will be exalted." Hospitality allows space for Christ to come to us on His terms rather than our own.[50]

Could the kind of waiting we find ourselves in be an invitation from Christ, asking us to join Him in Christian hospitality? He is waiting on us to accept; when we do, He begins to wash our feet too. He tells us to take off our worn sandals and to place our weary feet into a basin of water. Then, using His hands, He dips a cloth into the water that is already turning murky from the dust and the dirt that embedded itself between our toes and into our heels, and He begins to cleanse us. At first we object, but then we oblige. His showing of love is the lowliest of duties, but there He sits, washing and cleaning us one by one. By the end of it, we feel pampered, heard, and refreshed to continue onward and outward.

If hope comes after suffering, perseverance, and character building, then that must mean it is worth the wait. Hope is spring after a long winter, life after a season of death. Hope blooms and dances like tulips that grace a corner lot. Hope says, "I know you've been tested, but can't you see that your suffering has not been in vain?" Hope gives our struggles purpose: a reason to draw us closer to one another and to receive the love of Christ in the hardest of times.

Raleigh's granddad passed away just a few days before the twins turned three.

It was almost May, and we'd just celebrated their birthday the weekend before he took a hard fall. We visited and brought him a slice of chocolate cake, but he wasn't able to get out of bed. Crouching next to him, the twins put their dainty little hands over his weathered ones. We let the twins tell him about their ice cream party, and they describe in escalating voices how they each got chocolate, strawberry, and vanilla ice cream—with *sprinkles!*—and gummy bears and marshmallows on top. His eyes lit up, and we stayed for a while longer. As we left, Raleigh bent down to hug his grandfather. Even though he was weak, Granddad wrapped his arms around him too, and then patted his back, assuring his grandson that he was going to be okay. We said good-bye without words.

Raleigh's granddad was a small but strong man from years of farming and war. He was a member of the Great Generation, and he had lived a long life as a war veteran, entrepreneur, and a family man. Martin loved God and Auburn football, oysters and a cold beer, and his Kennette, the woman who, at the mention of her name, brought a smile to his face. On the eve of his funeral, we stood at the front of the room, along with the rest of the family, forty of us total, as Martin's friends, coworkers, church family, and neighbors came to pay their respects. Everyone had a story to tell, and I remember how Granddad used to share with Raleigh and me that he dreamed in black and white instead of color. He'd smile wistfully of a simpler time, when the world didn't seem so stimulated and fast. Rocking with him on that back porch made me feel like maybe we were getting a taste of the good ol' days, if only for a moment, but maybe this moment was also a taste of something more, something yet to come. These stories serve as a gentle expression that life is short, but a life well lived makes a great impact on the people who partake with us in community.

At his funeral, I'm reminded that God desires for us to live the deep, long life and not the short, shallow life. To live and love deeply, we will suffer, but this pain has the power of bringing us closer to Christ. Peter says that we will suffer grief in all kinds of trials so that our faith may be proved genuine and may result in praise, glory, and honor when Jesus Christ is revealed. He goes on to state, "Though you have not seen him, you love him, and even though you do not see him now, you believe in him and are filled with an inexpressible and glorious joy for you are receiving the end result of your faith, the salvation of your souls" (1 Peter 1:8–9 NIV).

After he's buried in the cemetery just a few fields over from his farm, the family fixed plates of food brought in by Granddad's friends. It's hospitality, this food—fried chicken, pasta salad, green bean casserole, freshly baked bread, seven-layer cakes, apple pies—and we ate what we knew to be good for our souls. His house sat on six acres of land, and the children ran wild in the green grass. To the right of the house lay a pecan orchard, and the backyard had blueberry bushes, muscadine vines, and a clementine tree. We ate our food on the back porch with the other Dothan cousins and caught up with news about work and kids. Inside, Raleigh's uncle from Tennessee and aunt from South Carolina sat across from one another on couches in the narrow living room, while other family members crammed into the kitchen and dining room tables. Nobody sat in Granddad's leather chair. As I took our plates toward the trash, I heard someone ask, "What do you think will happen to this place?"

If there is a time for everything, that must mean there is a time for us to experience winter and spring, death and life. In Ecclesiastes, Solomon writes, "When times are good be happy; but when times are bad consider this: God has made the one as well as the other" (Ecclesiastes 7:14 NIV). Throughout this book of the Bible, the author so often uses the phrase "Everything is meaningless." But, I don't think that is entirely true. Our happy and bad times teach us thankfulness.

Our times of waiting refine us. Our times of suffering connect us to Christ. Our lives do have purpose and meaning, but we can't understand it without experiencing the good and the bad times.

In the months after Granddad's passing, his house was slowly packed up and belongings were divided among the siblings. We walked through it with Raleigh's parents and picked out suit coats and table linens that we wished to keep. The house was vacant but alive with memories passing through the walls like wind. Walking down the paneled hallway, I imagined Raleigh's uncle chasing his dad to play with miniature soldiers in the back room. Kennette would be in the kitchen, barefoot and frying chicken, and her daughter would be in her room with the crown molding, making her youngest brother play dolls with her. I imagined Martin coming in through the back door, leaving his boots in the car port. Their family turned this house into a home, and now the family home was bare, unwillingly preparing itself to be sold.

The kids race through the back door and sit at the kitchen table for a snack. The walls are still papered with bright yellow lemons, but as they pull chairs to the table, I sense that this place could be a home for us to raise our family. *We* could continue the legacy that Martin and Kennette had left behind. Later that evening, Raleigh and I get excited as we dream about making that house into our home. It just felt *right*. We hadn't considered this an option, but now, somewhere deep inside our souls, we both knew that this was the place we'd been dreaming about for so many years. It was crazy, because it looked nothing like the Craftsman-style home in my head with a large front porch, but we both knew that this was the next best thing for us, it was where we belonged, what we must do.

Soon after that day, we bought the farm from the family. Raleigh and I celebrated and felt alive again. After the darkest of days, we could now see the light.

Finally, we would have a place to call our home.

What have you had to wait for?

The ache of your wait has the capacity to change you from the inside out. Your wait can become a time of despair or delight, depending on your attitude and actions. The choice to persevere through hope is yours.

Now that we live in Granddad's house, I can so clearly see how God was preparing us during our season of waiting. All the tears, frustration, and doubts led me to a tiny corner in an unkempt office just so I could be still. God planted us in the Wood House to discover His presence in a season of change. Throughout the book of Psalms, Scripture assures us that the Lord is with us, our stronghold in times of trouble, so that we may rest in His peace instead of fretting with anxiety. Every time I lost sight of this truth, I lost my peace and struggled with discontent, anger, and fear. Living in a rental house taught me how waiting ushers in a well soul.

Of course, I couldn't see all of that while I was waiting, and neither can you. Not knowing what the rewards are for our waiting drives us crazy, but when we have hope that it will come and be better than we imagined, we can rest our minds on the promise during our present circumstances. As believers, we too are waiting for the fulfillment of Christ's kingdom, the New Jerusalem, Zion, to be inhabited. When that day arrives, we will shout for joy, burst into song, raise banners, and pass through the gates and into the courts of God's sanctuary. Waiting leads to celebrating. Finally, we will experience the day we have been waiting for, and it will be a party that we'll never forget.

But Jesus is still preparing this place for us. The time has not yet come. So we must wait.

As we wait, we pray for our Father's kingdom to come, His will be done, on earth as it is in heaven. We ask for God to give us our daily bread, just what we need today so that we may wait with expectancy. Hope allows us to see heaven amid floral wallpaper, Formica countertops, and shag carpet. The promise is true, heaven lives inside of us, and our longings will soon be fulfilled.

Don't let the waiting crush you, friend. Persevere through your sufferings and let it build your character, so that you may live a life of hope, promise, and light. Wait for it. It's going to be worth it.

Delight yourself in the LORD and he will give you the desires of your heart.

~ Psalm 37:4 ESV

Chapter 15:

BIRTHDAY PARTY

{3 WAYS TO BREAK THE ANXIETY CYCLE}

Life should not only be lived, it should be celebrated.

~ Osho

"THIS . . . WILL be . . . the year of *fun!*" my eyes dance as I share my birthday wish with Raleigh after I blow out the candles that had just illuminated the room. Giggling, I grab a candle from the cake and lick the icing off the bottom. At twenty-nine, I was tired of the vicious cycle of fear, anxiety, and worry that I'd been living in since we'd moved home. It was time to start over and stop my thoughts from being consumed with unnecessary feelings. The following year, I was going to be thirty, and I didn't want this milestone birthday to pressure me into living the next year frantically.

For a lot of my friends, thirty is the new forty, making us question if we are on the right track to live the life we've always imagined. The *Huffington Post* has coined this feeling of anxiety a "Pre-30 Crisis." Carolyn Gregoire, senior writer for the *Post,* writes, "Much like the quarter-life crisis, a pre-30 crisis seems to stem from the misconception that you have to have everything figured out by a certain age—causing confusion, anxiety and insecurity about the ways that your life might have veered off course or fails to measure up to your expectations."[51]

Thirty seems like the age when everyone thinks of you as an adult and not a kid, and even though I should probably already think of myself that way . . . I don't really like to. I want to grab hold of my twenties and hold on tightly for one more year. I want to get lost in a city away from home, buy outrageously priced clothes just because I finally have a paycheck, and go on last-minute weekend excursions. Being a twenty-something is thrilling and fun. Who would want to pass those kind of moments by?

Then, at other times, I want to let my twenties go. My twenties have been years of growing pains. These have been the years where I've loved and lost friends, been accepted and rejected for employment, and have spent countless hours awake at two a.m., not because I'm out partying but because I can't get the baby on my chest to go back to sleep. I've lost and found hope more times than I can count, questioning why my goals still seem forever in the future.

If God knows every hair on my head and all the days of my life, then why do I care so much about knowing what's next for my life? Is this angst that I constantly experience a question of trust or control? Am I really living by faith, believing in something I can never see, or am I disguising my need for direction behind handcrafted lenses? Have I already experienced all the glory for my days here on earth?

When I was graduating from college, I honestly thought I would have my life figured out by the time I was thirty. But as I was about to turn thirty, I realized that I'm just getting started, still asking God what He wants me to do with my life. I read about how other people my age are trying to figure out their life purpose too. The Barna Group writes that 48% of Christian Millennials say they believe God is calling them to different work, yet they haven't yet made such a change.[52] *Why not?* I muse to myself. Are we afraid, or do we lack trust? Or, is it just not the right time?

Somewhere in my twenties, I chose perfection over party. I worked so hard to achieve the goals I had set for myself that I was always looking ahead instead of living in the moment. I thought that once I'd achieve that next thing, *then* I would be happy and where God wanted me to be. Many of my most celebrated moments are eclipsed with angst because something happened that made the event a little less perfect. In the midst of planning a perfect life, I lost the happy that should accompany my birthday. How could I change as I entered a new decade of my life?

A week after my birthday, Raleigh and I are in his truck, heading east. It's our anniversary, and we make our way to South Carolina through the back roads of Georgia. While driving, the past year slowly fades in the rearview mirror as we talk about our trip, our work, our future. I touch my stomach, still amazed that there is now a baby growing inside of me. *A baby!* We found out just weeks ago after the fourth of July, when I went to the doctor, sick from strep throat. He asked if I was pregnant, and I said no, but we were trying. We did a test, and while I waited for the results, I read the poster that hung on the wall that quoted Jeremiah 29:11 (NIV). "For I know the plans I have for you, declares the Lord, plans to prosper you and not to harm you, plans to give you hope and a future." It was a favorite, one that I had heard a thousand times, now growing almost numb to the declaration. But, when the doctor walked in with a smile and said the two words that I didn't expect to hear, I cried, right there in the exam room.

I was going to have a baby.

I'd waited for months to hear those words, and now they were a reality. Life was formed inside of me after a season of darkness, and the words of Jeremiah 29:11 could not prove to be truer. God had plans for us to have a hope and a future, even though I couldn't always clearly see what those plans were. I had to wait for hope, but at last it had come, and I couldn't be happier. After a season of sorrow, this pregnancy was such a sweet gift.

Isn't that how God works? We experience loss so that we may be given life. Rick Warren writes that the Bible compares spiritual growth to a seed, a building, and a child growing up.[53] Spiritual growth happens one day at a time and is a long, slow process. We grow through our life experiences, circumstances, people, and places. Growth happens as we change from a seed to a flower, a structure to a home, and a child to an adult. We grow through love and loss, darkness and light, good and bad times. We can't have one without the other.

In the book of Psalms, David speaks often of the heart and how we grow. Under Psalm 16 are the words, "A *miktam* of David." In my research, I discover the meaning of the term is unexplained, and this psalm is a prayer for safekeeping, written to point out that faith/trust is a characteristic of those who bring God their prayers. David writes:

> "I will praise the Lord, who counsels me; even at night my heart instructs me. I keep my eyes always on the Lord. With him at my right hand, I will not be shaken. Therefore my heart is glad and my tongue rejoices; my body also will rest

secure, because you will not abandon me to the realm of the dead, nor will you let your faithful one see decay. You make known to me the path of life; you will fill me with joy in your presence, with eternal pleasures at your right hand (NIV)."

Isn't faith like a miktam, unexplainable at times? We trust in a God we do not see but who keeps us safe. Faith is not a weather forecast, but we do know that our futures are secure when we believe in the promises of God. On my twenty-ninth birthday, I discover that my plans are not what make me happy.

Heaven is what makes me happy.

My twenties have been so much about growth and change. I've learned that as much as I plan the "perfect party," God always throws in the unexpected. His timing is truly His own, but He does sincerely care about the desires of my heart. He doesn't want me to live perfectly, because He knows that only leads to failure and then disappointment. I hate disappointment. He's asking me to open my eyes and thank Him for His provision and gifts, to love without an agenda. I don't have to have my life all figured out by the time I am thirty. Instead, I can live happily by pursuing holy-filled joy and gladness.

Heaven is home; it is hope fulfilled. With rooms that have already been prepared for us, all the striving and performing will be over, and our souls will finally be whole because we are living in a holy place. When we set our minds on heaven instead of earthly things, we see the temporariness of it all. Instead of pursuing perfection in our own lives, heaven beckons us to pursue the One who is perfect and serve Him in humility and with honor.

The pursuit of holiness is the path to experiencing true happiness as we grow older. But, holiness does not come without help. The way to holiness begins with remembering who we are in Christ and pondering the great events of our salvation—reflecting on them, holding them before our minds, and counting on them.[54] We have to resist questioning our paths so that we can live out our salvation to the fullest potential.

The story of Mary and Martha is well-known in the world of hospitality. Most women categorize themselves as either a Mary (aka "the spiritual one") or a Martha (aka "the worker bee"). Martha is the sister who gets the bad rap, distracted by all the preparation of hosting Jesus and His disciples, while Mary is the sister who chooses to focus on Jesus and gets celebrated for it (Luke 10:38–41).

But I have to give Martha some credit. Even though she was hosting Jesus, who she recognized as the Immanuel, she knew Him well enough to ask, "Lord, don't you care that my sister has left me to do the work by myself? Tell her to help me!"

I don't believe that Martha wanted to be distracted while Jesus was in her home, but all the planning just got the best of her. Every hostess has that moment when she realizes she is in over her head. Most of us don't admit that we are flustered and not fine, but Martha clearly recognized that she needed help.

Sarah Young writes in *Jesus Calling* that when we feel ourselves sinking in the sea of circumstances, we are to say, "Help me, Jesus!" She encourages us that even if we have to say that thousands of times daily, don't be discouraged, because Jesus knows our weakness and meets us in that very place.

Jesus understood that hospitality was both strength and a weakness for Martha. He also knew that this was one of the last meals that He would be sharing with His beloved friends, and He didn't want her to waste time running around like a crazy person in the kitchen.

A genuine posture of hospitality is humility. Mary chose "the better way" because she was able to predict that this moment with Jesus was unique. After the meal, she took a pint of her most expensive perfume, poured it on Jesus' feet, and then wiped His feet with her hair. While perfume was used mainly for festivities, it was also used for burials. Others objected to her actions, but Mary anticipated that her time with Jesus would soon end.

We can be both a Mary and a Martha. We can serve and open our homes while also sitting and savoring the special occasions that we are celebrating with our loved ones. The world needs more hostesses who can practice hospitality from a posture of humility. Hebrews 12:2 NASB tells us to "fix our eyes on Jesus, the author and perfecter of our faith."

Dr. Alice Domar writes, "Women are unhappy because, even if eleven out of twelve things are going well, they zero in on the one that isn't, and they get miserable about it." She explains that so often the women who seem to have a perfect life are unhappy because they don't feel good enough. Perfectionism chains my inner critic with demands to produce like Martha, leaving me dreadfully unhappy. To break this cycle of unworthiness, shame, and sadness, I've got to find Jesus sitting at the table. When I focus on Him, my problems no longer remain my focus. I can better serve the world around me when I confess my imperfections to Christ, the perfecter of my faith.

When we practice the most fundamental principle of hospitality—serving others the way Christ loved us—we no longer make our lives about ourselves. Philippians 2:3–4 NIV says, "Do nothing out of selfish ambition or vain conceit. Rather, in humility value others above yourselves, not looking to your own interests but each of you to the interests of the others." Might we become hostesses who confess we need help and serve with humility?

Nancy DeMoss states, "We are who we are becoming."[55] A term used in commentaries about the process of salvation is *vivication*, which is coming to spiritual life.[56] We become transformed into the likeness of Jesus, giving God glory with every aspect of our being. The way to peace and prosperity is God, through and through. God's present as we grow older is His presence. From the day we were born, God has been with us. He has invited us to be with Him, to live lives holy and in anticipation of heaven.

I want to be a woman who believes in the promises of God, don't you? Hospitality helps us fight back against perfectionism and plans. We can accept that life will never be perfect, we will always be battling some form of darkness, but Jesus is with us and the light of His presence brings us peace.

So let go.

Let go of the things that are holding you back from enjoying the moments worth celebrating.

When you blow out your birthday candles, what are you wishing for?

Love?

A youthful spirit?

Happiness?

With every birthday, I believe we want to wish for the best. We want to live the good life, laugh often, and love much. Nobody wishes for anxiety, stress, or frustration, do they? Growing older is supposed to make us wiser, but it's also a reminder that we've lived another year, which brings up the never-ending question of purpose. Are we living the life we want to live, or do things need to change this year?

Let's face it. As women, we get worked up, worried, and overwhelmed about all that we have to do, especially special events. Inside our heads, we have a vision for the party we're planning. We've dreamed about it, pinned inspirational boards about it, and spent months working on it. We want the party to be perfect. Our motives aren't for our own glory; deep down, we want the party to be perfect so we can let our people know just how special they truly are.

With this responsibility, it's natural to experience added stress, anxiety, and exhaustion. But breaking down in an effort to build someone else up is not the solution. There are three ways to break the fear cycle that causes meltdowns. We must know our triggers, accept that we have limits, and have faith. When we can keep these things at the forefront of our minds, we are less likely to lose it (can I get a hallelujah?!) and truly enjoy celebrating with the people we love.

Think about the last time you had a breakdown. It could be before a party or simply because it was a crazy week. What made you cry? Was something that you ordered not shipped on time? Or, did you overcommit to doing too many craft projects yourself? Were you up late making party food that looked nothing like the picture on Pinterest? Or, did you have no help with the kids and had to take them with you to Target only to have them spill the popcorn that they *had to have* all over the party plate aisle and then throw a tantrum for a toy? (Ahem, that's *never* happened with my kids.)

The main triggers for breakdowns are anxiety, exhaustion, and loss of daily routine. A main portion of pre-party anxiety comes from worrying about things that are out of our control, such as who is coming. We can stress so much about our guest list and who isn't at the party that we forget to focus on who *does* show up. Sometimes the best parties are the smallest parties. Big or small, the point is to celebrate with the people who show up to celebrate with you, not to worry about those who were unable to attend.

When exhausted, we can lose our perspective on the purpose of having a party. What was intended to be a special day of celebration turns into an event that we are ready to complete so we can collapse on our couch in our comfy clothes and eat leftover cake. The joy is lost when we are running ourselves ragged with pre-party planning. We don't know our limits or set realistic expectations for ourselves. Statistics show that women between the ages of 18-44 are twice as likely to feel very tired or exhausted. No duh. These are the main party planning years! Graduation, engagements, baby showers, birthday parties . . . we go, go, go, and exhaustion creeps in when we don't give ourselves enough margin. We break when we don't have breaks.

Last-minute prep work is expected the week of the party, but when we allow this work to consume us, we lose our daily routine and don't go to bed on time, eat well, or exercise. Lack of sleep causes us to be irritable and snappy, then we run late and grab a sugary muffin, leaving us starved by mid-day. We become "hangry," which is a recipe for disaster (someone please sit us on the bench and give us a Snickers bar)! Poor eating habits make us notice how tight our jeans are, and we want to go work out but can't because we've got so much party planning work to do—so we grab more fast food and feel the stress in our backs for the rest of the week.

Consider your schedule during your last party or major life event. Look back through your planner, and I bet you will find that you had a lot going on that week. Because, on top of this special occasion, you more than likely still had responsibilities in other parts of your life such as work, housekeeping, helping kids with homework, church, or you accidentally scheduled your yearly check-up for that week (yuck). You clearly have a lot going on, so it's no wonder that the pressure of party planning got the best of you.

With Pinterest, Instagram, and attending our friends' parties, we put too much pressure on ourselves to have a perfect party. This pressure causes us to put more work into a party than necessary, thus causing us to be exhausted. The week of any party is bound to be busy, but if we can prioritize what is important, we can put less pressure on ourselves to have it all together. Breaking the cycle begins with holding our plans loosely. A friend recently told me that she overcame her breakdowns by admitting that she had to let some things go.

So, what gives?

This is a tough question to answer, but I have learned from personal experience that it's best to focus on only one big project at a time. One thing that I am going to start doing on my calendar is marking "red weeks" like Disney World. If it is going to be a busy week because of events that are already planned, I don't need to plan anything else for that week. We have a maximum capacity, and if we go over our limit, we are bound to break.

No matter how hard we try to be perfect, we are going to experience pain. Breakdowns are bound to happen, and we are made to feel emotions like anger, frustration, and resentment. But, these emotions can be dangerous and easily lead us to experiencing doubt. We have the option to listen to the whispers of doubt inside our heads telling us to blame and belittle, or we can focus on the light of Christ and remember that He says, "Beloved, you are dearly loved." That means that even though we will experience raw moments of emotion, we don't have to live in the shame of our breakdowns. That shame was buried in the grave. All of our blaming and belittling has already been put to death. God has given us the gift of salvation and has invited us to accept this gift. Romans 8:12–17 says, "Therefore, brothers and sisters, we have an obligation—but it is not to the flesh, to live according to it. For if you live according to the flesh, you will die; but if by the Spirit you put to death the misdeeds of the body, you will live. For those who are led by the Spirit of God are the children of God. The Spirit you received does not make you slaves, so that you live in fear again; rather, the Spirit you received brought about your adoption to sonship (and daughtership). And by him we cry, 'Abba, Father.' The Spirit himself testifies with our spirit that we are God's children. Now if we are children, then we are heirs—heirs of God and co-heirs with Christ, if indeed we share in his sufferings in order that we may also share in his glory (NIV)."

To share in His glory is to live the resurrected life of faith. It means choosing to think about things that are lovely, refusing to be anxious about anything, and rejoicing in the Lord always. When we think about these things, the God of peace will be with us, especially as we are planning parties.

If you are tired of letting your breakdowns get the best of you, it's time to fully accept the gift of salvation. You are saved by faith. It's simple. It's complex. It's beautiful. This is God's invitation, His call to bring you into His community where you are accepted, loved, and forgiven.

In the book of Galatians, Paul reminds the people of Galilee that it is for freedom that Christ set us free (Galations 5:1). These people were Gentiles who had accepted that Jesus was the Christ, but now Paul finds them practicing the ancient laws of the Jews. He says, "Formerly, when you did not know God, you were slaves to those who by nature are not gods. But now that you know God—or rather are known by God—how is it that you are turning back to those weak and miserable forces? Do you wish to be enslaved by them all over again? You are observing special days and months and seasons and years!" (4:8–10 NIV).

These people had fallen into a trap of slavery, trying to practice rituals that didn't even apply to them. They were captives because they didn't fully believe that Christ had set them free. Paul states that the only way for them to break their chains is to stand firm against the bonds of slavery (5:1).

Live like you have been forgiven. Believe in your freedom when you breakdown. It's time to break the cycle. With God, anything is truly possible.

Over the course of the next year, Raleigh and I did have more fun and fewer breakdowns. On our anniversary, we stopped in Hilton

Head to eat shrimp fresh off the boat and then arrived at our bed and breakfast in Beaufort just after twilight. Our room was behind the house in the courtyard, and it was as charming as I hoped a bed and breakfast would be. We spent the weekend holding hands while touring historic homes, swimming in the Atlantic Ocean, and eating dinner by music and candlelight in the warm summer evenings. Afterward, Raleigh would put his hand to my stomach, and we'd share a secret smile, knowing that a new chapter of our lives had begun.

With each birthday, we get the chance to grow deeper in love with Christ and the people He's given us to serve. Even if we don't have our lives all figured out, we can still love the life we are living today. It's okay to ask for help and to remind ourselves continually to live as free people, not slaves to perfectionism. Birthdays are beautiful reminders to have fun and trust that God has a plan for our lives. Our lives are an invitation for celebration, a reckoning that we were created to love—not just God and others—but love ourselves.

Chapter 16:

THANKFUL GATHERING

{WHEN GOOD THINGS GROW}

When women gather, great things will happen.

~ Leymah Gbowee

CONFESSION: I'M A NETFLIX DOCUMENTARY junkie.

I've watched all kinds of documentaries, but my favorite ones are always about food. Right now, I'm hooked on *Chef's Table*. Each episode of this docu-series highlights a world-renowned chef taking us into their restaurants and their thoughts, allowing the viewer a first-hand glimpse into the process for creating art on a plate. During season one, *Chef's Table* showcased Dan Barber, a celebrated chef, dedicated farmer, and food industry revolutionary who is leading a fight to change the way we think about—and grow—our food. His restaurant, Blue Hill, is highly recognized as one of the first restaurants of the farm-to-table movement in the United States. In this documentary, Barber says this regarding his ideas about food: "As Wes Jackson likes to say, 'If you are thinking about an idea you can solve in your lifetime, you're thinking too small.' That gives me great hope and great energy because I don't know where else all these ideas come together. Where's the connection? A plate of food. And that's the power of a chef."[57]

Watching how Dan pursued his calling for cooking, I am inspired about my own ideas for bringing people together. I might not be a world-renowned chef, but I agree that we all hunger for connection. I like to plan parties so people can have a reason to gather. Just like the farm-to-table movement, gatherings connect local people, giving them an opportunity to commune over a festivity or for a specific purpose.

In the Old Testament, people would gather together for three annual feasts: the Feast of the Unleavened Bread, the Feast of the Harvest, and the Feast of the Tabernacles. Deuteronomy 16:13-14 (NIV) says, "Celebrate the Festival of Tabernacles for seven days after you have gathered the produce of your threshing floor and your winepress. Be joyful at your festival—you, your sons and daughters, your male and female servants, and the Levites, the foreigners, the fatherless and the widows who live in your towns."

Modern-day Christianity doesn't have a need to celebrate these feasts since Christ brought an end to the systems of types and ceremonies that pointed toward His great sacrifice, but we can take note of the joy that comes from harvesting. Before Dan ever puts a plate of food in front of his guests, he has been working with the farmers in the field to prepare the food for harvest. Once the food is ready to be picked, he then trains his kitchen staff on how to prepare the food and his waiters on how to present the food to the diners. From watching him take the food from farm to table, we see how the food represents a labor of love. Dan's joy is found in the process, from the food being picked to finally being plated.

We all have our unique God-given gifts that, when discovered, may contribute to a world in need. If we pursue these gifts as our professions, we find people serving as chefs, musicians, architects, nurses, teachers, writers, etc. The list continues, but the point is we all have a gift that has the ability to connect us to living in community. When we use these gifts, we are harvesting our own grain and wine, and we find joy in the work of our hands. If a chef has the power to connect people over a plate of food, how can we, as disciples of Christ, connect to one another for a specific purpose?

Hospitality.

While our stomachs hunger for food, our souls hunger for God. Women gather together by opening our lives and homes to one another. Leymah Gbowee, leader of the women's peace movement in Liberia and Nobel Peace Prize winner, states, "When women gather, great things will happen." There are no boundaries to God's hospitality. Imagine what could happen if you and I extended His love to the world. What would this look like? How would we even begin?

The definition of hospitality is to love our guests, visitors, and strangers. The thing that I've noticed about the Holy Spirit is once it is inside of us, it sure messes with our idea of a comfortable life. Like the wind, it leads us to a life beyond borders of the flesh. The Spirit has the unusual ability to extend our idea of family and connects us as the body of Christ. Biblical counselor Jason Hsieh says that as Christians, we are called not just to love our own flesh and blood but to love the stranger, care for someone who can't repay us, and to assist gospel workers to spread the name of Jesus.[58]

So how do we love someone outside of our immediate family? We invite the stranger into our lives the same way we love our family members—with sincerity. My family loves to share a meal together. Whenever we invite our family into our home, three people always have to sit on the bench at our farmhouse kitchen table. The bench serves as not only a place to sit, but it acts as a place to engage in conversation with the person sitting directly next to you. Emily P. Freeman says that benches are places for people to relate and live in community and converse and be together.[59] Benches are a simple way to ask sincerely someone you don't know to join you at the table.

Luke shares how Jesus was invited to eat at the home of a prominent Pharisee one Sabbath. At this meal, He said to His host, "When you give a luncheon or dinner, do not invite your friends, your brothers or relatives, or your rich neighbors; if you do they may invite you back and so you will be repaid. But when you give a banquet, invite the poor, the crippled, the lame, the blind, and you will be blessed. Although they cannot repay you, you will be repaid at the resurrection of the righteous" (Luke 14:12–14).

After I served as the Children's Ministry Director, my pastor asked me to transition into a new role to connect the women of our church. This job was a perfect fit for me and my desire to join women to one another through relationships built around the Word of God. It was also my party planning dream-come-true, because I'd be planning at least two big events each year—one for the fall and one for the spring. Because I knew the importance of fellowship, my fall event was the Thankful Gathering, an evening where we shared a meal together and gave thanks for what God was doing through the women of our church.

While planning the Thankful Gathering, I invited several women who were living in a transitional home from prison to attend. When I had first signed up to be part of the mentoring program at this transitional home, I was cautioned not to get too close to these women. They'd experienced a life that I'd only seen on Netflix, and some people close to me were afraid of what could happen if I engaged in this kind of relationship.

Showing up at the home for the first time, I sat in a chair beside my friend instead of on the couch with these women. During introductions, I just shared my first name and kept the details of myself to a minimum. My palms began to sweat, and I tried to think of every excuse to leave before the program began because *clearly* this whole mentoring idea was a mistake. Something made me stay in my chair, and as the women who were incarcerated began to share their stories, I realized that just one wrong move can alter the course of your life forever. Some women had been in prison because of poor decisions that they made, but others were victims or defending their children from harm. These women were released from prison and now in a transitional home because they had shown their ability to listen and obey while serving time. I learned that to live in the transitional home, all women had to pay rent and volunteer while they looked for a job. By the time the first mentoring session had ended, I felt like these women had mentored me, teaching me how to love someone completely outside my comfort zone.

While preparing for the Thankful Gathering, the Holy Spirit gave me the courage to invite those women to sit on my bench and share a meal with the women of my church. Our church sanctuaries are full of benches, and our communities are ripe with individuals who want to be asked to sit on the bench next to us. Robert Schnase, the Bishop of the Missouri Annual Conference of the United Methodist Church, says, "A congregation changes its culture one person at a time. Radical hospitality begins with a single heart, a growing openness, a prayerful desire for the highest good of a stranger."

Philoxenia, the Greek word for *hospitality,* means "love of the stranger." Who can you invite to sit beside you at your table?

When Jesus arrived at the Pharisee's house, all the guests watched Him, waiting to see what He would do. Have you ever almost not attended a party because you were afraid of all eyes being on you? You want to be noticed but not noticed at the same time, right? When I was in college, girls would always cluster together at parties on the weekends, and it was always uncomfortable being a girl without a group. Often, when we are invited to attend a party, we do our best to blend into the crowd, noticed but not noticed too much.

Not Jesus.

Immediately upon arrival, Jesus encounters a man who was sick and asks the experts, "Is it lawful to heal on the Sabbath or not?"

Everyone remained silent.

Jesus took the man's hand, healed him, and sent him away.

Even though the Pharisees had nothing to say, I can imagine that everyone at that party was in shock. I'm sure there were many darting eyes and hushed murmurs behind closed doors. The people at the party didn't understand why Jesus performed a miracle on a day of rest. He showed love to the sick man.

A quote that I hung in my college dorm room said, "It's easy to stand with the crowd. It takes courage to stand alone." When we begin to view hospitality as loving strangers or those who can't repay us, we run the risk of standing out from the crowd. We will feel uncomfortable. Our invitation might be rejected or questioned. It's so much easier to open ourselves to family and friends we already know and love. While this is the cost of being a disciple of Christ, Jesus assures us that we will be blessed.

To extend an invitation to guests with whom we wouldn't usually associate ourselves, a great indicator of who to invite should be our tears. What makes you cry?

Teenage pregnancies? Call your local pregnancy center and ask how you can mentor a young mom.

Military moms? Invite them to your play group more than once. Offer to babysit her kids while her deployed husband is away.

The disabled classmate? Take her to dinner or invite her to attend your small group.

Keep on loving each other as brothers and sisters. Don't forget to show hospitality to strangers, for some who have done this have entertained angels without realizing it! (Hebrews 12:13).

When we become brave and invite strangers to sit beside us on our benches, we enter into a realm of hospitality where we are no longer the ones serving, but we become the ones who receive. I have a friend who teaches a Bible study to homeless women, and she says, "I understand the message of Hebrews 13:1-2 now. These women are teaching me how to love the way Christ intended for us to love."

After the Thankful Gathering, I'm given a stack of comment cards to sort through on which women have written down their prayer requests, ways they wanted to get involved, or what they liked/disliked about the event. With over a hundred cards, I begin the tedious task of scanning the information on the card. I quickly stop scanning as I read their vulnerable words, prayers for infertility, jobs, health, marriages, and prodigal children. Women write and write and write words of insecurity, fear, comparison, failure, guilt, and suffering. These women didn't need to be sorted in a pile that would eventually be placed in a drawer. No, these women needed prayer.

Silently, I sort with more attention and care, asking God to continue revealing Himself in the lives of these women. For some, this was their first time attending a spiritual conference, and they were desperate for continued study, any sort of group they could belong to. When we are included, we so easily neglect to extend an invitation to others. It could be from fear or not wanting new people to make the familiarity feel awkward, or we don't invite simply because we don't think outside of our own current needs and desires. But, from the messages written on these cards, it was evident that many women wanted to be part of a community with other women. They needed help identifying where they would best belong, a guide to direct them toward spiritual growth.

As my piles grew larger, I found a comment from one woman that instantly captivated my attention. She wrote, "Thank you for the free ticket to this event. A member of your church and her daughter eat at the fast-food restaurant that I work at regularly, and I was blessed to receive a ticket from her. She knew I couldn't afford something like this, but I needed it." Pausing, I imagine this woman who works in the hospitality industry. Did she take orders from customers, or was she in the back, preparing the food? Was she a manager sorting through bottles of ketchup and mustard, or did she work at the drive-thru window, placing deliciously greasy bags into the hands of strangers? Was she a woman who smiled happily, or did her smile wear the lines of a life hard lived? Day in and day out, she serves both the grateful and the ungrateful. But for one night, she was on the receiving end of hospitality; given a chance to experience true joy that comes from life lived with Christ . . . all because someone noticed her and extended an invitation to come.

It's so easy for women who know Christ to become jaded in our experience of Christ. We recognize the Bible stories, or we plan events to fill dates on calendars. Our intentions can so easily shift from Christ to performance-based praise. We can lose our fervor and fall into the trap of familiarity. If you've ever been in this place, trust me when I say that I've been there too. The only cure for carrying on is found in Christ. He does not want our performance; He wants us to bask in His presence. This is where we are given the fullness of joy. Joy diminishes our jaded perception, giving us power to see Scripture with fresh eyes and continue the good work that God has called us to do.

We serve one another in love because we are commanded first to love God and then to love others. Celebrations are the moments that allow us to give and receive, bless and be blessed. It's a simple way to put aside our self-serving tendencies to show our people that we care about them more than ourselves. In *The Case for Character*, Drayton Nabers says, "We cannot love others or have faith or hope in God if we put ourselves first. Nor can we be humble, wise, just, courageous, or self-controlled while we are at the same time selfish."[60]

We don't serve one another out of selfishness.

We don't serve one another out of our need to be known.

We don't serve one another because we feel obligated.

We don't serve one another as a way to reach our goals.

We serve one another because serving brings us *joy*.

That's how it is with faith, really. It's not about me or us or anything that *we* do. Faith doesn't ask us to perform or plan or live a perfect life. Instead, faith begins with believing that there once was a perfect man, the Son of God, who accepted that His purpose in being born of the flesh of Adam was to redeem the actions of His ancestors and all of mankind. He took our disobedience and doubt to death so that we'd no longer have to bear the weight of disgrace. This gift is eternal and ours to take.

If we believe in the truth of salvation, our ultimate goal in life should be to empower those we live in community with to glorify God and enjoy Him forever. This is a gift of a lifetime. Who will you ask to receive it?

Good things grow when people gather. We all have the power of a chef to connect people, but we must believe that we have the power to serve and connect people to Christ. If we live in fear of strangers, shame of our homes, or are afraid that our ideas aren't special enough to create a movement, we lose the chance to offer our God-given gift of serving others in love. Let's create a social movement of service, displaying how to be a hallelujah hostess one invitation at a time. When we have great hope and great energy that God will bring our ideas together, we will gather and celebrate, joyfully and without fear. *This* is the power of a woman who loves through serving.

May good things grow.

Chapter 17:

GALENTINE'S DAY

{WHAT HAPPENS WHEN A GROUP
NEVER BECOMES FULL}

We need to remember what's important in life: friends, waffles, work, or waffles, friends, work. Doesn't matter, but work is third.

~ Ann from *Parks and Recreation*

WHEN ANDI TURNS THIRTY, THE girls from small group come over to my house for a fiesta. Sarah makes a banner from scrap paper and Sharpie markers, and I casually set out daisies, a plastic tablecloth, and multi-colored plates. Rachel brings the chips and salsa, and Allison bakes a chocolate cobbler that we eat after dinner with vanilla ice cream. Once Andi arrives, we take a picture at my bar before it's time for enchiladas. Allison, Sarah, and Andi are sitting on bar stools in the front row, Rachel is in the back, and I squeeze in on the side just before the camera timer snaps. The picture catches us between pose and laughter, my favorite kind, and it is now one that I cherish.

We had begun meeting outside of small group last summer once a month. Our group uses the conversation cards from If:Table to help us get to know one another better and to encourage our discussions to dig deep. Our first meeting had been at Andi's, just five of us, and I showed up late and uncertain of myself. I smiled as she opened the door, and I attempted to add points to the conversation once we sat down. Andi picked up the first card. "How does a change of place and pace affect your heart in seeing God at work?"

Sarah responded first, saying how being in a small group has helped her acknowledge that God was with her throughout her day, whereas before she just thought of Him being with her on occasion. Allison, living at her in-laws house after moving from another city, explained how different her life was now that she was in between homes. Clearing her throat, Melissa pondered the question, not truly able to see God at work with the role she was playing in her company. When it was my turn, I tried to come up with an upbeat response, but I was broken inside, and tears began to trickle down my cheek. I tried to brush them away and blinked furiously, embarrassed by my response to the question. The table grew silent, and they let me talk. Words gushed out of me, questions rising to the surface. The desire of a change of place and pace made me burn but also swept me up into the promise that God was at work. I unloaded all from within, right there on Andi's table, and noticed how the girls smiled sympathetically back at me. It was then that I knew this place, this pace, was safe and God was at work.

It's interesting to me that the Holy Spirit came to the disciples during a feast on the day of Pentecost (Acts 2:1–4). Soon after the Holy Spirit came, the disciples began to teach, and a fellowship of believers formed. They broke bread in their homes and ate together with glad and sincere hearts, praising God and enjoying the favor of all the people (Acts 2:46–47). It's almost like God wanted them to celebrate while living as a community, isn't it?

Pulling into the restaurant parking lot, I see my friends' cars already there. It's Saturday, and the girls from small group are meeting for brunch to celebrate Galentine's Day. This month Laura is joining us at the Table. She and her husband had just started attending our small group. Always dressed classically, she's quiet at first, and I wonder if she is enjoying being with us. Today, my question is answered after we order our waffles, eggs benedict, bacon, and grits. Laura shyly hands each of us a heart that she's cut out of red construction paper herself, and inside we find a handwritten note, wishing us a happy Valentine's Day. It's touching, this gesture, and I gently place the card in my purse as I thank her. While digging into our food, we do our best to answer the question of "How can we, as women, do a better job of seeing each other more clearly, breaking down barriers that separate us?"

No one answered immediately, but then Melissa spoke up. "I just wish I asked for help more. My husband is always out of town traveling for work, and I'm constantly juggling my job, taking care of our kids and our house. I live in my yoga pants, and my hair hasn't seen a straightening iron at all this week. I'm lucky if I can apply mascara in the mornings before we leave the house. I'm in survival mode." We all knew her husband had been out of town since he began his new job, but none of us had offered to help. I knew she had parents and in-laws in town, like me, so just assumed she was getting the help she needed from them. She was a friend, yet we still had barriers to our friendship.

Andi replied, "I don't think we are truly living in community the way we are supposed to do. We still have barriers because we are all like you and don't ask for help. You know, I'd be happy to take your kids home from school, but I haven't thought once to ask you because you seem to be doing everything so well."

After this meeting, we begin to text more frequently. Being in a group text, I find my phone popping up with a new message, then five more as responses. We text about church, our kids, and ask if anyone wants to grab lunch on Wednesday. The group text is filled with wide-eyed, yellow-faced emojis, the girl in the red dress dancing, and other symbols that speak louder than words. Inside this text, we circle through high and low points of our day, completely random questions, and gut-wrenching honesty. This text is like a magazine, but written by friends sharing secret relationship tips, how-to cleaning advice, and love that warms my soul. It is here, in this text, that Rachel is welcomed into the Table. Her husband and Andi's are friends, and they are looking for a group to join. They slide right into ours, and Rachel brings a positive strength to the Table, sharing her weaknesses and detachment with tenderness. We talk about hospitality over pad thai in the back corner of a Thai restaurant, and how growing up military, Rachel didn't fully know how to be a hostess or how much value to place on friendships and home furnishings. This leads to us each talking about our mothers, and how we learn and question the rules and relationships that come out of hospitality. It seems that each of us has a story to tell, of how our mothers celebrated, what they did, what they didn't do, what we were taught, and what we wished to do differently now as women. The call to not only show but also practice hospitality courses throughout our conversation, and we end up staying until closing time, finally leaving the table with carry-out boxes and the promise to show love simply, beautifully, intentionally to our people.

For "Friends-giving" a friend of Laura's who is going through a season of change joins us at Allison's house. Her wit and honesty fit right in, and we serve our meal family-style with platters of charcuterie, bacon, and blueberry jam pork tenderloin, roasted root vegetables, fried cornbread, and sweet potato bread pudding for dessert. On each of our place settings was a Mason jar filled with homemade muscadine jam as well as a little wooden pencil for writing on paper leaves what we were thankful for this year. Tonight, we share some of the more unexpected or surprising gifts of this past year. Each of us has our own struggle and success, but then Rachel states, "It is by God's grace that we are here and we have each other."

We toast and say amen.

The kind of community that the early disciples experienced in Acts 2 was generous fellowship. Sharing beyond the walls of their homes, the followers of Christ gathered together to tell the message of Jesus to the people. They were not exclusive—no—daily God increased the number of people who were being saved. The breaking of the bread and extending of grace was an open invitation. All were welcome to listen, eat, drink, and receive the gift of the Holy Spirit.

If God is inviting us to a table that is always open and never reserved, who are we inviting to sit at the table with us?

When I first began to be in fellowship with the girls from my small group, I felt like for the group to stay safe, it needed to be inclusive. Surely, the more people we added to the Table, the more surface our conversations would become. I feared disconnection, people not showing up or getting along, the time for each to talk decreasing. Selfishly, I liked the smallness. But, as our group grew, the complete opposite happened. A fellowship of friendship formed, a kind that would never have happened if not for our group being centered on Spirit-led conversation. Adding more seats to the Table has only increased our joy, not diminished it, which leads me to believe in the efficacy of an open table.

When a group is exclusive, there is a certain amount of trust and camaraderie between friends, but it can make those not part of the group feel very unwelcome, unwanted. If you've ever been on the outside of a group of friends, it's easy to ask yourself, *"What do I have to do to fit in, be invited, and belong with these people?"* It's like in the movie *The Help*, when Celia Foote shows up at Elizabeth's house with a pie, and instead of inviting her in, Hilly tells all the girls from Junior League to hide and be quiet. Friendship becomes a game of cards, luck, and elitism. But fellowship is different. Fellowship is unity, something that binds people together from the inside out.

When the Holy Spirit was ushered in after Christ's ascension, there were people from every nation in Jerusalem who began to declare the wonders of God and accepted that Jesus was both Lord and Christ. The Spirit did not discriminate or disown anyone who was not of Jewish descent. No, the Spirit welcomed all to the table. As the modern-day church, we too are called to live lives of invitation. Let us not fear the loss of exclusivity by widening our circles for more to join us at the table.

Fellowship is not just about friends being together, it is about friends coming together to do God's will. The early church went out each day to teach the truth about Jesus, help the sick, and share what they owned with the apostles. Fellowship was an action shown through generosity, hospitality, and serving. To be a fellowship of believers, we too must use our gifts to love others.

For us to live like this today, God requires us to listen to the world around us. To love our people, we must be present. Love doesn't have to be through a meal. Extended love asks earnestly how we can help our family, friends, or people that frighten us. How can we love simply and from the heart?

When listening to a friend, ask yourself, "How can I help her through love?" Maybe you love her through babysitting, hosting a girl's night, or sending her a funny quote with a smiley face emoji next to it. As you observe the people you surround yourself with in small groups or book clubs or PTO, who do you see that is in need? How can you help that person spiritually, practically, or physically?

We are all busy, but we shouldn't be too busy and self-absorbed to love beyond the people who live in our home. If you are in a season of stress like my friend, don't be afraid to be the one who asks for help. Let other people love you, provide meals for you, or babysit for you. Because at one time or another, we are all going to need someone to extend this kind of love to us in return. That is what makes being in a group an essential part of our existence.

When we break down barriers that separate us, we receive the fruits of the Spirit. Love, joy, peace, patience, goodness, gentleness, kindness, and self-control—these are the benefits of a disciple who embraces the action of inviting others into community. Being a fellowship of believers, we each play our part in the body of Christ, but we also exist to connect to one another so that we display His perfection together. We are champions for Christ, displaying His radiant beauty through the extension of an open table.

There are so many women who are practicing biblical hospitality but don't even realize it or want to admit that the root of how they love comes back to how God made them to love. They throw amazing parties, are creative entrepreneurs, and give gifts that make others feel special. Some are moms who have never gone to church but show love by cheering you on as a mother every time you get together for a playdate. Some are college girls who bring such laughter and fun to everyone else on their dorm room hall. Some are women who clean homes, feed children in the lunchroom, drive buses to school, who always seem to have a smile on their faces. Some are beautiful women who admit their flaws, making the rest of us love instead of envy them.

Is this you? If so, have you ever asked yourself where the root of your love comes from?

Salvation is a gift that God wants you to receive, but the key to accepting this gift is free will. I can't *make* you love Jesus just because I love Jesus. You might have been burned by the church and are in the process of healing. You might not believe Christ is the Redeemer and you've got to wrestle and sift through the questions of faith. Sometimes this happens quickly, but it is often a process. That's why I think Christ hasn't come back yet, because He sees that the fellowship of believers is still being formed, that there are still people who are making their decision.

I want to invite you to sit at the table with me. Ask the questions and let them linger inside of you, long after the breaking of bread. There is goodness to be found in community. We all need connection, to look into one another's eyes and see a friend who loves us without pretense. You need to know that you are not in this alone. Friends help friends, lift one another up, and cheer each other onward and upward. We are in this together.

I envision heaven having one really long table filled with platters of food and adorned with breathtakingly beautiful centerpieces. God will be sitting at the head, and Jesus at His right hand, and there will be a seat for each of us, if we choose to accept. At the table, we will sit with family, friends, and people who said yes when offered a place. We will all know one another, even if we've never met, because we are brothers, sisters, the body finally united. All of our hearts will be glad, our tongues rejoicing, and our souls filled with joy. God will raise His glass, and He will welcome us with His perfect love.

Fellowship and friendship are like the Eucharist, something we were made to receive so that we may live richly, whole, forgiven. Apart from it, we will always feel a bit broken, disjointed, unsettled. The body is made for connection so that we may realize the perfection that is to be found in Jesus. When all the parts are united, glory is sung, bottles are uncorked, and the saints celebrate.

God with skin on looks a lot like the girls who sit with me at the Table. We each come with our own struggles, but being together helps us see the *beauty* that covers our imperfections. Confession and communion draw us in, connecting us to one another as the body of Christ. After each meal, I always walk away feeling like heaven came down and I've sat at God's table, welcomed and loved.

Chapter 18:

A SPECIAL DELIVERY

{UNWRAPPING THE GIFT OF GRACE}

Grace upon grace, upon grace, until we have made our way home.

~ T.B. LaBerge

AS MY BELLY ROUNDS, THE air becomes crisp once again.

On Sundays, we put on our boots and pack snacks and head to the country to spend our afternoon on the farm. Pulling into the drive, I still can't believe that Granddad's house will soon be our home. It's looking less and less like the ranch-style home we have visited over the years. The inside is torn apart, bare and empty, with sawdust piled on the floor. We stop first in the living room, and I'm amazed that this once-narrow room with low ceilings has now gained square footage with a few walls knocked down and the roof raised. We've connected the kitchen to the living room by removing a wall that held upper cabinets, and I can now visualize entertaining in our home. Raleigh walks me through the house, explaining the renovations that he has been working on with our contractor. He shows me walls that will soon be removed, the new layout for the dining room and home office, and how we are reconfiguring the bed and bathrooms to function for our growing family. The last room we walk through is the nursery. At our gender reveal party earlier this week, we all bit into cupcakes filled with blue icing. Soon, a little boy will call this room home.

After the house tour, we make our way to the backyard. The twins help Raleigh pick up pecans that have fallen from the trees, and I sit in a rocking chair facing the peanut field to shell the pecans from their outer coat. The sky is full of puffy white clouds, and the field is not dusty yet from the tractors picking peanuts. Our dog, Obi, is smiling with slobber as he chases squirrels and sniffs birds from the trees. After helping their dad, the girls play house on the back patio steps. As I sit watching and working, I notice some of the pecans slide easily out of their skin while others are more stubborn, causing dirt to collect under my nails as I pry them apart. Who would have thought when we moved home that I'd be sitting in a back field, pregnant and shelling pecans?! I'm being transformed, not just into a country girl, but into someone who sees glory through grimy fingernails. God has been wooing me with His prevenient grace from the beginning, going before me, covering my imperfect plans of what home looks like in His perfection. I haven't always recognized His trail of breadcrumbs, but He's led us here, to a place where we can dwell. To move, He's had to gut me from the inside out, just like our house. He's stripping me of the unnecessary fear, selfishness, and performance-based anxiety through confession. With every misstep, He's continued to declare me as someone to receive His gift of grace.

Understanding perfection has been a process, one where I've discovered that perfection is less about me becoming perfect and more about me serving God wholeheartedly. Because Jesus has made me His own, I have been given His Spirit, which helps me to give God glory. God's power has been made perfect in my weakness, and His grace has provided for me so that I am able to see His glory. Even though my body is growing larger every day of my pregnancy, I feel lighter on the inside. While this can easily be viewed as a season of *overwhelm*—picking out paint colors, appliances, baby bedding—it's also a season where I am overwhelmed by God's goodness. So many prayers are finally being answered in the most delightful of ways. Hope is so very near; I feel it in the fall breeze, whispering to me that there was weight in the wait. Now was the time for me to receive and rejoice in grace and peace. The wait has led me to celebrate.

Spiritual growth begins with knowing the message of salvation by grace that God delivered us from sin through Jesus Christ. Faith is not about anything that we *do*. But, if we keep His Word, His love is made perfect in us (1 John 2:5). Like fireworks bursting in the night sky, God showcases His glory to us so that we may see His goodness. God acts for us by providing everything we need so that we can also participate in holiness. God gives so that we may receive. What we receive, we too can give.

If our lives flow in a similar fashion as an event planning cycle, might there be something to this giving and receiving? As friends prepare a baby shower for me, won't I in return prepare a party for their next big life event? We get what we give, and we give what we get. If faith is not about our performance but more about living life with the virtues of Christ, we can give to others what we've been given through the power of the Holy Spirit. The deeper our faith grows, the more we can add qualities to our faith like goodness, knowledge, self-control, perseverance, godliness, kindness, and love to share with others. These virtues not only renovate our souls but also give life to those we love.

It's so easy to let these fruits rot so that we become spiritually dead and inhospitable. Love can grow cold in the once-hospitable heart; it starts with an ache, which leads to anger, and then we find ourselves alone. We become easily offended by the actions of others and voice our opinion even when we aren't asked to give it. We believe we are right and everyone else is wrong. Instead of inviting people to stay in our presence, we turn them away. We say we are Christians, but if Christ is the vine, are we behaving as His branches?

A hostess is a woman who has added fruit to her faith. She extends love by inviting guests into her home. Joy escapes from her mouth as she laughs with her guests. Peace wins the anxiety battle for her heart when she declares that the unplanned will *not* spoil the party. She is patient while preparing the food with a kitchen full of cooks and exerts self-control by holding her tongue when she could so easily refute. Kindness resides in her, and goodness flows out of her by serving others.[61] She rids herself of pride by becoming gentle with both her words and her manners. Hostesses give because they have received.

I've found myself lacking in virtue, not only as a party planner but also as a wife and a mom. I've practiced the exact opposite characteristics of a hostess toward my family and have instead shown hostility when my life has not gone according to my plans. Perfection has driven me away from grace. I see this now, out in the wild, away from the clamor. The boy in my belly kicks in agreement.

But grace has not turned her back on me.

Grace has not turned her back on you, either.

Grace grows like wildflowers in the field. We are given grace in abundance from a glorious God who is so very good to His children. His deepest desire is for us to remain in Him so that we may live fruitful lives. He knows how displaced we feel when we detach ourselves from Him. To woo us back to the garden where His love for us began, He gives us the gift of grace in the most unexpected of ways. We don't deserve it, but He gives it to us anyway, so that we might encounter a life where we know we are loved.

God uses both our people and our place so that we may live lives of purpose. God's plan for you and for me is to have faith in Him, trusting that He has given us everything we need for a fruitful life. This is the party that He has invited us too. Will we accept His invitation to attend?

If we eagerly accept, we will receive a rich welcome into the eternal kingdom of our Lord and Savior Jesus Christ.[62] Oh, that is a party I do not wish for us to miss!

To work out our salvation, we have to work on ourselves, removing what is dead so that we can continue to be made new. Paul writes in Philippians, "Do everything without grumbling or arguing, so that you may become blameless and pure, 'children of God without fault in a warped and crooked generation.' Then you will shine among them like stars in the sky." (Philippians 2:14–15 NIV). The Message version of this passage tells us to do everything cheerfully and without bickering or second-guessing. Eugene Peterson writes that when we do this, we will be "a breath of fresh air, providing people with a glimpse of the good living and of the living God."[63] Isn't that what the highest pursuit of a hostess should be? Might we become women who encourage others to live the good life by saying yes to the invitation from our living God?

Not only am I pregnant and am renovating our home, but I'm also planning a women's conference at church in February, a month before my due date.

One might assume that I was hypnotized with cupcakes to think this was a good idea.

Nope, not the case.

Instead, I felt the Holy Spirit urging my soul to take a risk.

Party planning was a talent that God had given me, and He didn't want me to bury it just because other parts of my life were busy. He wanted to multiply that talent to bless others and to give me happiness. I feel most alive when I'm working toward a date circled on my calendar. Planning a women's conference wasn't just one more thing on my already long to-do list; it was an invitation from God to continue growing spiritually.

There is nothing more exciting than witnessing a woman using her gifts to give God glory. Preparing for this conference, I worked with volunteers who had hearts of hostesses. Because of the size and the amount of planning involved, women were recruited to serve in the areas where their talents could shine. My detailed girls who were good with numbers became registration volunteers. The woman with the red hair who was always smiling at our meetings? She became my greeter team leader. Two friends who never hear the word *no* drove all over town collecting art, gift certificates, and all sorts of wonderful goodies to go in our gift baskets that we gave away. The interior designer who owns a furniture store led our decorating committee.

On and on, volunteer positions were filled, and women continued to say yes to the challenge, some with schedules much busier than mine. Because my team said yes, we were able to bless.

Brennan Manning sums up the parable of the talents in his book, *The Ragamuffin Gospel,* by explaining how the three servants were called to share with their master how they used the gifts he entrusted to them. "The first two used their talents boldly and resourcefully while the third prudently wraps his money and buries it, typifying the Christian who limps through life on childhood memories of Sunday school and refuses the challenge of growth and spiritual maturity. Unwilling to take risks, this person loses the talent entrusted to him or her." "The master wanted his servants to take risks. He wanted them to gamble with his money."[64]

While accepting the gospel of truth has nothing to do with our performance, spiritual growth is about moving forward in our journey of knowing God. Moving requires action. Ephesians 2:10 says that we are not saved by good works, but we are saved for them. God has prepared the party of our lives, but if we don't accept the portions that He has given us, He will use others to bring Him glory.

When we begin to allow doubt to direct our thoughts and actions, we stray from faith. God wants us to say yes to our talents! Yet so often, we cast them aside in the name of busyness. I get it, but we are all busy, and if God is calling you to do something, He will provide the time and resources so you can focus on serving Him with your gifts. If we are to "shine like stars," Paul says that we are to work out our salvation with fear and trembling (Philippians 2:12–13), not doubt and anxiety. While faith is a gift, it is also an ongoing process of growth.

The week of the women's conference, my calendar is covered with scribbled last-minute items to check off my to-do list, along with lists for the house and baby. I attend planning meetings and doctor's appointments, and then meet my husband at Lowe's after work to pick out doorknobs (a very important decision). I had my to-do list organized by each day of the week, with the beginning of the week being my last-minute prep work and the end of the week being where I coordinated volunteers to assist with tasks. All of the t-shirts and event bags were scheduled to come in on Wednesday before our event on Saturday, so we planned on volunteers being at the church on Thursday and Friday to help decorate, make name tags, and stuff bags. I had the whole week planned out, giving us plenty of time to get it all done.

That is, until the "snowpocalypse" shut down the South.

While we knew that the forecast called for snow (a rarity in lower Alabama), we had no idea how this snowstorm would freeze the major metropolitan cities of the South, leaving people stranded in their cars on highways while their children had to sleep overnight at their schools. My Facebook feed was filled with friends sharing their stories, some happy and others very hard, of how they were affected by the snow. Our city did not experience as much chaos as Birmingham and Atlanta, but we did shut down for two days until the roads were less icy. Because of the snowstorm, all of my plans for the week were lost. Trucks were unable to deliver orders, and our speaker was unsure if she would be able to drive on the roads to get to the conference. Staring at the television screen, I began to doubt I had heard God right.

If You wanted me to take a risk, will this risk pay off?

Outside my window, snow was gently falling from the sky. Raleigh and the girls were curled up on the couch, a rarity for a Tuesday. Adeline asked for pancakes with chocolate chips for breakfast. In that moment, I could panic about my plans or have peace and eat pancakes.

I chose pancakes.

Flipping flapjacks in the Wood House, I pause to take in the white wonder just outside my kitchen window. Icicles have formed on tree branches, and roofs look like they have been dusted with confectioner's sugar. The neighbors have made a sled out of their trashcan and are sliding down their hill in giggles. Our girls are in their footed pajamas, and Raleigh's feet are cushioned in his heavy socks. My rounded belly goes before me as I stand at the stove, and I rub it with one hand, recognizing that the snow was a chance for me to retreat before the rush that would come if our event wasn't cancelled. I call my family into the kitchen, and we stack warm chocolate chip pancakes on our plates and drizzle syrup on top, making it cascade down the cakes like a sticky caramel waterfall. Together we eat at the table as a family of four for one of our last times, and then we spend the afternoon building snowmen, drinking hot chocolate, and watching movies in the den. I go to bed in the evening without anxiety (which is a rarity for event week) and with faith that God will provide.

On Wednesday, the weatherman cleared us from further danger from the storm, and I was back at the church, making new plans for how we would get all the last-minute details done on time. Volunteers stepped up to the challenge with me, and together we found solutions to any problems from the storm. Nobody buried their talents; instead, the talents of many were multiplied. We became the body with different parts, functioning as one. With clipboard in hand, I checked everything off the to-do list, and when the doors opened on Saturday, we were ready to receive. Women dressed in boots and scarves spilled inside, and the narthex was soon filled with chatter over coffee and people checking in at the registration table. At nine a.m., we gathered together for worship. I felt the room moving into deeper communion, a bond of recklessness that comes only from taking risk. It was demo day, and the walls came down as we raised our hands to give God glory.

We were vulnerable.

God was rebuilding us from the inside out, gently whispering away our doubts with His grace. While we are not saved by good works, God does reveal His goodness to those who take risks and rewards us with "Well done, my good and faithful servant" (Matthew 25:23).

He was good to us.

He is good to us still.

If we receive everything we want, right when we want it, we might be immediately satisfied, but then we would fix our eyes on what is next. But, when we have to wait for what we want to come to fruition, we are enlarged in the waiting with bodies yearning for deliverance. We are a pregnant creation, eagerly waiting in hope for new life.

A week after the women's conference, water spills from me at my doctor's office.

She remains calm while I lie panicking on her table. Once again, I would be having a premature baby, six weeks earlier than expected. My husband drives me from her office to the hospital one block over, and my body begins to prepare itself for labor. A grip takes hold of my stomach, twisting me tighter and tighter until I can't stand the pain. It then releases itself for a moment, and I catch my breath before it begins again. I give Raleigh my wedding band. Moments of our life together flash before me—our first date, engagement, wedding, Adeline and Maralee—and I momentarily fear for my life and our baby. I didn't want to lose what God had so graciously given me. What if this was my last moment with Raleigh?

Raleigh takes my naked fingers and holds my hand as the contractions begin again. He helps me through the pain, assuring me that I am strong and loved.

Once the contraction subsided, I was forced to let go of his hand to be wheeled back into surgery. It was a different room, but the sterile environment, bright lights, and blue sheet covering my stomach were all too familiar. Would this baby be healthy, or would we soon endure heartbreak once again?

Raleigh is ushered into the room and sits beside me while I feel the doctors tug at my skin. My doctor is a she-woman, directing the room with admirable leadership skills. She says, "Here we go!" and then the cold room goes silent as we wait for what seems like hours for her to slide the baby out of me and into this world. But then, the room erupts with wailing.

Our son has arrived.

He's placed in Raleigh's arms, still red and splotchy with eyes closed, and I meet John Ridley. He's crying and I'm crying and Raleigh is crying; we are all crying at the gloriousness of this moment. We have a healthy baby boy.

A few days later, we leave the hospital and drive to our almost-finished house, taking a picture with Ridley on the front steps of the porch. The twins are dressed in big sister shirts and turquoise striped leggings, happy to be a family again. We then drive back to the Wood House and bring Ridley home to a house filled with moving boxes. Suddenly our toddlers have grown into girls as they take turns holding their baby brother in the blue chair. We've all grown up during our time in this house, learning the true lesson of perfection and grace.

The difficult times of pain that we experience are like birth pangs as we wait for what we do not yet have. But hope is the promise through the pain, urging us to keep going because in due time, we will experience glorious freedom. There is peace in knowing that "It is finished"—the difficult circumstances, pain, and trials—and that we can be at home today through the inheritance we've been given. First Peter 1:3–4 NLT celebrates this by stating:

> All praise to God, the Father of our Lord Jesus Christ. It is by his great mercy that we have been born again, because God raised Jesus Christ from the dead. Now we live with great expectation, and we have a priceless inheritance—an inheritance that is kept in heaven for you, pure and undefiled, beyond the reach of change and decay.

Gratitude blooms from the bud of patience. We come into this world with eyes closed and spend most of our lives not truly seeing the work of God in our lives. But when we open our eyes like a newborn child and see the goodness of our great Father, we unwrap grace, the gift of life.

Chapter 19:

EASTER

{HOW TO CELEBRATE YOUR
PEOPLE AND YOUR PLACE}

Let not the emphasis of hospitality lie in bed and board;
but let truth and love and honor and courtesy flow in all thy deeds.

~Ralph Waldo Emerson

IT'S MOVING DAY.

Boxes filled with pots and pans, toys, books, and makeup are piled in hallways of the Wood House. All that is left to be packed is our bedding, Ridley's bassinet, and a stack of diapers and wipes. Looking around the Wood House once more, I quietly say my good-bye.

While the men load the truck, I strap the baby and the girls into their car seats. We roll out of the steep drive one last time and pull away from the house that brought us sanctuary for over a year. We always knew this would be our temporary home, but a twinge of sadness still stirs within me as it drifts into our rearview mirror. Following the moving truck, we make our way through the city and turn right, heading toward the country. It's March, and the fields are bare. Cows huddle together near a watering hole on our left, and a windmill slowly turns its hands to our right. It's wide open, this land, and it welcomes my heart to be still amid moving and packing. When our drive approaches, I turn in and smile, knowing that we are finally home.

Our parents are here, helping us unload and unpack. We each take a room, and the boxes with their labels begin to pile up around us, ready to find their place in our new space. I work, then feed Ridley, and then work some more while he sleeps. Friends bring us food, and our mothers take turns helping us both with the baby and with settling into our new home. This routine becomes my life for the next few weeks, and I can remember how instead of feeling at peace, I needed more than anything to get out of the house, away from the boxes. "It's just too much," I tell my mom as I bounce Ridley while wiping away tears.

On Ash Wednesday, I throw on mascara and a shawl, wrap the baby in his cap and blanket, and march into our church. We sit in the back—me, Raleigh, and the baby—with our small group. It is here that I temporarily forget about the mess of unpacking.

I can't remember what our preacher spoke on that evening, but I do remember that I felt a deep sense of stability sitting in the pew with our friends. When it was time to receive our ashes, Raleigh and I took turns, and as I sat with my knees against the embroidered cushion, I was ashamed of my selfishness. After so many years of yearning for home, I am still unsettled; my heart beats faster at the sight of disarray, desiring perfection but not wanting to deal with the imperfect mess that comes with daily living. I want to rid myself of this feeling, once and for all, but I am helpless. How do I love my people, my place well?

When Paul was speaking to the church of Corinth, he shared how he pleaded with God not once or twice, but three times to take away a thorn that was in his flesh. We don't know what Paul's thorn was but it must have been great for him to ask God multiple times to rid him of it.

We, too, have our thorns. Some of us are in a season where life is just making us feel sad. Incredibly sad. We might be smiling on the outside, but we are living with an aching soul on the inside. This sadness makes us feel unhinged, especially when we have people in our lives that we love and so much to be thankful for. So many young women feel sad for the things unknown, unfulfilled hope, the yearning for a life lived fully and completely. Like Paul, we ask God to take away our pain, believing that if we can just rid ourselves of our thorns, then we can be whole.

If Lent is a season of release, shouldn't God release us of our pain?

But He said to Paul, "My grace is sufficient for you, for my power is made perfect in weakness" (2 Corinthians 12:9 NIV). God did not rid Paul of his pain; instead He offered Paul His goodwill, the promise of being with him through his affliction so that Paul would give God glory through his suffering.

Just as the deer pants for streams of water, so our souls have to pant for God (Psalm 42:1). When the sadness creeps in and we don't understand why we are feeling so down, we can go to God with the deepest of our sorrows through prayer.

"Deep calls to deep in the roar of your waterfalls; all your waves and breakers have swept over me" (Psalm 42:7 NIV). Perhaps our thorns are leading us to the throne of grace.

Throughout the season of Lent, I kneel at the throne of grace often. I desperately want our house to feel like everything is in its place, and perfectionism pricks against my skin daily. After Ridley's morning feed, I slip on my rain boots and housecoat to walk around our home. Outside, the world seems more serene, and as my feet make a path across the dewy lawn, I press into prayer. There is power here, walking and talking to Jesus, and once I'm done spilling my guts, I stare up at the sky, just above the pecan orchard. It has changed from lavender to light blue, and a yellow school bus barrels down the road.

Inhaling deeply once more, I know it's time to turn back and begin again. Inside, the living room has vases and books haphazardly placed in the bookcase, and the pink chair from the twins' nursery sits in the corner. Our hallway is lined with suitcases, and the office is still stacked high with Tupperware. I attempt to delight in my weakness to become strong, like Paul, but I desperately want a brown paper bag instead.

When Jesus first asked Peter, Andrew, James, and John to follow Him, the early disciples knew that this command would lead them to self-denial. Following Jesus, these men chose to turn away from being fishermen so that they could learn the ways of Jesus. John writes, "The next day John saw Jesus coming toward him and said, 'Look the Lamb of God, who takes away the sin of the world'" (John 1:29, NIV)! They watched Him in wonder as He poured out grace upon grace, even to those who cursed His name. Jesus devoted Himself to these men in brotherly affection, teaching them the difference between the law and love, and how to share with those who are in need.

If Lent is a time for self-reflection and deepening our relationship with God in Jesus Christ, then you and I can also deny ourselves to follow Jesus. Christine Hoover writes that when we surrender to Jesus, we allow Him to crucify our flesh with its earthly passions and desires.[65] Jesus wore a crown of thorns so that His grace can cover our weaknesses. Self-denial is about recognizing our need for a Savior. Jesus' death and resurrection assures us that happiness can come out of any heartache. When we find ourselves feeling sad, we don't need to feel ashamed. We need to experience our sadness, give God our pain, and have hope that soon our lives will be restored. Crucifixion breaks the cycle of self so we can love our people and place with greater sincerity.

When Peter was first asked to follow Jesus, he didn't know that he'd soon deny Jesus three times. Peter's story of denial and devotion captivates me because it is such a clear example of how even the cornerstone of Christ's church had his own thorns, doubts, and imperfections. Yet Jesus knew Peter's heart. After His resurrection, Jesus appears to Peter by providing him a net full of fish. When Peter recognizes that it is Christ, he jumps out of the boat and heads toward the shore where Jesus is burning a fire.

"Come and have breakfast." Peter, Thomas, Nathanael, and a few more disciples sit down, and Jesus offers them bread. When they finish eating, Jesus turns to Peter and asks, "Simon, son of John, do you truly love me more than these?"

"Yes, Lord," he said, "you know that I love you."

Jesus asks him a second time. Peter's response is the same. Hurt the third time Jesus asks, Peter replies, "Lord, you know all things; you know that I love you" (John 21:1–17 NIV).

Three times Peter denies Christ, and three times Jesus asks Peter if he truly loves Him. While Jesus knew that Peter *did* love Him and had plans for Peter to take care of the early church, Peter needed to say the words "Lord, I love you" out loud. This was his apology, his chance to look Jesus in the eyes so he could see that he was forgiven.

If forgiveness comes in the offering of fish and bread to Peter, might Christ also be calling you to the shore? He knows your heart and how you long to follow Him . . . yet you quietly turn away again, and again, and again. You want to deny yourself and be obedient, but you are afraid of what that kind of sacrifice looks like. It's easier to follow the path that you've carefully planned and go after the life you've always dreamed of living. So, do you go to the shore and follow your Savior? Or, do you choose yourself?

Before Jesus' death, the crowds would often ask the disciples who Jesus *really* was. Most thought of Him as a prophet at best; He couldn't really be the Savior, could He? But Peter would tell them, "He's the Christ of God." "Then Jesus told them what they could expect for themselves: 'Anyone who intends to come with me has to let me lead. You're not in the driver's seat—I am. Don't run from suffering; embrace it. Follow me and I'll show you how. Self-help is no help at all. Self-sacrifice is the way, *my* way, to finding yourself, your true self. What good would it do to get everything you want and lose you, the real you'" (Luke 9:23–25, MSG)?

If you want to find yourself, your true self, you must sacrifice. Lenten tradition is to deny yourself, not so you lose who you are, but so you can delight yourself in the love of Christ. The core of who you are is to give God glory. You were created to love Him, serve Him, follow Him, and when you do this, you experience strength. You bear witness to a love so beautiful, a love that meets you on the shore and offers you grace.

Will you look Jesus in the eyes and follow Him?

You and I are fishing, casting our nets into the waters, hoping to pull up enough fish to satisfy our souls, so that we may feel complete, whole, worthy, loved, and alive. But, if we keep trying to fish on our own, we will always be wanting more, comparing what we have been given to what others have received, and always craving the life that we have planned for ourselves. So, we will keep trolling, baiting our lines with the pursuit of perfection, hoping to catch contentment—hook, line, and sinker.

Or, we can listen to the man who calls from the beach and throw our nets on the right side of the boat. Jesus sits at the right side of God, on the throne of grace, and that is where we will find what we've spent our whole lives fishing for—completeness.

The desire of my flesh is to have everything in my life perfect. My house, family, myself. But perfection is found only in crucifixion, when I connect myself to Christ on the cross. I meet Jesus in the small parts of my day; we sit together as I cradle Ridley, pull clothes out of suitcases to hang in closets, and journal words onto blank pages. The thorn still stabs, and the idealistic image stays, yet it has less power over my soul. I can see it for what it truly is—a desire of my flesh—and I embrace it. Perfection no longer holds me down because I die to it daily by following Christ.

For my power is made perfect in weakness.

God promises to restore our souls, even if we never rid ourselves of the things that cause us to suffer. Not only does He replace our sorrows with joy, but He also brings happiness back into our lives to the point where we are laughing and singing. Isn't that crazy?

Easter is almost here, and the azaleas are suddenly blooming bright white and magenta pink at our house. The country is becoming alive, awakening from winter, and grass, prickly and green, shoots up, making way for bare feet to tread. Our days are getting longer, warmer.

We are expectant.

Our first spring is sweet. Raleigh buys the girls baby chicks, and we have friends over for an Easter egg hunt. We pick flowers, wear sundresses, and eat chocolate. The real is mixed with the make-believe as we combine a sacred act with secular activities, teaching our children how to celebrate the cross. On Maundy Thursday, we attend our church's Seder meal, a Passover celebration of God's redemption of Israel from Egypt. Two candles are lit. The room is silent. Our leader begins:

"I pray that the brightness of these lights may inspire us and bring spiritual joy and promise to all of us.

"Tonight we celebrate the Passover, the feast of freedom and redemption, and we read from the Haggadah. *Haggadah* is a Hebrew word meaning 'story.' It is a special story. It relates to our history: enslavement in Egypt, freedom, the holy commitment at Mount Sinai, and the return to the Promised Land. The Haggadah ritual is called *Seder*, meaning 'order' in Hebrew. The various parts of the Seder are symbolized on the special plate on your table."

Our plate is in the center of our table, and on it is a shank bone of a lamb, a reminder of the lamb offered on Passover, an egg, which was offered at the Temple of Jerusalem at the Passover festival, bitter herbs (the hardship of slavery), a mixture of chopped apples, cinnamon, nuts, and wine, which symbolizes the mortar used by the forced Hebrew laborers in Egypt, and parsley, a reminder of springtime, a sign of gratitude to God for the goodness of the earth. We also had salt water, symbolic of Israel's slavery and used to dip the parsley, the matzot (a kind of dessert) that represents Abraham, Isaac, and Jacob, and four cups of grape juice, which outlines the four stages by which Israel was taken away from slavery, how God *freed* the Israelites, *delivered* them from bondage, *redeemed* them, and *took* them as His people. There was also a special wine cup, Elijah's cup, which is a symbol of hope in the coming of the kingdom of God upon our world.

We follow the example of our leaders and participate in the Seder meal by following the songs and script that coordinate with the four stages of Israel's deliverance. Our table is set with Andi's fine china and a white linen tablecloth. Everything is ceremonially wonderful in beauty, and the meal cadences from somber to celebratory. At the end, we break bread and are dismissed with a blessing.

When Jesus participated in the last supper, He said to His disciples, "I have eagerly desired to eat this Passover with you before I suffer." And He took bread, gave thanks, and broke it, saying, "This is my body given for you; do this in remembrance of me. Now is your time of grief, but I will see you again and you will rejoice, and no one will take away your joy" (John 16:22 NIV).

On Good Friday, the cross is lit with red lights in a black room.

Jesus compared His death to a woman giving birth to a child. He explained that she has pain because her time has come, but when her baby is born, she forgets the anguish because of her joy that a child is born into the world.[66] Ridley rests in my lap with his feet barely hanging over the edge. On his original due date, March 17, he's five weeks old and whistles as his chest draws in soft, tranquil breaths. The day that I had circled on my calendar for over a year turns out to be just another ordinary Monday. I went to the doctor, helped the girls work on a school project, and made chicken tacos for dinner. My goal was to keep him in my womb until this date, but life does not always go according to plan, does it?

While Ridley greeted us before expected, it's not unexpected that his life has been a gift, and he reset me in the most wonderful of ways. His peaceful demeanor beckoned me to be calm in the chaos of moving, and he brings me a special sort of joy, a cradling of time, space to love wholly. I find redemption in his tenderness, a reminder to trust in God's sovereignty.

God has a plan for Ridley, just like He has a plan for His kingdom.

We build up to Easter Sunday like a woman about to deliver a baby. We walk through the pain of the final days, remembering the torment of the nails and blood, so that we can celebrate the resurrection. Hope has finally come, and we are like a newborn, born new in Christ.

God's plan has always been to redeem the world through Christ. Nothing that we do is too much for Him. He has taken on all of our junk so we can have joy. We celebrate Easter like a new mother who holds her baby in her arms for the first time, forgetting the pain of delivery by rejoicing in the gift we have been given. As children of

God, we are welcomed into the family by grace. We don't do anything to deserve it. Grace is given to us by God through Christ. This is His good and perfect plan.

The arrival of Easter ushers in a new way of living, if we trust in God's plan. We boast in Christ, give Him praise, and follow Him along the perfect path of peace. Hope rests inside of us, the promise that our thorns are not permanent once we cross into Zion, allowing us to pass over the temporary for the eternal. Like the disciples, our eyes are opened at the breaking of the bread, and we see the life of resurrection, how to abide in Christ even when we break down and are overcome with anxiety. Let us move, pack up our boxes, and permanently dwell in the house of the Lord. Sort through the clutter, keeping what is good and throwing out what is bad. Welcome this new chapter of your life, and celebrate the new life that only spring can bring.

Happy Easter.

Chapter 20:

GRADUATION DAY

{CELEBRATE YOUR PURPOSE}

Always wear your thinking cap with your party shoes.

~ Denise Keller

I TOLD MYSELF I WASN'T going to cry.

Today is preschool graduation, and I'm waiting with the other mamas, trying to keep myself together. Sitting in the church pew, I have saved seats for the rest of our family and nervously fidget with my camera, making sure I've got it set just right to document this special day. Earlier this morning, Adeline and Maralee couldn't contain the giggles as they stood in front of the hydrangeas for the first of many pictures. Holding my camera steady, I focused my lens, taking in their maturing features. Their round baby faces look more like Raleigh's every day, long and angular with high cheekbones and delicate lips. When they began preschool, their hair was barely below their ears, blonde and wispy, and now it hangs halfway down their backs, manes of sun-kissed highlights and waves.

Standing before me in their lime green program shirts and tennis shoes, I remember how on their first day of school they wore red checkered dresses with smocked apples, matching bows, and squeaky shoes. I was just as much of a mess then as I am now, unsure of what the future holds and yearning for moments I could not rewind. Never again would my girls be babies, one, two, three, four, or five. Did we make the most of the time we've spent together? Have we prepared a way for them? Are we ready to begin a new chapter of our lives?

The sanctuary begins to fill with family members. I'm at the end of our pew, and next to me is my dad and mom, then Raleigh and his parents. We've got our cell phones set to video. As the piano begins to play, children walk down the aisle toward the stage, one by one. I watch as the friends of my girls pass by me, little people who now seem so big, and then I spot our girls ready at the back of the room. Adeline makes her way down the red carpet first, keeping her eyes down until she spots me. Walking past our row, she darts a glance our way, and I give her a wink as she triumphantly walks up the stairs and finds her place on the stage. Behind her, Maralee is all smiles and gives us a thumbs-up as she meets her sister at the front of the room. Together they stand, side by side, and sing the words they've committed to memory the past few weeks.

Watching them, a wave of happiness cascades inside of me. As our girls clap their hands, stomp their feet, and shout words of joy, I am overwhelmed with pride. At the end of the program, as their preschool director calls their names, Adeline and Maralee walk off the stage to receive their diplomas from their teacher. I do not try to hide the tears that shimmer in my eyes. *They did it!*

Once the program ends, the parents are herded like sheep to the classroom where our children await. Adeline and Maralee jump into my and Raleigh's arms, and we hug them tightly amid all the people. At their seats, they've been given a celebratory snack of a sugar cookie shaped like a graduation hat with the words "Congrats!" scrolled in white. They each have a yearbook filled with pictures on colorful pages of laminated construction paper, and I hold these tightly against my chest, waiting to flip through once we've said our good-byes. The girls bounce between grandparents and give their friends one last hug before summer break. We then tell the teachers good-bye, and the tears begin to fall from my eyes again. It's crazy how you drop off your children with strangers at the beginning of the year and by the end, you have become friends, co-champions wanting the best for these kids. Glancing around the cheerful room one last time, we walk away hand-in-hand and head out into the world of possibility.

When I first graduated high school and college, I understood only the pride of personal success, but after watching Adeline and Maralee graduate, I now understand deeper what it means to have parental pride. Parental pride comes not from our own victories but from celebrating the victories of our children. Growing from baby to toddler to preschooler, I've watched our girls win every little victory—coming home from the NICU, walking, talking, potty-training, learning their ABCs and how to write their name—and I stand in amazement at their growth and development. I want to cheer them on, but part of me wants to hold them close in hopes that they will stay little forever. It's a tug of war within my heart, this growing and going.

Just as I was a proud parent at our twins' graduation, God is such a proud father of His children. He is with us, helping us navigate every unexpected obstacle that we face, teaching us how to develop in character so that we may graduate and move on to the next stage of life. Not only is He with us, He is good to us. Gracious, compassionate, slow to anger and abounding in love, He is our Heavenly Host, the calm parent who assures us that we are always welcome at home. As our Father, God is sitting front and center, giving us the thumbs-up encouragement to keep our heads up. He yells, "That a girl!" He whistles through His teeth and lifts us up in a papa bear hug, celebrating our achievements. With grace, love, and mercy, He helps us correct course when we've gone astray. Tenderly, He mothers us through the lens of Creator—how He carefully designed you and me from conception to completion, hoping that we will turn our hearts toward His.

From the time a child is born until age eighteen, a parent has 936 weeks before that child becomes an adult. On my nightstand sits a jar of marbles, based on a concept from a ministry called Orange, and each week I take out one marble. Autumn Ward, a curriculum writer for Orange, explains it this way: "The idea is that when you count the weeks you have left with a kid, you stand a better chance of making your weeks count."[67]

After kindergarten graduation, my jar for Adeline and Maralee is three quarters full, with only 624 marbles left. Have I made the 312 weeks from their birth until now count? When they look back at their preschool years, will they remember their rushed and frantic mommy hurrying them to school in time for their tea party, or will they remember their mommy who laid a quilt in the backyard and ate Cheetos and Oreos with them on a beautiful fall day?

Probably both.

The weeks we have with our children are not always going to be perfect. We will make mistakes, be ridiculously tired, and say words we will regret. There are no perfect parents, just as there are no perfect kids. But, we can teach our kids about grace through our imperfections. We can apologize, bake cookies, and sing "Let It Go" at the top of our lungs. Tickle fights, back scratches, and girl talks are a great cure for any misstep. What I hope my children remember is that their mama loved them to the moon and back, just like she loved Jesus. I hope they remember how much fun we had together, how we believed in teamwork, and how we celebrated each other with candles, cake, and ice cream.

Let's make our marbles count and focus on connection, not perfection, with our kids. Our goal as parents should be that when we have no marbles left in our jars, our kids know that they are loved and belong to Christ (and they are always welcome at home). Are we not supposed to train up a child in the way she should go so that she may not depart from it?[68] Let us train with grace through our imperfections and with lots and lots of laughter. As our boys and girls grow up into young men and women, our mission as parents is to guide them in their discipleship journey so that they may discover who God has made them to be. When we model His goodness and grace in our own lives, they see the value and worth of following Christ in their lives.

If school is designed to educate and grow us, might we fix ourselves on learning how to imitate the behavior of God our Father? Shouldn't our goal in life be to exemplify His truth, beauty, and goodness to the world around us? Could this not come in the form of hospitality?

Incorporating a posture of hospitality into our minds and hearts, we are no longer worried about pleasing the world through perfection. When we are no longer striving to attain the unattainable goal of human perfection, we become students of Christ, learning the ways of the heart, mind, and soul. Instead, when we accept the freedom of being in Christ, we become whole, complete, not lacking in anything. Truth is spoken in love like Christ, beauty is the centerpiece of our tables when we serve like Christ, and goodness is found when we extend an invitation to others like Christ.

It's not uncommon to exclaim "Hallelujah!" as we receive our diploma in hand and move our tassel from the right to the left. A simple scroll and a small gesture symbolize great value and worth. Paper and string are an outward display of the work of our minds and hearts, the hours spent formulating equations, writing essays, and giving verbal presentations. Nine hundred and thirty-six weeks of growth and development are wrapped up in one grand ceremony. As we throw our hats in the air, are we giving God the glory? Is He not the master and we the servant? Hallelujah—"God be praised"—is an expression of rejoicing, a way to worship. To praise God is to be a hallelujah hostess, giving Him the glory for every achievement we earn, every obstacle we face, and every victory we win. After all, He is the author and perfecter of our faith.

Our time on Earth is so short. As young graduates, we think we have the rest of our lives ahead of us, with plans to accomplish and dreams to fulfill. We want to eat, drink, and be merry with no regrets or thoughts to our actions. Youth is but a blink of the eye, and we want to make memories now instead of later. We don't know what the future holds, but we all expect to live long and have plenty of time to figure out what we want.

But for some of us, life ends before we ever truly begin living.

At my ten-year high school reunion, we lifted up our glasses as we remembered the classmates we had lost. One girl died in college from a tragic overdose. Another was killed instantly in a car accident. A close friend let sadness steal his smile. Still another classmate passed away from cancer. Each of these deaths was unexpected and unplanned, leaving us with more questions than answers. We dressed ourselves in our mourning clothes, and with a loss of words, all we could manage was to hug their mothers and fathers and sisters and brothers. After each of these funerals, I would come home and wrap myself in the arms of my husband and gather my children close to my chest, hoping and praying that we will be spared from that kind of pain. While there is a time for everything, there is a time when we will each draw our final breath. Where will your spirit go when your body is lowered into the depths of the earth?

We live in a world of options when it comes to religion. Some people believe we were made just for pleasure; others announce that our purpose is for productivity or consumerism. New Age philosophers suggest that we are part of the universe and will become dust once more. Muslims believe that Allah is the source of evil as well as good, and even the source of human sin, for Allah himself leads people astray. Then, there are people who believe we were created by chance, part of the evolution of this world, while others doubt whether our existence even matters. The Greeks believed that we were made to reach our full potential in art, music, technology, and the life of the mind.[69]

But the first book of the Bible says, "Let us make human beings in our image, to be like us. They will reign over the fish in the sea, the birds in the sky, the livestock, all the wild animals on the earth, and the small animals that scurry along the ground. " (Genesis 1:26). The word *us* refers to the Triune-God speaking to both Jesus and the Holy Spirit, which means that the three of them worked together to make man. When man was made in the image of God, we were made to be perfect like him—loving and serving without sin.

Since the beginning, we broke away from perfection in disobedience. But our desire for perfection stems from the sixth day of Creation. And for those of us who believe in the salvation offered to us through the death and resurrection of Jesus, we will once again return to a state of perfection and liberation from sin. In the last book of the Bible, the disciple John writes about heaven, saying, "I looked and there before me was a great multitude that no one could count, from every nation, tribe, people, and language, standing before the throne and in front of the Lamb. They were wearing white robes and were holding palm branches in their hands. And they cried out in a loud voice: 'Salvation belongs to our God, who sits on the throne, and to the Lamb.'"

John did not write that salvation comes to the communist, capitalist, or the humanist. He did not speak of the Islamist or the Buddhist. He said salvation belongs to God and Jesus. The people he saw worshipping were God's new people, His children who believed that Christ died for their sins and lived with the hope of heaven until they drew their last breath. They were salvation people. Sinclair Ferguson writes,

God lifts us not only from what we are by nature to what Adam was in the Garden of Eden, but to what Adam was to become in the presence of God, and would have been had he persevered in obedience. The gospel does not make us like Adam in his innocence—it makes us like Christ, in all perfection of his reflection of God. This is the essence of the salvation Christ provides.[70]

If your heart longs for perfection, for a day when you no longer have to plan but receive promise, consider deeply that you were made like Christ, a perfect reflection of God. Believing in the truth of salvation, you believe that you were created for a purpose from a God of love, not of evil, a God of redemption, not a byproduct of the universe. You were made for more than work or merriment or shopping or nothing-ness—you were made for glorification, to join a party of celebration.

Please don't wait to accept God's invitation to join the party.

A party decoration that I've always loved is confetti. Like gradua-tion hats tossed into the air, confetti captures the heart of celebration. To watch these paper fireworks flutter in the air is enchanting. For a moment, we don't care about the mess that the explosion of brightly colored paper brings; we just want to lift up our hands and let it rain down on us, shedding our sufferings and pain.

God's love is like a confetti cannon, bursting in our hearts with happiness and joy. Instead of living by our calendars (that we think we can control), confetti invites us to look up, pause, and receive His gifts of grace and peace. Confetti is the grand finale, inviting us to celebrate life everlasting. After Christ's second coming, all of the bodies of believers will be reunited with our souls in heaven. We will complete the process of salvation, receiving robes of white linen to clothe our new bodies in a new universe. We will see Jesus face-to-face and join a body of believers in celebration. On this great day, everyone who trusts in Christ as their Redeemer will appear with Him in glory. This will be the party of eternity.

To graduate from earth into the glorious, we need to grab some confetti instead of a clipboard. God is going to keep on surprising us with His plans, but we can rest in knowing that He will provide for us. He's got all the details covered, the timeline laid out, and the entertainment scheduled. We need to let go and let God work within us, refining us through suffering, perseverance, and hope. The salvation people were saved by grace but not saved from heartache. But God was with them through the pain, and He is with us now. All we must do is have faith.

While we might have diplomas hanging on our walls to show the world our education accolades, I'd like to hope that today you celebrate your own sort of graduation. My prayer with this book is that God has grown you since the start, turning you into a woman who is not only unafraid of practicing hospitality but who is also ready to extend the invitation of salvation to others. Let us be hostesses who make others feel welcome, whether over wedding celebrations, women's retreats, or while waiting in the trenches for hope to be fulfilled. Might we overcome our fears of missing out, anxieties of the heart, and deception of the mind so that we may show kindness and love and grace to people we encounter. As we begin to plan our next party, let us focus on connection, not perfection, bringing people into community and celebrating the occasions that are truly special.

To live a life of invitation, we are living in Christ, the perfecter of our faith. When we give our expectations to God and realize that perfection is found only in Christ, we are less disappointed, discontent, and depressed. True happiness is found when we are living in community with other Christ followers and giving His love to others. We can spend our whole lives trying to "have it all," but God simply wants us to accept His invitation and enjoy the people, places, and purpose that He has planned for us. You are invited to join the party. Come, gather, feast your eyes on the abundance of life everlasting! Throw your hat in the air.

Celebrate the life you've been given.

 *Epilogue:*

CHEERS

MAY WE BE HOSTESSES WHO are kind and gentle, welcoming our guests into our homes not to marvel at our pretty things but to share our sacred space of hospitality. As we invite, let us extend an invitation with a smile, a warm hello, and sincerity.

Here's to celebrating the happy and the hard, cheering instead of comparing, connection instead of perfection, and cupcakes eaten in community. Let us love our people well, always making them feel special. Let us love our place and learn how to make whatever city we live in our home. Let us love our purpose, for we were created to give God glory.

Cheers to a life well lived!

Invited

PARTY PLANNING HANDBOOK

Welcome, Y'all!

I LOVE TO ATTEND A good party.

Not necessarily a let's-go-crazy-and-roll-a-house kind of party (although those can be fun)! No, the kind of parties I like to throw are the ones that stretch into the evening and leave me so happy that by the end of the night I'm humming as I do the dishes. When I think back to some of my favorite parties, I remember the karaoke night with my sorority sisters right before college graduation, how we all sang our hearts out to the latest country music songs while hugging necks and promising to always remain friends, or my friend Laura's wedding on St. George Island, where I wore an emerald green dress that whipped around me as my husband spun me on the dance floor. I think about playing rock band in our living room in Montgomery with our small group friends, and how loved I felt after my baby shower at my sister-in-law's house for our twins. Some parties were simple while others grand, but they were all with people I love.

Throughout this book, we've shared the importance of celebrating, being in community, and living a life of connection, not perfection. Now, I'd like to give you a glimpse of some of my favorite party planning tips, comforting and quick recipes for entertaining family and friends, and simple decorating tips to make your home feel inviting. The goal for this section is to provide you inspiration for entertaining, no matter what the occasion. In the pages that follow, I've laid out sample parties inspired by the chapters of this book that you can recreate with your family and friends at home. I've also given you a glimpse inside my event planning toolkit, with the essentials to make your corporate function, church event, or community fundraiser a success. Take these ideas and make them your own, adapting the party depending on the size and location of your event.

The idea of planning back-to-basic parties is what defines how I entertain—serving family-style, picking flowers from my own backyard, and saying yes when others offer to bring a dish. Even though parties can range from two people celebrating an anniversary to two hundred people gathering for a special event, the purpose is the same: to celebrate. The best parties are the ones where the hostess is enjoying the party as much as her guests and she doesn't allow the stress of planning the perfect party to ruin the fun. The antidote to perfection is when we as hostesses can be mindful of others, making our homes less about us and more about serving our guests in love. To get back-to-basics as a hostess, I like to remember this party acronym:

P – Make a **plan**

A – Have a positive **attitude**

R – Create a **rain** plan

T – **Thank** people often

Y – Remember, it's not about **you**

Instead of spending all of our time cleaning floorboards, dusting windowsills, and crafting party decorations, we focus on the keys of any great party: eating, drinking, and entertaining. Serve really amazing food made with fresh, seasonal ingredients (whether prepared by you, take-out, or from a caterer) and pair it with drinks that make guests feel festive, like holiday sangria for a Christmas party. Entertainment for parties depends on the occasion, but don't plan so many games that people tire from playing them. Music is a must for creating a celebratory mood for your party, whether it is a band, a friend who brought their guitar, or background music. If you want to decorate, light some candles and make a simple centerpiece that correlates with the theme of your party from flowers that can be snipped from your own backyard. Add a wreath and some balloons and call it done. Remember, for us to celebrate our people well, we have to release our ideas and let the party unfold naturally. The unexpected will happen, I guarantee it, but don't let it spoil your fun.

Parties are celebrations that we share with the people who matter in our lives. We save the date, buy the present, pick out the dress. We should hate to decline an invitation to attend a party, because parties are a reason to wear heels, catch up with friends, and forget for a little while all the things that weigh

I would love to see how you use these examples to plan your own party! Feel free to tag me @chrisioprice or use the hashtag #invitedbook to show us your party on social media.

us down. I guess that's why parties are called special occasions—it's a reason to be free and merry. When we celebrate our people with intention, they feel as special as the occasion, and we, the hostesses, feel pretty warm and fuzzy too.

To download your free Party Planning sheets, head to www.invitedbook.com/freebies.

Planning:

Every great party begins with planning and preparation. Before a bride ever says "I do!" or a baby smashes his first birthday cake, there has been a party planner working behind the scenes to make the party unforgettable. The party planner has been dreaming of this party for months now—scribbling to-do lists, making phone calls, and staying up past her bedtime ordering who knows what online. The party planner masters the art of entertaining by making sure the details of the day are covered so that she and her guests can enjoy the day with as little stress as possible.

As a party planner, it is easy to feel overwhelmed with all the party preparation. To keep all my plans together, I like to have worksheets in a three-ring binder or use my *Happy Hostess* party planner. The key to not getting overwhelmed is to have a theme and prioritize the essentials for the party.

Here are the five essentials you need to throw a great party:

- Theme
- Invitations/Guest List
- Decorations & Set-Up

- Food & Drink

- Activities

Let's take a closer look at how these essentials can help you create a party that is fun and inviting:

THEME:

Party themes are like a business brand, it's the unspoken message that is relayed throughout your celebration, highlighting what you love and want to share with your people. A well-planned theme is what draws your guests in and keeps them talking long after the party has ended. Most often, a theme is formed from an idea of how you want your party to look, feel, and taste. After some initial thought and research, the concept is transformed into a design/color palette and can be found in the details of the day–invitations, napkins, cupcake toppers, food, decorations, and party favors.

I like to jot down ideas for party themes inside my *Happy Hostess* party planner and create Pinterest boards online. If I go to a wedding or birthday party where I love the look and feel of the event, I save invitations, napkins, and party favors in a box so I can use them as examples while planning my next event. Because parties are visually appealing, I often take pictures with my phone of party supplies that I find around town to help me create a party that is cohesive from concept to completion.

When planning a party for others, it is so much fun to interview them on what they envision for their party. Even though my children are young, they love for me to ask them what kind of party they want. One year, my twins wanted a *Frozen* themed birthday party, and we had the best time scrolling through Pinterest together to get ideas for their cake, decorations, and activities. During your "interview," be sure to ask the guest of honor her favorite foods, colors, and the message that she wants to share with her guests.

Whenever you get stuck in party planning, always refer back to the theme. Let the theme guide you as you pick out party supplies, food, and decorations. Themes help you bring your celebration to life so you can create an atmosphere that will be enjoyed by you and your party goers.

INVITATIONS/GUEST LIST:

I couldn't agree with Letitia Baldrige more when she states, "The invitation is what makes people come to your party." Call me old-fashioned, but one of my favorite things is to walk out to my mailbox and open an invitation with my name on it. I'm like a kid, checking the return address to see who sent it! As I slide the invitation out of the envelope, I take note of the weight of the card, the design, and the type of font used to inscribe the details of the party. Sending an invitation in the mail takes extra time for the hostess, but it is truly a delight for the recipient to know that she was on the guest list.

Now, don't get me wrong, I'll gladly accept an invitation to a party that is sent electronically or through a text/phone call. The type of invitation sent sets the standard for the type of party you are throwing. It is your guests' first taste of your theme and gives them an idea of what kind of function they are attending. If your party is more formal, like a wedding or dinner party, it is nice to choose a heavier weight paper, and consider custom calligraphy, embossed text, or letterpress invitations. If you are hosting a more laid-back event, such as a barbecue or shrimp boil, you can choose a lighter weight paper (I recommend a bright white cardstock) and use fonts and icons that coordinate with your theme. I also love handmade invitations. My friend Stephanie always hosts a Christmas brunch with Santa, and one year she sent my kids an invitation that looked like a snowman and was created with toilet paper rolls, construction paper, and glitter. She sent the invitation in a long tube and I had just as much fun opening it up as my kids! Other friends have also sent us birthday party invitations that were created with glitter paper and stickers from a craft store, and I've even seen scratch and sniff invitations for bachelorette parties. If you are having a festive theme, don't be afraid to throw some confetti or glitter inside the invitation too.

Since our children were born, my husband and I have started to create party invitations for their birthdays and for other special occasions like engagement dinners, bridal luncheons, and baby showers. You can shop our invitations online at www.christenprice.com/shop-the-studio. It is easy to get lost in the choices of invitations, and my advice for creating back-to-basics style invitations is to start with these necessities:

- Who is the event for? Who is hosting it? Who do the guests need to rsvp or regret to?

- What type of party is it? What type of attire should your guests wear?

- Where will the party be held?

- When will the party take place?

No matter what your invitation looks like, these necessities will give your guests the information they need to determine if they can attend or not. Once you've laid out the necessities, you can use these tips to design an invitation that is classic instead of cliché:

Use no more than three fonts. I recommend using a serif or sans serif for the basic information and using a calligraphy or more festive font for the details you want to highlight, like who the party is for. Use larger fonts for the main message of the party and smaller fonts for the details like who to reply to and gift registries.

Use the same colors and design in your invitation as your party theme. For example, if your invitation has a bright pink chevron background, use bright pink chevron plates or napkins at your party.

If you hand-make your invitations, consider using multiple layers like glitter paper and cardstock or stickers and ribbon. Also, hand calligraphy is so lovely but remember to write neatly.

DECORATIONS & SET-UP:

I have spent so much money on decorations over the years, and I've learned through trial and error that back-to-basics decorating is all about using what you have, keeping it simple, and not being afraid of throwing a little whimsy in the party mix. Imagine your party being like decorating your living room–keep the base simple and use color as your accent pieces. Invest in some really nice Edison string lights for your backyard patio, white tablecloths, and a fun set of acrylic serving dishes, plates, and cups that you can reuse for almost any home party. Use seasonal flowers, vegetables, and fruit for centerpieces, mix and match chairs, and then choose accessories that are timeless, such as white votive candles in clear containers, seashells, pecans, or magnolia leaves, and burlap runners to complete the tablescape.

Purchase the "color" items for your party to tie together your theme. Buy colorful balloons, napkins, banners, straws, food labels, cupcake toppers, and food. Let these be your "throw-away" items, the things that entice people to eat, play games, or directional signs that help them know where to go.

It's nice to have help setting up, but remember to mind your manners, even if your help is your husband, mom, or best friend. As you read throughout the book, the decorations and set-up easily cause me the most anxiety. The best solution is to be kind, get enough rest before the event, and remember that the party is about connection, not perfection. And hey, there's nothing that a roll of duct tape can't fix!

FOOD & DRINK:

Y'all, people come to parties to eat and drink, so don't go skimpy with some Cheetos and tap water. As I mentioned in Chapter Five, *Weddings*, people eat with their eyes first, so offer food that is colorful, coordinates with your theme, and is easy to cut. Food and drinks are the stations that people gravitate to and are a great way to give your guests something to hold. When you are meeting new people or have invited people who are more introverted, putting something in your guests' hands can set them more at ease. This may be a plate of appetizers or something to drink. Isn't it easier to talk when you can fidget with something in your hands?

If you enjoy cooking, then cook! If you are hosting a birthday party or shower, I suggest preparing the food the day before or bringing your food to the hostess's house ready to plate. For dinner parties, crawfish boils, and tailgates, you are fine throwing the food in the oven or on the grill after your guests arrive, but be sure to have some appetizers, cheese boards, or some nuts for people to munch on while the food is cooking. If you don't like to cook, don't let that stop you from throwing a party. Go to a local caterer or meat store and shop their fresh cheeses, dips, and frozen casseroles.

One thing that has helped me go back-to-basics with preparing food over the years is to keep children's birthday parties simple. Pinterest is full of beautiful ideas for food tables that are filled with candy, gum balls, and cupcake pops, but all kids really want are pizza or chicken nuggets, a store-bought cupcake, goldfish, and some sliced apples. I know that doesn't seem fun, but if you stick a custom cupcake topper in the cupcake and serve the drink with a striped straw, the kids (and parents!) are really just fine and dandy.

For drinks, I prefer drinks that are both tart and sweet, like lemonade, margaritas, and sangrias. At adult parties, I always have a non-alcoholic beverage and enjoy dressing it up with freshly cut lemons, limes, and oranges, or use cucumbers, strawberries, lavender, or rosemary as extra flavor. It's also a lot of fun to get creative with your ice cubes and place fruit inside ice cubes or buy ice cube trays that make ice into different shapes and sizes. At children's parties, buy old-fashioned Cokes, personalized water bottle labels, and all-natural fruit drinks with straws to keep spills at bay.

ACTIVITIES:

Activities serve as a great way for people to get to know one another or as a way to keep children busy at different stations. If you are hosting a "Friends-giving," let your guests write down what they are thankful for on a paper leaf and hang all the leaves together from your centerpiece of sticks taken from the yard. For wedding showers, let the bride and groom play trivia games on how well they know each other, and for baby showers allow guests to use a stamp pad to leave their thumbprint on an art print for the nursery.

Activities can even involve food, where guests can make their own mashed or sweet potatoes or desserts like fondue, chocolate truffles, or frosted sugar cookies.

Parties should have no more than three activities, so the guests can have enough time to mingle without feeling pressured to do something. Have a friendly hostess explain the activity and get into playing the game so it makes everyone else excited about playing too.

Creating an Event Timeline

Before any party or event begins, it is important to have a timetable to help you organize all of your tasks. What type of event you are planning determines how far out you need to timeline. Here are my suggestions:

- Casual Get-Together with Friends (tailgate party, summer cookouts, girls' nights) – 1-2 weeks

- Dinner Party – 1 month

- Holiday Party – 1-2 months

- Birthday Party – 2 months

- Showers (engagement, bridal, baby) – 3 months

- Church, Community, or Corporate Fun Nights (paint parties, ice cream socials, May Days, movie nights) – 2 months (I like to plan these quarterly)

- Corporate Fundraiser Dinners/Women's Gathering Dinners – 4-6 months

- Charity Events, Conferences – 6-10 months

- Weddings – 8 months-1 year

While all these events vary in the amount of time it takes to plan them, they all begin by determining the essentials. If you are planning an event that takes six or more months, it is so important to reserve a date at your venue. That will determine when your timeline will need to begin.

Remember in your timeline to account for the six stages of the Event Planning Cycle which are:

- Stage One: The Beginning/Dreaming Phase

- Stage Two: Planning Phase

- Stage Three: Promotion Phase

- Stage Four: Month of Event (four weeks out, three weeks out, two weeks out, week of)

- Stage Five: Event Day!

- Stage Six: Wrap-Up

Setting a Budget

Before any event begins, it is important to set a budget. While budgeting, consider these costs:

- Number of Guests

- Invitations and Postage

- Venue Rental

- Food and Drinks

- Decorations

- Clothing

- Photography/Videography

- Music/Sound

- Transportation/Hotels

- Tables, Chairs, Tablecloths

- Promotion Materials (yard signs, t-shirts, banners, billboards, posters, radio or TV ads)

- Event Signage and Programs (registration, parking, programs, nametags)

- Gifts (wrapping and purchasing)

- Party Favors/Volunteer Thank You's

Planning a Corporate, Church, or Community Event

When you are making your timeline and setting a budget, use this simple event planning checklist to help you build your event:

- Mission/Purpose of Event

- Event Location

- Volunteers/Paid Staff Members

- Sponsors
- Special Guests, Keynote Speakers
- Planning Meetings – Date, Time, Location
- Event Schedule
- Prayer
- Facilities
- Marketing
- Tickets/Registration
- Decorating
- Giveaways
- Production (lights, sound, stage, video)
- Musicians—screen them and get samples of their work
- Specific photos you want captured
- Set-up and break-down team
- Food & Drinks
- Transportation
- Hospitality Coordinator
- Special Needs
- Product Table
- Awards

Planning a corporate event takes extra attention to detail. I can't stress enough how important it is to pray over your event and to gather a great group of people to help you make the event a success. As I shared in Chapter Eighteen, *A Special Delivery,* I did not plan the women's conference at my church alone. I had teams of people who were gifted in different areas of service to help me with these categories. As the coordinator of the event, it was my job to work with these volunteers to complete the tasks leading up to the event.

Working with volunteers can be a challenge at times, but it can also be very rewarding. Whenever I have a new event that I want to plan, I first develop a relationship with my volunteers. I stop by their office, take them to coffee, or invite them to a retreat so I can learn more about their passions, work, family, and faith. I love to find out what makes them laugh, what their favorite candy is, and how full their schedules are so I can evaluate how much time I should expect them to be able to commit. Volunteers become "your people" while planning an event, and building a relationship is crucial to working together well.

To create an event that people want to come back to year after year, your team will need to invite their friends, family, neighbors, and coworkers to attend with them. Typically, people are drawn to events that have a festive atmosphere, are family friendly, and have great food.

While planning your event, take note of your event logistics. How many bathrooms do you have? Will people have to wait in line? If so, where does the line begin, and what can people do while standing in line? How far will people have to walk from the parking lot to the entrance? Is there childcare? What kind of first impression do you want your visitors to have when they enter your event venue? How does your event smell and sound? The events that plan out these details are the events that continue to draw people in year after year. The ones that don't plan for logistics are the events where people will stand in line to complain, want a refund, or gossip about at next month's book club. When an event is executed well, it truly is magical.

It's easy to get lost in the event planning cycle while planning a corporate, church, or community event, especially when the unexpected happens right before your event is to begin. I think it is imperative to keep the planning fun, give yourself and volunteers' incentives and rewards, and to remember the reason why you are working so hard. Keeping the mission as the focus of the event helps you to stay motivated so you can keep others going. Remember, planning these types of events is all about bringing people together to create community. So dream big, gather your people, and take a risk!

Planning a Social Party

As I shared in Chapter Three, *A Call for Community*, whenever I host a party at my house, I use Ina Garten's advice and work backwards from the time the party starts. On the day of a party, I also like to keep an entertaining checklist that reminds me or whoever is helping of last-minute items that need to be completed like cleaning, lighting candles, turning on the music, putting ice in the ice bucket, laying out serving spoons and utensils, putting extra toilet paper in bathrooms, taking out the trash, and fluffing pillows.

As you timeline your event, ask yourself these five questions:

1. What is the party schedule?
2. What do I need to order?
3. What do I need to make?

4. What needs to be delivered and picked up? Time? Location?

5. Who is helping me?

As I begin planning my party, I love to find inspiration online and in my favorite party planning books. Here are some of my favorite sites:

- www.thetomkatstudio.com

- www.amyatlas.com

- www.shopsweetlulu.com

- www.marthastewart.com

- www.cakeeventsblog.com

- www.ohhappyday.com

Favorite Books:

- *New Manners for New Times* by Letitia Baldrige

- *Celebrations* by Real Simple

While I think all these resources create parties that qualify as "Pinterest parties," they are not always easily adaptable for real-life parties. Rather, I like to use Pinterest parties to get my creativity churning. I use the concept to plan parties that work for my own space and people. Remember the purpose of celebrating is to show your friends and family how much they mean to you!

To download your free Party Planning *sheets, head to www.invitedbook.com/freebies.*

Parties:

In this section, you'll find the details of the parties, holiday celebrations, and community gatherings that were shared throughout the book. Each celebration has examples of invitations, food and drinks, decorations, and activities to help you throw a simple but amazing party. Enjoy!

Bridal Showers

Being a bride is one of the happiest (and most stressful!) seasons of a girl's life. There are so many details to plan for the wedding, so to have friends be hostesses who take care of all the planning of the bridal shower is truly delightful. More than likely, your bride will have a theme for her wedding–rustic, sophisticated, retro–and you can use that theme to plan your bridal shower or choose to go all out girly with a pink, white, and gold theme. Going gold will make the shower sparkle with classic elegance and won't replicate what the bride is working so hard on for her wedding and reception.

Invitations/Guest List

Three months out, ask the bride for her guest list and gather a group to help you host.

If your bride is a sparkle and glitter girl, go for the bling, but if she is more demure, stick with a white or baby pink luxe cardstock with a gold embossed font. Bridal showers work well on a Saturday morning or Sunday afternoon. (I prefer parties on Sundays because I'm already dressed for church!) Mail invitations three weeks to one month before the shower and make sure to note where the bride is registered.

Decorations & Set-Up

My favorite bridal showers are the ones hosted in a home, but you can always reserve a party room at a local clubhouse, hotel, or tea room. If you are hosting the shower in your home, decorate your front porch with flowers and ferns, and hang a wreath or door hanger that incorporates the bride's soon-to-be last name. Have a small table at your entryway for the guests to sign the guest book. Place a mirrored decorative tray that has a gold rim on the table and ask the bride for some engagement pictures that you can place in gold picture frames on the tray and have a Mason jar or small vase with pink flowers next to the pictures.

For the food table, ask your hostesses if they have any gold-plated serving platters that they can bring. Annieglass has a beautiful line that you can invest in and use for dinner and holiday parties, or you can find trays on Wayfair.com or shop acrylic trays at Target. If the gold trays are too much of an investment, use glass or white porcelain platters. Place a large vase of pink flowers in the center of your table (garden or spray roses, pink ranunculus, or lilies).

Food & Drink

Whipped Cream Pound Cake

Raleigh's grandmother, Okalee Gunter, is known for her cakes. This pound cake is best when it is firm. I like to make a traditional and chocolate pound cake and serve with fresh berries, whipped cream, and chocolate sauce. To make a three-tiered naked cake, double this recipe and cook in 8" round pans (you will have some batter leftover that can be made into muffins). Make a buttercream icing that goes between each layer (I prefer Wilton's Buttercream Icing with butter extract and water instead of milk).

Ingredients:

- 2½ sticks butter
- 3 cups sugar

- 6 eggs
- 3 cups flour (plain)
- 1 teaspoon vanilla
- ½ pint whipping cream

To make this a chocolate pound cake, add ½ cup chocolate cocoa powder to mixture

Instructions:

Combine butter and sugar, and add eggs one at a time to mixture. Add flour and vanilla. Mix well and add whipping cream (already whipped) gradually with a blender. Pour into a Fleur De Lys or crown Bundt cake pan and bake at 300 degrees for approximately 1½ hours.

Palmetto Cheese with Wheat Thins

Pawley's Island makes an amazing palmetto cheese that you can find in the grocery store. It is creamy and comes in a variety of flavors and is served great with Wheat Thins or Ritz crackers.

Stephanie's Pink Punch

My friend Stephanie and I worked together at the American Cancer Society, and we helped host a bridal shower for a mutual friend. She served this pink punch at the shower, and it's been my go-to party punch ever since!

Ingredients:

(double the ingredients if you are hosting a party for more than twelve people)

- 12 ounce can frozen pink lemonade concentrate, thawed
- 4 cups white cranberry juice or white grape juice
- 1 quart club soda, chilled

Instructions:

Stir together lemonade and juice and let chill for one hour or up to 24 hours. Just before serving, pour the club soda into the punch to give it fizz. Serve in slender tall glasses with a gold striped straw.

Activities

Place a "tip" jar in the living room where guests will be sitting and pass around slips of paper and pens for the bride's family and friends to write down their best marriage tips. Ask one of the hostesses to read the tips as the bride is unwrapping presents to help spark conversation in the room.

Baby Showers

In the Introduction, I shared the baby shower Michelle and I helped host for Hannah. The colors for the party coordinated with Hannah's nursery for Sydney Grace, which were lilac, cardinal pink, and lime green. The flowers made the baby shower feel extra girly!

Invitations/Guest List

Stick with the floral theme on your invitations, and make sure to share the baby's name so guests can purchase monogrammed items. Host a baby shower on a Thursday evening or weekend afternoon, and send invitations three weeks prior to the party.

Decorations & Set-Up

On your front door, create a door hanger with the baby's name on it and make sure there is space to write the baby's weight and birth date beneath it. Give this to the mom-to-be as a hostess gift.

Create a hanging floral chandelier to go over your food table with a wire wreath, glue gun, realistic silk flowers, scissors, and twine, ribbon, or fishing wire.

On the fireplace mantel, spell out the baby's name with alphabet balloons or hang a banner. In the center of the fireplace, create a collage of nursery-inspired art prints, Bible verses, and baby pictures from the mom and dad, as well as the sonogram pictures of the soon-to-be newborn.

Food & Drink

Mrs. Tucker's Cheese Straws

Michelle's mama made these cheese straws for Hannah's baby shower, and the secret ingredient is Rice Krispies! They are so good, y'all!

Ingredients:
- 2 cups self-rising flour
- 2 cups Rice Krispies

- 2 sticks real butter
- 2 cups grated sharp or extra sharp cheese
- Cayenne pepper to taste

Instructions:

Mix all the ingredients together and roll into balls. Place on lined or greased baking sheet and use a fork to flatten them. Cook at 350 degrees for 20 to 30 minutes.

Veggie Pizza

Ingredients:

- (2) 8-ounce cans pre-packaged refrigerated crescent rolls
- 8 ounces cream cheese, softened
- 1 cup sour cream
- 1 envelope ranch salad dressing
- 3 tablespoons mayonnaise
- 3 cups finely chopped mixed vegetables (broccoli and shredded carrots work great together)
- 1 cup finely shredded sharp cheddar cheese
- 1 cup grated Parmesan cheese

Instructions:

Preheat oven to 350 degrees and line a greased baking sheet with the crescent rolls to form a rectangular crust, making sure the seams are pressed together tightly. Place in the oven and let the rolls bake for 10-12 minutes until cooked and then place on the counter to cool. In a medium sized bowl, mix together the cream cheese, sour cream, ranch dressing, and mayonnaise until smooth. Spread over the crust with a spatula and sprinkle with vegetables and cheese. Cut into squares and serve.

Strawberry Cupcakes

Order them! Order them! Order them! It's worth every penny!

Water with Flower, Fruit, and Herb Ice Cubes

Who says water has to be served with plain ice cubes? Dress up your water by placing edible flowers like violas and pansies, along with raspberries, blueberries, rosemary, and mint into ice cube trays. Right before guests arrive, arrange the ice cubes in a decorative bowl next to your water pitcher and let your guests choose which ice cubes they want placed in their cups. Make sure to have some ice tongs next to the bowl.

Activities

Print a calendar for the month the baby is expected to arrive and write the due date inside the appropriate square. Have the guests write their own guesses in the days on the calendar.

Birthday Party

In Chapter One, I shared the ups and downs of planning my son's first birthday party, which was an "Up, Up, and Away" theme. Naturally, I used more of a blue color palette since it was Ridley's birthday, but you could easily use this theme for a girl party too by using aqua, pink, and yellow.

Invitations/Guest List

Hot air balloons were the focus of my theme, and I found some adorable vintage invitations from a company called Anders Ruff Custom Designs. For this party, we kept the guest list to our extended family and my best friend (who is like family). I hand-delivered the majority of the invitations two weeks prior to the party.

Decorations & Set-Up

There are so many fun things you can do for a child's birthday party! As I mentioned in Chapter One, I made a "hot air balloon" out of a wicker basket that I bought at Target and some blue and white balloons attached to the basket's handles.

For a guest book, I had family members write a note to Ridley in Dr. Seuss's *Oh, the Places You Will Go* book. On our kitchen table, I placed three flower pots in the center that each had paper pinwheels and paper kites glued on lollipop sticks. For his 12-month collage, I blew up twelve miniature balloons with helium and tied them with striped craft ribbon which was taped to each of his monthly growth pictures.

For my walls, I cut out clouds from white poster paper and hung green, yellow, and blue streamers from the clouds.

Ridley sat in a vintage white high chair when we sang the happy birthday song. We blew up a big blue balloon (it was honestly too big but super fun!). I made blue, white, and gold tassels out of tissue paper that hung from his high chair table. It was adorable.

Food & Drink

Milk Chocolate Birthday Cupcakes
(adapted from Georgetown Cupcakes)

Yes, these were the cupcakes that hit the floor! I was in luck and able to save a few for his party!

Cupcake Ingredients:

- 2½ cups all-purpose flour
- 2½ teaspoons baking powder
- ¼ teaspoon salt
- 8 tablespoons unsalted butter, at room temperature (European style recommended)
- 1¾ cups sugar
- 2 large eggs, at room temperature
- 2¼ teaspoons pure vanilla extract seeds from one vanilla bean (I did not have a vanilla bean so I just used two teaspoons of nice vanilla extract that I found at Whole Foods)
- 1¼ cups whole milk, at room temperature

Milk Chocolate Buttercream Frosting Ingredients:

(I usually have plenty of icing left over from this recipe. Because it has milk in it, the icing does not freeze well so I would suggest making more cupcakes or even a small smash cake to use all of the icing.)

- ⅔ cup milk, at room temperature
- 5 cups confectioners' sugar (I used six, so have some extra handy)
- 12 tablespoons (1½ sticks) butter, at room temperature
- 5 teaspoons pure vanilla extract

- ½ teaspoon salt
- 2½ cups (two bags) chocolate chips, melted and then cooled to room temperature
- ¼ cup Crisco (I added this to my frosting to help form peaks)
- Rainbow sprinkles (optional)

Instructions for the cupcakes:

Preheat the oven to 350 degrees. Line a standard cupcake pan with twelve paper baking cups, or grease the pan with butter if not using baking cups.

Sift together the flour, baking powder, and salt in a bowl and set aside.

In the bowl of a stand mixer or in a bowl with a handheld electric mixer, cream together the butter and sugar for 3 to 5 minutes, or until light and fluffy.

Add the eggs one at a time, mixing slowly after each addition.

Add the vanilla and vanilla bean seeds to the milk in a large measuring cup.

Add one third of the dry ingredients to the bowl of creamed butter and sugar, followed by one third of the milk, and mix thoroughly. Repeat. Stop to scrape down the bowl as needed. Add the last third of the dry ingredients followed by the last third of the milk, mixing slowly until well incorporated.

Scoop the batter into the cupcake pan using a standard-size ice-cream scoop and bake for 16-18 minutes (rotate cupcakes halfway through) and start checking at 15 minutes or until a toothpick comes out clean. Transfer the pan to a wire rack to cool completely.

Instructions for the frosting:

Combine the milk, confectioners' sugar, butter, vanilla, Crisco, and salt at high speed until light and airy, approximately 3-5 minutes. Slowly add the melted chocolate until well incorporated. Frost and top with rainbow sprinkles.

Sugar Cookies

Ask a local baker to make iced sugar cookies in the shapes of clouds and hot air balloons. Ridley's hot air balloon sugar cookies were created with yellow and blue icing. So adorable!

Activities

A simple party activity for preschoolers is to have them decorate their own hot air balloons out of paper plates (set up a coloring station with stickers and crayons) and attach the paper plates to plastic cups with string (go ahead and hole punch the plates and cups before the party).

For party favors, we gave each kid a kite, and we went outside to let them fly it. Simple and easy but oh so fun!

Holidays and Special Occasions:

Christmas

I often feel like December is a sprint to Christmas Eve, packed full with holiday parties for kids and adults. While all the celebrating is loaded with holly and jolly, my favorite part of Christmas is attending the Christmas Eve candlelight service at church and then watching my kids race to the den in their pajamas on Christmas morning. The pause before the party helps my heart to soak in the season.

Below are two kinds of parties–one themed more for kids and the other for adults–but you could easily hire a couple of babysitters to help the kids do their activities at one house while the parents get together at another.

Invitations/Guest List for Kids' Cookie Decorating Party

One of the traditions my girls and I have started is to invite a few of their friends from school over to decorate Christmas cookies during the month of December. We've found that inviting 4-6 friends works best, and younger siblings are welcome if the mamas are staying to help! For invitations, we've done a super fun and simple card that has gingerbread cookies at the top, and then there are places to fill in the child's name and what they need to bring. For example, it would be worded:

Cookies, Cocoa, and Holiday Cheer,
Adeline and Maralee invite

(Handwrite the guest's name here)

to join us in decorating Christmas cookies this year!

Wednesday, December 15th

12:30 – 2:00

Adeline and Maralee's House

Please bring (list an item that the child needs to bring, such

as sprinkles, colored icing, etc.)

We'll provide the cookies!

RSVP to Christen at abc@gmail.com or 123-4567

Decorations & Set-Up

Since it's Christmas time, you've probably already set up your holiday décor, so that part is finished! When we host cookie decorating parties, I spread a red or green plastic tablecloth on my kitchen table and then place three topsy-turvy metal Christmas trees across the center of the table. At a local craft store, I purchase two Santa serving plates to place the cookies at each end of the table. Then, in the center, I place a wooden Christmas bowl for all of the different colored icings to sit in. At each child's place, I put a festive Christmas plate, napkin, and wooden craft knife to help them spread the icing on the cookie. If you are feeling extra merry, purchase child size aprons for the kids to wear so they don't get icing on their Christmas outfits. Baby wipes are close by to help with sticky hands.

Food & Drink

I'll be honest, when it comes to making sugar cookies from scratch and then cutting them out in Christmas shapes, my cookies always are too thin and expand in the oven. Instead of stressing over the baking, I purchase my sugar cookies from a local bakery in town that sells Christmas cookies shaped like gingerbread men, Christmas trees, and stars. I usually buy enough for each child to decorate three cookies (each style) and a few extra for siblings and moms to munch on (for six kids that would be one dozen of each).

For the icing, it is super easy to ask each kid to bring a color (try to have two of each color to help with sharing) and you supply the white icing. (Sometimes, I'll make a big batch of cream cheese or buttercream icing and then put them in Ziploc bags and cut an end off just before the kids begin to use it). Ask the kids to bring sprinkles, red hots, and gumdrops to complete the decorating ensemble.

Once the kids decorate their cookies, go ahead and have cookie craft boxes for them to put their cookies in and a Sharpie marker to write their name on the outside of the box. I like boxes with handles to make it easy for their small hands to carry.

Kid's Cookie Decorating Party – Food and Drinks

The kids are excited to decorate their cookies, so we usually start with that craft and then let them keep one cookie to eat with their snack lunch. For a salty snack to go with the sweet cookies, I like to make pigs in a blanket (*Sister Schubert* has a delicious frozen version), Strawberry Santas, chips, hot chocolate, and juice boxes.

Hot Chocolate with Homemade Whipped Cream
(adapted from Paula Deen)

Ingredients:

(I double this for more than four people):

- 2½ cups whole milk
- 2 cups half & half

- 4 ounces bittersweet chocolate chips
- 4 ounces milk chocolate
- 1 tablespoon sugar
- 1 teaspoon pure vanilla extract
- 1 teaspoon instant espresso

Instructions:

Heat milk and half and half just below simmering point. Remove pan from oven and add chocolate. When melted, add sugar, vanilla, and espresso, and whisk. Reheat gently and serve with homemade whipped cream.

Homemade Whipped Cream

(Homemade whipped cream beats frozen whipped cream and is so simple and quick to make!)

Ingredients:
- One pint of heavy whipping cream
- Two tablespoons confectioners' sugar

Instructions:

Pour the heavy whipping cream into a mixer and start it on low to prevent splattering and then turn the mixer to high speed to create air in the cream. Mix until soft peaks begin to form. Turn off mixer and sprinkle in the confectioners' sugar. Mix again until incorporated. Pour into a serving bowl and place next to the hot chocolate with a candy cane to help mix the cream into the chocolate.

Strawberry Santas

(adapted from Giada de Laurentis)

Wash your strawberries and cut off the leaves, creating a base for your strawberries. Next, cut off the bottom of the strawberry (which is now the top) to create a Santa hat. Let the strawberries sit in the refrigerator for about thirty minutes to allow the slice where the Santa hat was cut to dry out. Then, take your white icing for cookies and spread it on the strawberry and place the "hat" back on top. Make two Santa eyes with mini chocolate chips. Keep in refrigerator until ready to serve!

Adult Christmas Party

This menu is perfect for a party with friends or family. Elegant and festive, it is best served as a sit-down dinner with Christmas china, but it can easily be adapted to sandwiches for a mix-and-mingle party.

Decorations & Set-Up

If you choose to have a sit-down dinner, place some Christmas tree trimmings across the center of your table to serve as your runner. Lay a 12-inch decorative wreath in the center of your table and place a large candle or a candle inside a tall vase inside the wreath. Add small tea lights on either side (I love tea light vases that have snowflake cut-outs to give it a holiday touch). Visit your local nursery and search for some sage green ceramic sculptures of birds or use other holiday inspired decorative pieces to place inside the greenery to give your tablescape another dimension. Finally, place scented pine cones (three to five on each side of the center table) and small twigs of faux red or gold glittered berries as accents in the greenery.

Christmas Sangria (Cake-n-Knife.com)

Ingredients:

- 2 bottles Pinot Grigio or Chardonnay
- ¾ cup sparkling apple cider
- ¼ cup sugar
- ¼ cup cranberries, halved
- ¾ cup cranberries, whole
- 1 Granny Smith apple, chopped
- 3 rosemary sprigs

Instructions:

Combine all ingredients in a large pitcher and stir together with a large wooden spoon to help the sugar dissolve. Refrigerate for at least 4 hours before serving. Serve chilled or over ice.

Roasted Beef Tenderloin (The Pioneer Woman)

Ingredients:

- 1 whole (4 to 5 pounds) beef tenderloin (butt)
- 4 tablespoons salted butter, or more to taste
- ⅓ cup whole peppercorns, more or less to taste
- Lawry's Seasoned Salt (or your favorite salt blend)
- Lemon pepper seasoning
- Olive oil

Instructions:

Preheat oven to 475 degrees.

Rinse meat well. Trim away some of the fat to remove the silvery cartilage underneath. With a very sharp knife, begin taking the fat off the top, revealing the silver cartilage underneath. You definitely don't want to take every last bit of fat off—not at all. As with any cut of meat, a little bit of fat adds to the flavor. (Hint: you can also ask the butcher to do this trimming for you if the process seems intimidating.)

Sprinkle meat generously with Lawry's. You can much more liberally season a tenderloin, because you're having to pack more of a punch in order for the seasoning to make an impact. Start with Lawry's Seasoned Salt. Rub it in with your fingers. Sprinkle both sides generously with lemon & pepper seasoning. (There are no measurements because it depends on your taste, but be sure to season liberally.) Place the peppercorns in a Ziploc bag, and then with a mallet, hammer, or large, heavy can, begin smashing the peppercorns to break them up a bit. Set aside. Heat some olive oil in a heavy skillet. When the oil is to the smoking point, place the tenderloin in the very hot pan to sear it. Throw a couple of tablespoons of butter into the skillet to give it a nice little butter injection before going in the oven. A minute or two later, when one side is starting to turn nice and brown, flip and repeat.

Place the tenderloin on an oven pan with a rack. Sprinkle the pummeled peppercorns all over the meat. Press the pepper onto the surface of the meat. Put several tablespoons of butter all over the meat. Stick the long needle of the thermometer lengthwise into the meat. Place it in a 475-degree oven until the temperature reaches just under 140 degrees, about fifteen to twenty minutes. Stay near the oven and keep checking the meat thermometer to make sure it doesn't overcook.

Let meat stand ten minutes or so before slicing so the meat will have a chance to rest a bit. To serve, you can spoon the olive oil/butter juices from the skillet onto the top of the meat for a little extra flavor.

Prosciutto Wrapped Asparagus

Rinse asparagus and break off the white ends. Lay the asparagus on a sheet pan and drizzle with extra virgin olive oil, and sprinkle with salt and pepper. Use your hands to mix until asparagus is coated. Have your deli cut one pound of thinly sliced prosciutto and wrap it around a bundle of three asparagus. Place your bundles on a sheet pan and bake at 375 degrees for 10-12 minutes or until the prosciutto is crispy. If you are serving this at a mix-and-mingle party, cut your asparagus into smaller bundles to resemble cut green beans and then place them on a white serving platter with red decorative flourishes.

Stuffed Italian Herb Cheese Potatoes

Ingredients:

- One large bag of new potatoes
- ⅓ stick of butter
- 8 ounces sour cream
- 8 slices of bacon, crumbled
- ½ pound Colby-Jack shredded cheese
- 2 tablespoons milk
- Salt and pepper to taste
- Italian style bread crumbs
- Extra Virgin Olive Oil

Instructions:

Slice the new potatoes in half and let them boil in a pot of water until they are soft in the center but still firm around the skin. Pour out the new potatoes and let them cool on your counter. Once cooled, take a spoon and scoop out the potatoes from the inside of the halves, careful to leave the skins whole. After the potatoes have been carved, mix the sour cream, butter, cheese, and milk with the scooped out part of the potato, adding salt and pepper to taste. The potatoes should not be completely mashed or runny, but should be stuck together well. Add in the bacon bits and extra milk and butter if the mixture is too dry.

Take the skins and gently coat them with olive oil, salt, and pepper, and then place on a baking sheet. Using your spoon, place the potato mixture inside the skins. Once all the skins have been filled, sprinkle the breadcrumbs on top of the potatoes and drizzle olive oil to create a crust. Bake in the oven at 375 degrees for 25 minutes or until the breadcrumbs are golden brown.

Grandpa's Chocolate Cake

This is the chocolate cake that I mention in Chapter One that my grandpa always had waiting on us when we visited for the holidays in New Orleans. It's not Christmas without a slice of his cake! My family usually serves this cake in a sheet pan, but for mix-and-mingle parties, I like to place the cake in clear push pop containers making layers of the cake and icing.

Cake Ingredients:

- 2 cups flour
- 2 cups sugar
- 2 sticks butter
- 1 cup water
- ¼ cup cocoa
- ¼ cup buttermilk
- 2 eggs, slightly beaten
- 1 teaspoon baking soda
- 1 teaspoon vanilla
- 1 teaspoon cinnamon

Cake Instructions:

Flour a sheet pan and spray to prevent sticking. Mix flour, sugar, cinnamon, and baking soda together in a bowl. Then place in a blender. On the stovetop, bring butter, water, and cocoa to a rapid boil and then pour over the flour and sugar. Mix well and let the mixture cool slightly before beating in the eggs. Mix in the buttermilk and vanilla. Bake at 375 degrees for thirty minutes (this cake is best when it is moist).

Frosting Ingredients:

- 1 stick butter
- 2 teaspoons cocoa
- ½ cup (four ounces) Pet Condensed Milk
- 1 pound confectioners' sugar (sifted twice)
- 1 teaspoon vanilla

Frosting Instructions:

Combine the butter, cocoa, and milk, and heat slowly to a boil. Pour into a mixer and slowly add in the confectioners' sugar, careful not to form lumps. Add in the vanilla and mix until smooth. The icing should be runny and will set once it is poured over the cake. Best served with a cold glass of milk!

Activities

After dinner, have some fun with your friends and family by playing the Jingle Bell Shake! The Jingle Bell Shake is the Christmas version of Minute-to-Win-It, where contestants have one minute to get all of the ping pong balls out of a Kleenex box that is tied around their waist with ribbon. All you need are six empty Kleenex boxes, sixty ping pong balls, and some Christmas music to get your jingle on! Trust me, you'll need the extra Kleenex to wipe away your tears from laughing so hard while people play this game!

Galentine's Day

"What's Galentine's Day? Oh, it's only the best day of the year. Every February 13th my lady friends and I leave our husbands and boyfriends at home and we just come and kick it breakfast style. Ladies celebrating ladies. It's like Lilith Fair, minus the angst. Plus frittatas."

~Leslie Knope, Parks and Recreation

In Chapter Seventeen, *Galentine's Day*, I gave you a glimpse into the conversations that happen with the girls I do If:Table with once a month. These dinners are some of my favorite nights out of the whole month, and I love it when we go overboard with a theme like Galentine's Day. Nothing beats having a group of girls to do life with, so gather your ladies together and have some fun, Leslie Knope style!

Invitations/Guest List

Keep your Galentine's Day party to your close group of friends, or use this idea at your church for a Valentine's party where your members invite their best friend to come to a brunch with them, listen to an inspirational message, and play some fun games. For electronic invitations, consider sending a funny meme of Leslie Knope from Parks and Rec. If you send a card in the mail, go old school and cut a heart out of red cardboard paper and write in hand calligraphy the Galentine's Day details.

Decorations & Set-Up

Since we are celebrating friendship with our gals, mix pastel pink, bright white, and red together for your table and decorations. The Tom Kat Studio has some really cute Valentine's Day inspired t-shirts, party plates, and heart-shaped miniature balloons and stickers. For the food table, cover it with a white tablecloth and write x's and o's on it with a black Sharpie. Download a free blank placemat at www.invitedbook.com/freebies to use at each place setting, and handwrite your guests' name in the center of the placemat. Instead of going with the traditional red roses of Valentine's Day, consider placing candy hearts in clear vases at different heights as your centerpiece and hang a garland of paper hearts from your chandelier.

Food & Drink

Heart-Shaped Waffles

Shop online or at a local kitchen store for a heart-shaped waffle maker. It's not necessary but sure does make for a festive waffle!

You can make waffles from scratch, but to cut time there is nothing wrong with using a boxed waffle mix. My favorite is Krusteaz Belgian Waffle mix. Once you make the waffles, dot them with butter that has been cut into tiny hearts with a cookie cutter and have a variety of specialty syrups and toppings like pecans, bacon, and chocolate chips for the ladies to sprinkle and drizzle on top.

Yogurt Bar

A yogurt bar brings girly sophistication and lightness to the brunch. Purchase vanilla and strawberry yogurt and spoon them into glass parfait glasses for your guests. Set up a yogurt station with fresh strawberries, raspberries, and blueberries, granola, local honey, and coconut flakes.

Gorilla Bread (Paula Deen)

Ingredients:

- 1 cup granulated sugar
- 1 tablespoon ground cinnamon
- ½ cup (1 stick) butter
- 1 cup packed brown sugar
- One 8-ounce package cream cheese
- Two 7.5-ounce cans refrigerated biscuits (10 count)
- 1½ cups coarsely chopped walnuts

Instructions:

Preheat the oven to 350 degrees. Spray a Bundt pan with vegetable oil cooking spray. Mix the granulated sugar and cinnamon. In a saucepan, melt the butter and brown sugar over low heat, stirring well; set aside. Cut the cream cheese into 20 equal cubes. Press the biscuits out with your fingers and sprinkle each with ½ teaspoon of cinnamon sugar. Place a cube of cream cheese in the center of each biscuit, wrapping and sealing the dough around the cream cheese. Sprinkle ½ cup of the nuts into the bottom of the Bundt pan. Place half of the prepared biscuits in the pan. Sprinkle with cinnamon sugar, pour half of the melted butter mixture over the biscuits, and sprinkle on ½ cup of nuts. Layer the remaining biscuits on top, sprinkle with the remaining cinnamon sugar, pour the remaining butter mixture over the biscuits, and sprinkle with the remaining ½ cup of nuts. Bake for 30 minutes. Remove from the oven and let cool for 5 minutes. Place a plate on top and invert. Serve warm.

Ham and Swiss Quiche and Spinach and Bacon Quiche

To save time, you can always purchase two 9-inch frozen pie crusts

Pie Crust Ingredients:

(double this for two quiches):

- 1½ cups flour
- ½ teaspoon salt
- 1 stick cold butter, cut into ½ inch cubes
- 2 tablespoons solid vegetable shortening
- 3 tablespoons ice water

Pie Crust Instructions:

In a food processor, combine flour and salt. Cut in butter until mixture resembles coarse crumbs. Stir in water, a tablespoon at a time, until mixture forms a ball. Wrap in plastic and refrigerate for 4 hours or overnight. Roll dough out to fit a 9-inch pie plate. Place crust in pie plate. Press the dough evenly into the bottom and sides of the pie plate. Run a fork up and down across the bottom of the dough to keep it from bubbling while baking and use the fork to create a decorative crust.

Quiche Ingredients:

(double this for two quiches):

- 2 tablespoons small diced onions
- 3 eggs

- 1 cup milk
- Salt and pepper to taste

   For Ham and Cheese Bacon Quiche add in:
- 1 cup shredded Swiss cheese or Colby-Jack cheese
- ⅔ cup deli sliced ham, shredded

   For Spinach and Bacon Quiche add in:

- Crumbled bacon
- 1½ cups of baby spinach (for spinach and bacon quiche)

Instructions:

Place the onions in a skillet with butter until lightly browned. Mix eggs and milk together and add the onions, salt, and pepper to taste. Divide the mixture into two bowls. Add in the cheese and toppings and pour mixtures into pie crusts. Bake at 350 degrees for 40-45 minutes.

Cappuccino Brownies

Ingredients:

- ½ cup (1 stick) unsalted butter, softened
- 1½ cups sugar
- 2 teaspoons vanilla extract
- 1 cup all-purpose flour
- ½ teaspoon ground nutmeg
- ¾ cup semisweet chocolate chips
- 3 ounces unsweetened chocolate, coarsely chopped
- 1 tablespoon espresso powder
- 4 large eggs, lightly beaten

- ¾ teaspoon ground cinnamon
- ¼ teaspoon salt
- 2 tablespoons confectioners' sugar

Instructions:

Preheat oven to 325 degrees, with rack in the center. Butter a 9-inch square baking pan, and spray with vegetable cooking spray. In a large heatproof bowl, combine the butter and unsweetened chocolate, and place in microwave to melt. Let the chocolate mixture cool slightly and whisk in sugar, espresso powder, vanilla, and eggs. In a small bowl, whisk together flour, cinnamon, nutmeg, and salt. Add to the chocolate mixture, and stir until just combined (do not overmix). Fold in chocolate chips. Pour into pan and bake until a toothpick inserted in the center comes out slightly wet, 25-30 minutes. Let the brownies cool completely and cut using a damp, warm knife into 16 squares (wipe knife blade after each cut). Sprinkle with confectioners' sugar before serving.

Activities

Ask your friends to come over in their pajamas and bring their favorite fingernail polish. Once you've finished eating, paint nails and have a classic television show like *I Love Lucy* playing in the background. When it is time for everyone to leave, send them home with a bottle of nail polish and gift tags that say "Happy Galentine's" and sign your name with "XO."

Easter

Ever since we moved to the country, one of my favorite traditions is to host an Easter egg hunt for our friends. We have lots of azaleas blooming and a large front yard for the dads to hide the Easter eggs in while the children are around back painting real eggs. To keep things simple, we have all of our friends bring a spring-inspired appetizer or dessert like fruit pizzas, Easter egg Rice Krispies, cups of ranch dip with carrots and celery, and turkey wraps. After the Easter egg hunt, we let the kids hold our baby chicks and tour the chicken coop to see where the chickens sleep and lay eggs. We've even had friends let us borrow real bunnies for the kids to take their pictures with!

Since this party is outside, we let the kids decorate eggs on our backyard picnic bench and let the parents eat with their food in their laps while sitting in rocking chairs or on big quilts on the grass. I place candles and a small arrangement of flowers on the patio and hang our Hallelujah banner across the back porch to complete the look. Food is served buffet style on another rustic picnic table that is set with a centerpiece of wheatgrass, freckled eggs, and sprigs of Queen Ann's lace in Mason jars.

Carrot-Shaped Goldfish

My girls love goldfish, and I'm sure your children do too. Purchase a clear, plastic bag from the party section of your home goods store and tape the back so it is in the shape of a cone. Fill the bag 3/4 full with goldfish. Tie it off with some pretty green ribbon and your child has their very own carrot snack to enjoy!

Easter Fruit

To make fruit a bit more fun, try cutting it out with some Easter-shaped cookie cutters. I found a mini cookie cutter package filled with shapes such as eggs, crosses, bunnies, flowers, and ducks at my local craft store that made the perfect size treat for my children. Let your child pick out the shape that they want and help them press the cutter into their favorite fruit. We used cantaloupe, pineapple, and honeydew as our fruits and they were just as much fun to eat as they were to make!

Bake Pretzels

One of the traditions of Lent—which some religions still practice—was fasting. This was very strict in the Middle Ages. You can tell your children the story of how the pretzel began (see below) and how it relates to Lent. You can make dough and let them make homemade pretzels, buy them soft pretzels, or get a bag of the regular kind to enjoy.

A very long time ago (in the early 600s), there was a man who worked for God. His job was being a monk. A monk does everything in his life for God. He lives in a special place with other monks, who pray and read the Bible many times during the day. They usually live in a building or group of buildings for this purpose. It is called a monastery. Monks usually make and/or grow their own food.

This monk had been in the kitchen where other monks were baking a special bread for Lent, and he saw some leftover pieces of dough. This monk decided to use the leftover pieces of dough for something special. The monk formed the dough into thin strips crossed into a looped twist to be like the folded arms of **children in prayer**.

Let's all try crossing our arms like the children in the early church. (Like a pretzel for prayer.)

This treat was given to the children as they learned their prayers. They began calling the treat *Pretiola*, which means "little reward" in Latin (a common language of the monks). (A *different version of the story calls them* bracellae, *a German word that eventually became* pretzel.)

Soon it was known the world over as a pretzel. The simple shape of the pretzel, arms folded in prayer, reminds us to pray every day. Every time you see a pretzel, remember **prayer!** What do we do with our hands and arms when we pray? We should fold our hands and bow our heads! Would it be okay to pray with our arms folded? Yes it would, but some people who do not know what you know might think it was strange!

The pretzel really has its origins as an official food of Lent. Lent is known as the forty days before Easter. Lent is a time when we should be thinking of what Jesus gave up for us—His body and blood, His life—so we could go to heaven. Lent is a time when we could think of what we could give up in honor of God or Jesus. Long ago, in some churches, you had to decide on something to give up for the forty days of Lent (a personal sacrifice). Some ideas would have been chocolate or some other candy, cookies, or pizza!

The monk in our story lived in a time when you could not eat meat or milk or eggs during Lent! So he and his brother monks had to figure out a special bread that did not use eggs or milk. The monks were preparing a special Lenten bread of water, flour, and salt—which is what pretzels are still made out of today. Pretzels then began to be enjoyed by all people. They became a symbol of good luck and long life. They were also a common food given to the poor and hungry. They were cheap and easy to make and satisfied hunger.

Questions:

1. Have you ever had a pretzel like this?
2. Who can tell what it tastes like?
3. If you were asked to give up a favorite food from now until Easter, what would it be? (Ask each child)
4. Would it be easy or hard not to have that food until Easter?

Let's pray with our arms folded like the pretzel:

Dear God,

We thank You for Your Son, Jesus. We thank You for caring about us and loving us. Amen.

Activities

Bury the Alleluia

I know classic church services do traditional Lenten music during Lent, but it's tradition that you don't sing alleluias during Lent because it's a time of reflection, and it's supposed to make it that much more impressive when you break forth with music and alleluias on Easter Sunday. One activity for parents to do with kids at home to reflect on this tradition is to have your kids each make a banner using yarn and triangles of construction paper. Each triangle will have a letter from the word *Alleluia* or *Hallelujah*, whichever you prefer. Once finished, tell them to hide it (you can make one and hide as well), and Easter Sunday they can find it and hang it somewhere prominent like the front door or on their bedroom door. On Easter Sunday, make a game out of how many alleluias they hear the church saying or singing.

To download your free Hallelujah banner, go to www.invitedbook.com/freebies.

Tea Party – Mother's Day

Tea parties are so ladylike. Why not host one for Mother's Day? While the theme of a tea party is . . . well . . . tea, you can create a tea party that is London-style (very prim and proper) or more *Alice in Wonderland* whimsical. No matter what direction you take, allow your tea party to serve as a time where you can sit, eat sweets, and savor the conversation.

Invitations/Guest List

Consider hosting a tea party with your friends and their daughters, or invite your relatives or women who have been like a mother to you for tea. Create handmade invitations by cutting out teapots on flowered stationery paper or have an invitation made that has a ribbon threaded through a hole punch and is attached to a piece of cardstock to resemble a tea bag. Tea time is typically between 3:30 to 5:30 p.m. Invitations should be sent 2-3 weeks prior for a formal tea party.

Decorations & Set-Up

If you don't own a tea set, consider shopping at an antique mall to find tea cups and saucers. Owning a tea set allows you to use your set for decoration and can be something you pass down to your children. If your party is for small children, use the real tea cups for decoration and let them use plastic cups. Also, arrange a small table set for tea with large stuffed animals sitting in the chairs.

If possible, use a round table that seats no more than eight guests for your tea party. A lace tablecloth is a beautiful backdrop to the ornately designed tea cups. The centerpiece of the tea table should be a tiered tray with food (see below for food suggestions). In front of every other place setting you may place simple spruces of white gardenias or blush peonies inside small glass vases. Each place setting should be set with a salad plate. On the left side of the salad plate, fold a tea napkin and place a fork on top; place a tea cup and saucer in the upper left corner. On the right side of the salad plate, place a small spreader knife for jam. Set a spoon and a water glass in the upper right corner of the place setting.

Place cards are a great way to let your guests know where to sit. Another option for a place card is to have each guest's monogram embroidered on her tea napkin. This makes a sweet tea party keepsake for your guests.

Activities

Dress up for your tea party! One of my favorite trends of the past is big hats and gloves. Little girls will love dressing up in their mama's pearls, and it is so much fun to dress up even as an adult. Have a Polaroid camera at the tea party to take instant pictures that your guests can keep afterward.

If your tea party is with little ones, a wonderful activity is teaching them etiquette and manners through trivia games. If it is an adult-only party, play trivia games from your favorite British television shows like Downton Abbey.

Food & Drink

Scone Nibbles (King Arthur Flour)

My friend Megan is a school teacher, but her dream when she retires is to open a tea shop in town. Until then, she hosts our If:Table group for a tea at her home in the summertime and at Christmas. In the middle of her round table, she places a tiered serving dish that holds an assortment of cookies on the top tier and delicious scones on the bottom tier. For the cookies, I recommend purchasing some macaroons, thumb print cookies, cranberry walnut cookies, and sand tarts from a local bakery. These scone nibbles are one of her recommendations and can be served with jam by omitting the chocolate chips. Makes 32 mini scones.

Ingredients:

- 2¾ cups King Arthur Unbleached All-Purpose Flour
- ⅓ cup sugar
- ¾ teaspoon salt
- 1 tablespoon baking powder
- ½ cup (8 tablespoons) cold butter, cut in pats
- 1-2 cups mini chocolate chips
- 2 large eggs
- 2 teaspoons vanilla extract or the flavoring of your choice
- ½ cup to ⅔ cup half & half or milk

Glaze:

- 3½ cups confectioners' sugar
- 7 tablespoons water, enough to make a thin glaze
- 1 teaspoon vanilla, optional

Instructions:

In a large mixing bowl, whisk together all the dry ingredients.

Work in the butter just until the mixture is unevenly crumbly. It's okay for some larger chunks of butter to remain unincorporated.

Stir in the chips

In a separate mixing bowl, whisk together the eggs, vanilla, and ½ cup half and half or milk.

Add the liquid ingredients to the dry ingredients and stir until all is moistened and holds together. Stir in additional milk or half and half if the dough seems dry and doesn't come together.

Scrape the dough onto a well-floured work surface. Pat/roll it into an 8" to 8 ½" square, a scant ¾" thick. Make sure the surface underneath the dough is very well floured. If necessary, use a giant spatula to lift the square and sprinkle more flour underneath.

Cut the square into 2" squares; you'll have a total of 16 small squares. Now, cut each square in half diagonally, to make 32 small triangles. This is all easily accomplished with a rolling pizza wheel; if you're working on a silicone mat, be very careful not to press down too hard as you cut.

Transfer the scones to a parchment-lined or well-greased baking sheet. They can be set fairly close together; you should be able to crowd them all onto an 18 x 13 inch half-sheet pan.

For best texture and highest rise, place the pan of scones in the freezer for 30 minutes, uncovered. While the scones are chilling, preheat the oven to 425 degrees.

Bake the scones for 19 to 20 minutes, or until they're golden brown. Remove the pan from the oven and allow the scones to cool on the pan. When they're cool, cut each scone in half once again, to make a total of 64 tiny triangles. Don't be too particular here; in fact, if the scones are already a size you like, don't bother to cut them again. But if you decide to cut, don't stress about making them all the same size, or perfect triangles. Trust us; no one but you will care once they're glazed and on the table.

Make the glaze by stirring together the sugar, water, and vanilla. If the sugar seems particularly lumpy, sift it first for an extra-smooth glaze.

Now you're going to coat each scone with glaze. You can dip each one individually, which is quite time-consuming. Or line a baking sheet (with sides) with parchment and pour about half the glaze atop the parchment. Then set the scones atop the glaze, swirling them around a bit to coat their bottoms. Then drizzle the remaining glaze over the top. Use a pastry brush to brush the glaze over each scone to coat it entirely. The glaze is very thin, so this is easily done.

Transfer the scones to a rack set over parchment, to catch any drips. As you pick each scone up, run its sides over the glaze in the bottom of the pan, both to use up some of the extra glaze, and to make sure all sides are coated.

Allow the glaze to set before serving the scones.

Patsy's Grape Salad

My grandmother loves to make grape salad for ladies' luncheons. It is a light dish, in spite of the cream, and goes perfectly with the chicken salad and scones.

Ingredients:

- 1 eight-ounce cream cheese
- ⅓ cup mayonnaise
- ⅓ cup sour cream
- 5 tablespoons sugar
- 5 cups or one bag of seedless grapes (we like the purple ones!)
- 1½ cups roasted pecans, chopped
- ½ cup brown sugar

Instructions:

Combine cream cheese, mayonnaise, sour cream, and sugar together.

Toss grapes and one cup of pecans into the cream mixture and mix until coated.

Mix together the remaining pecans into the brown sugar.

Place grape salad in a clear trifle dish and top with the brown sugar pecan mixture.

Chicken Salad

To save time, I like to purchase my chicken salad and serve it with crackers or croissants. Megan also suggests using teacup cookie cutters to cut out sliced white bread to serve with the chicken salad.

Numi Organic Tea

The White Rose flavor of Numi Organic Tea is lovely served with sugar and cream.

If children are in attendance, serve them "Arnold Palmers" (a combination of sweet tea and lemonade) or pink lemonade.

Graduation

While graduation parties are traditionally black and gold, I think having a fiesta graduation party is much more fun! I mean, who doesn't love Mexican food, right? A fiesta party color scheme is bright and cheerful, using a mixture of aqua, pink, orange, lime green, and yellow.

Invitations/Guest List

If you are hosting the party before graduation, send invitations with colorful flowers on them for girls or stripes and a sombrero for guys. Or, if you plan on having family over after the graduation ceremony, just send them all a text with the time and location, along with the details of the ceremony.

Decorations & Set-Up

Along with colorful balloons full of confetti, paper lanterns, and poms, purchase gold Mylar balloons that spell out YAY! Put carnations in Mexican cans of tomato sauce, refried beans, or beer bottles (for a college graduate), and mini cactuses on runners that resemble Mexican rugs.

Food & Drink

If you are hosting the party after graduation, consider having the food catered by a local Mexican restaurant to cut down on set-up. Set up a taco bar with soft and hard shell tacos, ground beef and shredded chicken, and condiments such as shredded cheese, lettuce, Spanish rice, black beans, peppers, salsa, and cilantro. Don't forget to have chips, salsa, queso, and guacamole nearby! For dessert, purchase a key lime pie. For drinks, serve virgin margaritas and Mexican beer for college grads.

Other food ideas are mini quesadillas made with wontons instead of soft taco shells and individual cups layered with refried beans, ground beef, corn, sour cream, shredded cheese, salsa, and guacamole, served with tortilla chips on top. If you want to prepare the food, I suggest making salsa from scratch, the meat, and a tres leches cake.

Susanne's Salsa

Ingredients:

- 2 large chili peppers
- 2 large jalapeno peppers
- 1 yellow pepper
- 1 green bell pepper
- 6-8 green onions

- 4-5 sprigs of fresh cilantro
- 2 large cans of peeled tomatoes (16-20 ounce cans)
- 1-2 tablespoons of salt
- 1-2 teaspoons of black pepper
- 1-2 tablespoons of sugar

Instructions:

First, core all seeds from the peppers. Then cut up the peppers and put into a food processor and place into bowl. Next, cut the white part off the onions and put into food processor. Open cans of tomatoes and pour just the sauce into the bowl over the peppers and onions. Then place the whole peeled tomatoes into the processors and grind. Add salt, sugar, and pepper over the mixture. Stir with a spoon all together. Seal bowl and let chill in the refrigerator before serving.

Tres Leches Cake (adapted from Publix Greenwise Magazine)

Once you make this cake, put tiny gold glitter numbers of the graduation year on skewers and place in the center of the cake

Ingredients:

- 1 two-layer-size regular white cake mix
- ¾ cup butter, softened
- 6 eggs
- ½ cup water
- 2 tablespoons finely shredded lime peel
- 3 fresh mangoes, pitted, peeled, and chopped
- 1 Recipe Tres Leches Mixture (see below)

- 1 cup whipping cream
- ¾ cup granulated sugar
- 1 teaspoon vanilla

Tres Leches Mixture Ingredients:

Starting with 2 (14-ounce) cans, set aside ¼ cup of sweetened condensed milk. In a large saucepan combine one full 14-ounce can sweetened condensed milk, 2 (12-ounce) cans evaporated milk, and 2 cups milk. Cook over medium heat just until boiling, stirring frequently. Remove from heat. Transfer to a large bowl. Cover and cool 1 hour. Transfer to refrigerator and chill completely. Makes about 7¾ cups.

Instructions:

Preheat oven to 350 degrees. Grease and flour two 10-inch springform pans; set aside. In a very large mixing bowl, combine cake mix, butter, eggs, and water. Beat on low speed until combined. Beat on medium speed for 2 minutes (batter will be thick). Stir in the finely shredded lime peel. Spread batter in prepared pans. Back 50-55 minutes or until a wooden skewer inserted near the center comes out clean. Cool in pans on a wire rack for 10 minutes. (Cake may sink slightly during cooling.) Loosen cake from sides of pans; remove sides. Lift cake from pan bottoms using a wide spatula. Cool on wire rack.

Take a long serrated knife and trim off the top of each cake to create an even surface. Place one cake on the bottom of your prepared cake platter (choose a platter with a lip) and place four pieces of wax paper on the bottom of the platter that are large enough to pull out from underneath the cake. This will help catch the Tres Leches mixture and the icing to keep your cake stand pretty before serving). In a medium bowl combine mangoes with the ¼ cup reserved sweetened condensed milk from the Tres Leches Mixture recipe; spoon evenly atop the cake layer on platter. Next, flip your second cake layer where the top is on the bottom and place this layer on top of the mango filling, pressing down lightly. Using a wooden skewer, poke holes in cake layers across the whole surface. Slowly pour 4 cups of the Tres Leches mixture all over the cake. Cover and chill overnight. Cover and chill remaining Tres Leches mixture.

About 1 hour before serving, pour 1 cup of the remaining Tres Leches mixture slowly over cake. Cover and chill cake and remaining Tres Leches mixture until serving time.

To serve, in a chilled large bowl combine whipping cream, sugar, and vanilla. Beat with an electric mixer until stiff peaks form. Remove cake from refrigerator and uncover. Spread whipped cream mixture over top and sides of cake. Some of the Tres Leches mixture will seep out of the cake as it stands. Serve immediately with remaining Tres Leches mixture.

Activities

Have a photo booth set up with sombreros, mustaches on sticks, and colorful plastic sunglasses. Create fun sayings on the computer like "Taco 'bout a bright future," "Adios," "Buena Onda" (which means good vibes), and "Holy Guacamole!" Label the photo booth with the phrase "Grab a prop and say queso!"

Father's Day

Invitations/Guest List

There's really no need for fancy invitations for a small family gathering for Father's Day, but if you want to make some, consider using a Mason jar or a picture of a pig on the top of the invitation to invite family to a Father's Day Barbecue.

Decorations & Set-Up

Men don't need a lot of decorations to feel loved, but you might shop at your local craft store for any items that have pigs or barbecue on them. I found a pig-shaped cork board once and gave it to my dad with pictures of our family on it for Father's Day.

For your tablecloth, use a red and white gingham cloth and place Mason jars with fresh white, yellow, and red gerbera daisies in the center. Don't forget to have bug spray, candles, and fans close by to help with the heat and mosquitoes.

Food & Drink

BBQ Sandwiches

Slow cook at home or pick up from your favorite barbecue shack around town!

Aunt Janie's Cole Slaw

Ingredients:

- 1 head of cabbage, chopped
- 1 onion, chopped
- 1 green pepper, chopped fine
- Salt to taste
- ½ cup sugar
- 1 cup cooking oil
- 1 cup cider vinegar
- 1 teaspoon celery seed
- ½ teaspoon dry mustard

Instructions:

Chop the cabbage, onion, and green pepper and combine. Pour the sugar over the ingredients. Meanwhile, bring to a boil the cooking oil, cider vinegar, celery seed, and dry mustard. Pour the boiling mixture over the cabbage mixture (it will cook it) and then refrigerate and keep up to nine days. Best prepared the day before you want to serve it.

Baked Beans

Add cooked ground beef, maple syrup, and spicy mustard to two cans of baked beans and cook until done (around 25 minutes) in the oven at 350 degrees.

Layered Lemon Blueberry Cake
(Sally's Baking Addiction)

Ingredients:

Cake:

- 1 cup unsalted butter, softened to room temperature
- 1¼ cups granulated sugar
- ½ cup packed light brown sugar
- 4 large eggs, at room temperature
- 1 tablespoon vanilla extract
- 3 cups sifted all-purpose flour (spooned & leveled)
- 1 tablespoon baking powder
- ½ teaspoon salt
- 1 cup buttermilk
- zest + juice of 3 medium lemons
- 1½ cups blueberries, fresh or frozen (do not thaw)
- 1 tablespoon all-purpose flour

Cream Cheese Frosting:

- 8 ounces full-fat brick style cream cheese, softened to room temperature
- ½ cup unsalted butter, softened to room temperature
- 3½ cups confectioners' sugar
- 1-2 tablespoons heavy cream
- 1 teaspoon vanilla extract
- Pinch salt

Instructions:

Preheat the oven to 350 degrees. Grease and lightly flour three 9 x 12 inch cake pans with nonstick spray. Set aside.

Make the cake: Using a handheld or stand mixer with a paddle attachment, beat the butter on high until creamy, about 1 minute. Add granulated and brown sugars and beat on medium-high speed until creamed, about 2-3 minutes. Add eggs and vanilla. Beat on medium speed until everything is completely combined, about 2 full minutes. Scrape down the sides and bottom of the bowl as needed. Set aside.

In a large sized bowl, toss together the flour, baking powder, and salt. Slowly add the dry ingredients to the wet ingredients. Beat on low speed for 5 seconds, then add the milk, lemon zest, and lemon juice. Remove from the mixer and stir lightly until everything is just combined. Toss the blueberries in 1 tablespoon of flour and fold into the batter. Batter is extremely thick. Do not overmix at any point. Overmixing will create a tough, dense textured crumb.

Spoon batter evenly into three prepared cake pans. If using only two cake pans, your bake time will be longer. Bake the three layers for about 21-26 minutes or until a toothpick inserted in the center comes out clean. Mine took 21 minutes. Remove from the oven and allow to cool completely before frosting.

Make the frosting: Using a handheld or stand mixer with a paddle attachment, beat cream cheese and butter together on medium speed until no lumps remain, about 3 full minutes. Add confectioners' sugar, 1 tablespoon cream, vanilla extract, and salt with the mixer running on low. Increase to high speed and beat for 3 minutes. Add 1 more tablespoon of cream to thin out, if desired.

Assemble and frost: First, using a large serrated knife, trim the tops off the cake layers to create a flat surface. Place one layer on your cake stand. Evenly cover the top with cream cheese frosting. Top with second cake layer, more frosting, then the third cake layer. Top with frosting and spread around the sides. The recipe doesn't make a ton of frosting, just enough for a light frost. Top with blueberries or lemon garnish if desired. Refrigerate for at least 45 minutes before cutting or else the cake may fall apart as you cut.

Make ahead tip: Prepare cakes and frosting 1 day in advance. Keep cakes at room temperature, covered tightly. Refrigerate prepared frosting in an airtight container until ready to use. Frosted or unfrosted cakes may be frozen up to 2 months, thaw overnight in the refrigerator and bring to room temperature if desired before serving.

Drinks

The guys in my family love a good old-fashioned Coca-Cola, Root Beer, and Dr. Pepper. For the ladies, buy some bottles of Izze sparkling water.

Activities

Play a game of horseshoes, backyard Jenga, or corn hole. Men love having something to throw and compete with!

Building Community:
Southern Style Dinner Party

In Chapter Two, *The Art of Entertaining*, I prepared a meal in our first home for two of our best couple friends. Whenever I am hosting a dinner party, I like to keep my tablescape simple by using white dishes, linen napkins, and a placemat that coordinates with the season. I'm also fond of having lots of candles burning in the dining room to create a warm and glowing atmosphere. I also recommend downloading the *Dan in Real Life* soundtrack. Composed by Sondre Lerche, the music serves well in the background but also has some fun tracks like *Let My Love Open the Door*. My favorite quote from this movie is by Steve Carell's character, Dan, when he says, "Plan to be surprised." Plan to be surprised when you host a dinner party, but let your love open the door!

Arugula Salad with Lemon Vinaigrette Dressing

Whenever I make my dressings, I always eye-ball the ingredients into a jelly-sized Mason jar. I do equal parts extra virgin olive oil and apple cider vinegar, then I zest and squeeze the juice of one lemon, add salt and pepper, and sprinkle in Herbs de Provence and diced garlic. I screw on the lid and shake it all together until mixed well. Then it's ready to be poured over a fresh arugula and spinach mixture with thinly sliced Parmesan cheese. For an extra crunch, serve a slice of cheese bread with the salad that guests can also use to dip into the shrimp and grits.

Shrimp and Grits (adapted from Bubba's Shrimp and Grits and The Bay's Faux Ya Ya)

Grits Ingredients:

- 4 cups chicken stock
- 2 cups grits, such as Dixie Lily
- 1 cup heavy cream
- 4 ounces unsalted butter
- One 14-16 ounce can creamed corn
- Shredded smoked Gouda cheese

Shrimp Gravy Ingredients:

- 4 tablespoons butter
- 2 teaspoons salt, plus ½ teaspoon, divided
- 2 cups quick grits
- ¼ cup bacon, chopped
- ½ cup onion, diced
- 2 tablespoons diced red bell pepper
- 2 tablespoons diced green bell pepper
- ½ teaspoon garlic, minced
- 36 medium shrimp, tails removed, peeled, and deveined
- ¾ cup flour
- ½ cup dry white wine
- 1 quart heavy cream
- ½ teaspoon pepper
- ½ teaspoon garlic powder

For the grits, boil the chicken stock in a saucepan and stir in the grits. Reduce to a simmer and cook for 40 minutes, stirring occasionally and adding in cream if the grits need more liquid. Pour in the butter, creamed corn, cream, and stir until it is combined with the grits. Add in the shredded cheese and stir until smooth.

For the gravy, sauté the bacon in a large heavy saucepan over medium-high heat until the fat is rendered. Stir in the onion, peppers, and garlic, and cook until soft. Add the shrimp and stir to combine. Sprinkle in the flour and stir, making sure the flour is well incorporated. Add the wine and cream, stirring well until the sauce has thickened. In a small bottle or bowl, mix the ½ teaspoon salt, pepper, and garlic powder and season the gravy to taste. Serve the shrimp gravy over grits.

The Barefoot Contessa's Raspberry Cheesecake

Crust Ingredients:

- 1½ cups graham cracker crumbs (10 crackers)
- 1 tablespoon sugar
- 6 tablespoons (3/4 stick) unsalted butter, melted

Filling Ingredients:

- ½ pound cream cheese, at room temperature
- 1½ cups sugar
- 5 whole extra-large eggs, at room temperature
- 2 extra-large egg yolks, at room temperature
- ¼ cup sour cream

- 1 tablespoon grated lemon zest (2 lemons)
- 1½ teaspoons pure vanilla extract

For the topping (optional):

- 1 cup red jelly (not jam)
- 3 half-pints fresh raspberries

Instructions:

Preheat the oven to 350 degrees. To make the crust, combine the graham crackers, sugar, and melted butter in a bowl and stir until moistened. Pour into a 9-inch springform pan. With your hands, press the crumbs into the bottom of the pan and about 1 inch up the sides. Bake for 8 minutes. Cool to room temperature. Raise the oven temperature to 450 degrees. To make the filling, cream the cream cheese and sugar in the bowl of an electric mixer fitted with a paddle attachment on medium-high speed until light and fluffy, about 5 minutes. Reduce the speed of the mixer to medium and add the eggs and egg yolks, two at a time, mixing well. Scrape down the bowl and beater as necessary. With the mixer on low, add the sour cream, lemon zest, and vanilla. Mix thoroughly and pour into the cooled crust. Bake for 15 minutes. Turn the oven temperature down to 225 degrees and bake for another 1 hour and 15 minutes. Turn the oven off and open the door wide. The cake will not be completely set in the center. Allow the cake to sit in the oven with the door open for 30 minutes. Take the cake out of the oven and allow it to sit at room temperature for another 2 to 3 hours, until completely cooled. Wrap and refrigerate overnight. Remove the cake from the springform pan by carefully running a hot knife around the outside of the cake. Leave the cake on the bottom of the springform pan for serving. If you make the topping, melt the jelly in a small pan over low heat. In a bowl, toss the raspberries and the warm jelly gently until well mixed. Arrange the berry mixture on top of the cake. Refrigerate until ready to serve.

Thankful Gathering or Friends-giving Meal

Hosting a Thankful Gathering at your church or a Friends-giving meal in your home is all about creating an atmosphere that brings you joy and laughter. If you are planning this gathering at church, recruit women to be table hostesses and ask them to decorate their centerpiece and invite seven others to sit at their table. Invitations can be sent electronically so women can register online.

For a Friends-giving meal at your home, decorate your centerpiece with seasonal vegetables like asparagus, artichokes, and pumpkins, along with bright yellow sunflowers and fresh evergreens. Invite three couples over for dinner by sending invitations on brown craft paper.

During the meal, use conversation cards provided by If:Table to help create purposeful dialogue among the people at your table.

As a party favor, give guests a package of seeds with their name on it and a label that says "May Good Things Grow." (Download your free label at www.invitedbook.com/freebies).

Agenda:

5:15 – Table hostesses arrive to greet their table guests and set up last-minute decorations for table.

5:30-6:00 – Background music plays while women check in, fill out giveaway cards, and find their tables (Chris Tomlin mix with Christy Nockels and other female singers). Have each hostess bring a cheeseball and crackers for their table to munch on while waiting for program to begin.

6:00 – Welcome by Women's Ministry Hostess

- Share the evening's purpose – Hebrews 12:28

- Giveaways

6:10-6:13 – Worship (at the end of the worship set, ask the worship leader to lead the women in a prayer for the food)

- 10,000 Reasons

6:15 – Men bring out salad and fill glasses with water or spiced tea. Salad dressing, napkins, and silverware are already on table.

6:30 – Men bring out main dish and have busboys help them pick up salad plates.

6:50 – Men bring dessert and coffee to the table and have busboys help them pick up dinner plates.

6:55 – Women's Ministry Hostess introduces the keynote speaker.

7:00-7:20 – Keynote Speaker

7:20-7:30 – Closing Worship (have the women remain seated for the first song so they can reflect and write what they are thankful for and then stand for the second song).

- Lord, I Need You

- You Revive Me

7:35 – Closing Prayer and Dismissal for Women's Ministry Hostess

- Share upcoming event announcements and wish them a Happy Thanksgiving.

- Play upbeat background music like Meredith Andrews as women leave.

Thankful Gathering Volunteers

- Food Team (five people)

- Greeters (one greeter leader and four helpers)

- Registration Table (two to four people)

- Men and Busboys (one waiter and busboy for every two tables)

- Worship Leader and Band

- Church Info Table (one person)

- Pictures (one person)

- Keynote Speaker Hostess (one person)

Food

When preparing food for a large event at church, you will have a budget that typically allows for six dollars per person for the main meal. You might have to adapt the menu below to stay within budget. An adaption of this menu could be:

Cheese Ball and Crackers

House Salad

Roast Chicken

Rolls

Pie Table

(Have key volunteers bring pies—pecan, pumpkin, apple, chocolate—and set them on bark servingware.)

If you are hosting a version of Thankful Gathering in your home for a Friends-giving, ask friends to bring the charcuterie, wine, and roasted vegetables while you prepare the meat, fried cornbread, and sweet potato bread pudding.

Charcuterie Board

A charcuterie (shar-KOO-tuh-REE) is the art of salting, smoking, brining, and curing meats. Assemble your charcuterie board by purchasing meats, cheeses, crackers, nuts, fruit, and jam that can be artfully arranged. Some suggestions are handcrafted pepperoni, goat cheese, and strawberry jam.

Roasted Turkey with Blueberry Jam
(may substitute pork tenderloin for the turkey)

- 1 whole bone-in turkey breast, 6½ - 7 pounds
- 1 tablespoon minced garlic (3 cloves)
- 2 teaspoons dry mustard
- 1 tablespoon chopped fresh rosemary leaves

- 1 tablespoon chopped fresh sage leaves
- 1 teaspoon chopped fresh thyme leaves
- 2 teaspoons kosher salt
- 1 teaspoon freshly ground black pepper
- 2 tablespoons good olive oil
- 2 tablespoons freshly squeezed lemon juice
- 1 cup dry white wine
- Blueberry jam

Preheat the oven to 325 degrees. Place the turkey breast, skin side up, on a rack in a roasting pan.

In a small bowl, combine the garlic, mustard, herbs, salt, pepper, olive oil, and lemon juice to make a paste. Loosen the skin from the meat gently with your fingers and smear half of the paste directly on the meat. Spread the remaining paste evenly on the skin. Pour the wine into the bottom of the roasting pan.

Roast the turkey for 1¾ - 2 hours, until the skin is golden brown and an instant-read thermometer registers 165 degrees when inserted into the thickest and meatiest areas of the breast. (I test in several places.) If the skin is over-browning, cover the breast loosely with aluminum foil. When the turkey is done, cover with foil and allow it to rest at room temperature for 15 minutes. Pour the blueberry jam into a saucepan with 3 tablespoons of water to simmer. Slice and serve with the pan juices and blueberry jam spooned over the turkey.

Roasted Vegetables

- 1 large (4 pound) butternut squash, peeled, seeded, and 1-inch diced
- 4 carrots, cut
- 1 head of cauliflower, cut
- 4 zucchini, 1-inch diced
- 3 tablespoons good olive oil
- 1 tablespoon fresh thyme leaves
- 2 teaspoons kosher salt
- 1 teaspoon fresh black pepper

Preheat oven to 400 degrees. Place the vegetables on a sheet pan (I lined mine with parchment to help with cleanup). Add olive oil, thyme, salt and pepper and toss. Roast for 30-40 minutes until tender; toss once during cooking to help brown evenly.

Na Na's Fried Cornbread

My grandmother makes delicious fried cornbread but eyeballs her ingredients to make cornbread that is thick but still soup-like. To watch her make cornbread, go to this link on YouTube:

https://youtu.be/gWc25P9UmD0

Ingredients:

- 1 cup Adams Self-Rising Cornmeal
- 1 spoonful flour
- ¾ cup buttermilk
- 16 ounce can of Crisco all-vegetable shortening
- 1-2 teaspoons water
- Lawry's seasoning salt, to taste

Instructions:

Heat the vegetable shortening in a skillet until bubbling. Combine the cornmeal, flour, buttermilk, and water, taking care to make the mixture a thick but still soup-like consistency, similar to pancakes. Add the buttermilk in halves until the consistency is just right and spoon patties into the oil. Let the patties cook for 2-3 minutes on each side and flatten the patties once you flip them. The cornbread should be a golden brown color when cooked. Once the cornbread is finished cooking, place on a plate covered in a paper towel to pat dry. Sprinkle seasoning salt on top and serve warm.

Acre's Sweet Potato Bread Pudding and Whiskey Caramel Sauce

Acre is a restaurant in Auburn, Alabama, that celebrates southern hospitality. Their menu is inspired by the farm-to-table movement, and they are known for their pimento cheese, shrimp and grits, and carrot bread pudding. This is another version that is inspired by their bread pudding, using sweet potatoes and ingredients that are easily found in your local grocery store.

Ingredients:

- 10 Sister Schubert's Rolls
- 5 croissants
- ½ tablespoon kosher salt
- 1 cup brown sugar
- Dash of nutmeg
- 1 teaspoon cinnamon
- 1 cup sugar

- 3 eggs
- 1 teaspoon vanilla
- 2 cups heavy cream
- 3 cups milk
- 3 small baked sweet potatoes

Streusel Topping:
- 1½ cups crushed pecans
- ½ cup sugar
- 1 cup brown sugar
- 2 tablespoons flour
- ½ stick cold butter
- 1½ teaspoon kosher salt

Instructions:

For streusel: Add all ingredients to a mixing bowl. Begin crumbling the mixture together using your hands until the butter is incorporated evenly into the streusel. Keep chilled or at room temperature.

For Bread pudding: Preheat oven to 400 degrees. Take all breads and tear into silver-dollar sized chunks and place in a large mixing bowl. Add brown sugar, nutmeg, cinnamon, and salt. Peel baked sweet potatoes and crush into small pieces and add to bread mix. In a separate mixing bowl, whisk eggs and sugar together until smooth. Then add vanilla, milk, and heavy cream and whisk. Add your custard base to the bread and gently fold (do not crush or squeeze the bread) until custard is incorporated into the bread. Let bread pudding rest for 15 minutes.

Take one 2-inch-deep baking pan, spray with pan coating, and place bread mixture in the pan evenly. Crumble streusel topping evenly over the top layer. Bake in oven for 35 minutes or until bread pudding rises slightly in the center.

Remove and cover top with caramel sauce. Return to oven until caramel begins to bubble slightly (about 5-10 minutes).

Whiskey Caramel Sauce

Ingredients:

- 1 pound light brown sugar
- ½ cup whiskey
- 1 cup heavy cream
- 1 tablespoon kosher salt
- ½ pound unsalted butter

Instructions:

Add sugar and whiskey to sauce pot. Simmer on low heat for 4 minutes. Be careful not to turn heat too high, which could set fire and burn the sugar. If alcohol ignites, just place lid on pot. Next, add cream and salt. Bring to simmer and reduce by a fourth. Whisk in butter. Serve warm.

New in Town Basket or Welcome Home Baby Basket

In Chapter Eight, I spoke of how it feels to be the new girl in town and how much I appreciated a friend bringing my family dinner to welcome us home. This meal is great for new neighbors or for friends who have just had babies. I always make my meals in aluminum serving tins that are labeled with the meal and date so they can freeze the meal and don't have to worry with returning any Tupperware.

When you deliver the meal, bring a basket lined with a tea towel and filled with a local candle, soap, nut mixture, or honey. Also place some snacks and basic household toiletries in the basket. Download one of our recipe cards at www.christenprice.com/shop-the-studio and write your recipe on it, along with your phone number and e-mail address. When you deliver the meal, try to invite your friend to church, book club, or your mommy group to let her meet new people or get out of the house after being home with the baby for a few weeks. Your friend will appreciate your generosity and thoughtfulness!

Poppy Seed Chicken Casserole

Ingredients:

- 4 skinless chicken breasts
- 1 can cream of celery soup
- 8 ounces sour cream
- 2 rolls of Ritz crackers
- 1 can cream of mushroom soup
- 1½ sticks of butter
- 1 tablespoon poppy seeds

Instructions:

Boil and cube the chicken breasts. Combine the sour cream, poppy seeds, and cream of mushroom and celery soups into a bowl. Pour the melted butter over crumbled crackers in another bowl. In a 9 x 13 inch aluminum pan, pour ½ cup of the cracker mix on the bottom, then add the chicken and pour the soup mixture over the chicken. Sprinkle the remaining cracker mixture over the top and bake at 350 degrees for 30-45 minutes until golden brown.

Strawberry Shortcake Pound Cake

Use the pound cake recipe from the bridal shower and the homemade whipped cream recipe from the kids' Christmas party to make this from scratch.

Ingredients:

- 1 pound cake (store bought or freshly made)
- 1 pint of whipped cream
- 1 package of strawberries
- ½ cup dark brown sugar

Instructions:

Cut strawberries in half and place in a bowl. Add brown sugar to strawberries and let sit until incorporated (at least thirty minutes). Cut pound cake into cubes. In a Mason jar or aluminum pan, layer the pound cake, strawberries, and whipped cream.

Book Club Discussion & Menu

Discussion

(Pick four to six questions that fit well with your group conversation):

1. In *Invited,* Christen shares about how unplanned events have happened to her as she plans parties, like the time she dropped the cupcakes on the floor before her son's first birthday party. Can you share a time when you've had disaster strike just before a big event? How did the unexpected make you feel, and what did you do to recover?

2. Why do you think women struggle with perfection?

3. The definition of connection is "a relationship in which a person, thing, or idea is linked or associated with something else." Who are your "people," and how do you connect with them intentionally?

4. Have you ever been afraid of opening your home because you have compared it to someone else's?

5. Share a time when you have received hospitality from others. How did this make you feel?

6. What is your favorite memory of celebrating? Or, what is your favorite occasion to celebrate? What hospitality tips in the book could help you with celebrating your people?

7. As women, our calendars are often full with work, activities, and celebrations. Do you ever struggle with doing too much? What are some positives/negatives of being busy (ex: positive: fun memories; negative: running late, breakdowns)? How do you give yourself grace?

8. Have you ever been lonely or experienced a fear of missing out (FOMO)? Share about this experience and what helped you overcome your fear.

9. *Expect the unexpected* and *trust in God's plans* are a common theme in the book. When have you had to let go of your plans to follow God's plans?

10. A phrase used in *Invited* is for us to become "hallelujah hostesses." How can you put this idea into practice in your community?

11. Have you ever experienced anxiety? What are your triggers? How can you break the anxiety cycle?

Menu:

Pink Punch

Charcuterie Board

Barbecue Sliders

Veggie Pizza

Cappuccino Brownies

Starting an Invited Small Group, with party ideas

First friend, I want to say thank you!

Thank you for being so willing to lead a small group. You are a hostess, and our team will be praying for you as you invite other women to participate in this study with you. Below are a few helpful tips for creating a warm and welcoming atmosphere for your small group:

Getting Started:

- Go to www.invitedbook.com/supportthebook.

- Ask your group members to download our supplemental material that provides questions for application and discussion. You will need to download this material too, as it goes hand-in-hand with the leader guide.

- The supplemental material is divided into eight sessions, and you can find videos that correlate with each section on www.invitedbook.com/videos.

Leading a small group does not have to be scary. You do not have to be the smartest person in the room about anything. You just have to be willing to gather some friends, facilitate the discussion, and create a safe environment.

1. Gather some friends. You can do this! Just invite some friends from your work, church, or neighborhood. Pick a place and a time. Decide how often you want to meet. Once a month, twice a month, or weekly. If you need childcare, ask the church what days and times they can provide it for you.

2. Facilitate the discussion. This just takes a little prep work. Use the book's content and supplemental material. Pick out some things to discuss or use questions provided by the material.

3. Create a safe environment. Everyone needs to feel safe. This means you encourage them to share and are kind about everyone's answers. You also want people to feel like what they share in the group stays in the group. Discuss the issue of confidentiality and stick to it!

Who to invite and how to invite:

- A good size for small groups is anywhere from 6-12 people. Attendance can become slim if there are less than six and can feel impersonal if there are more than 12.

  - If a group is more than 12, consider breaking into "sub-groups" of six.

  - If a group is less than 6, consider meeting off campus at a coffee shop or another place better suited for one-on-one conversation

- People won't attend your group if you don't ask them. Phone calls work best because they make potential group members feel special that you took time to think to invite them. E-mail, Facebook, and texts work also, but a personal phone call is a great first step.

- Check in with group members outside of your meeting. If someone doesn't show for a few weeks, visit with them privately; don't call them out in front of everyone. Plan get-togethers for dinner, movies, girl weekends, etc. outside of small group!

Facilitating a group:

Before the first meeting, send an e-mail with time, location, and what they need to bring. Keep the first meeting light-hearted and personal. It's fun to play icebreaker games and have food.

Don't feel like you have to know it all or have it all together. It actually helps group members feel like they belong if you admit that life is crazy and you aren't superwoman! But, keep in mind that you should be prepared with a general schedule and an idea of what to cover in each meeting. Try to read the chapter and have some sample questions to get conversation started. (Don't be afraid to go off-topic. Sometimes, your group discussion will go in a completely opposite direction of the study guide. That is OKAY! It's also okay to just pray or catch up. Don't feel like you have to cover everything verbatim to the book/study guide.)

Here is a sample party menu to go along with an eight week schedule:

Party Ideas:

- Session One: Meet and Greet Bagel or Yogurt Bar, Coffee
- Session Two: Bridal Shower Pound Cake, Pink Punch
- Session Three: Baby Shower Veggie Pizza, Herbed Ice Cubed Water
- Session Four: Tea Party Scones, Herbal Tea
- Session Five: Galentine's Day Quiche, Christmas Hot Chocolate
- Session Six: Charcuterie, Flavored Tea
- Session Seven: Birthday Party Cupcakes, Izze Drinks
- Session Eight: Graduation Taco Bar, Chips and Salsa, Virgin Margaritas

Words of Advice:

- Small groups aren't scary; they are super special. Some of my best friends have come out of my small group friendships.
- Small groups are about community, connection, and content. It is totally cool to cry at small group and admit that you are stressed and desperately need an hour away from your kids, work, school, life.
- The more you go, the more you will like it. This is important for your group members to know in the beginning, and that is why we ask for a small commitment to the group.
- Give other group members responsibility. Ask someone else to pray, take attendance, plan socials, and remember

birthdays. The people that step up and help are future group leaders!

- Encourage your group members privately. Invite them to lunch and be a friend. You will see a hundred blessings come your way if you just take time to love on someone!

- If something isn't working, don't be afraid to change it.

- Most importantly, know that you are being a disciple of Christ by investing time in a small group. Well done, good and faithful servant! (This is me giving you a BIG pat on the back)

Love my people, not their performance.

Hold on to my plans loosely.

Be me, *beautifully*.

Celebrate the life I've been given.

It's easy to stand with the crowd. It takes courage to stand alone.

Expect the unexpected! *Take naps.*

Let go and let God move.

Parties are about *connection*, not *perfection*.

Live well, laugh often, love much.

Seek Christ. *Serve* my family. *Spread* God's truth to others.

Laugh without fear of the future.

the invited manifesto

Be a woman of noble character.

Celebrate simply, beautifully, and joyfully. *Give grace.*

Be *intentional.* Show kindness. Live invitationally.

Invite people not only into my home but into my *life.*

Be the *friend* I wish to have. Color outside the lines.

Surrender my plans and let God surprise me with His.

Believe that hope does not disappoint.

Give God the desires of my heart. Wait in patient expectation.

Believe that all the promises of God in Christ are Yes and in Christ, Amen, to the glory of God through us.

Be a pioneer. Having it all is a lie.

Let my light shine. Joyfully encourage others.

ENDNOTES

1. "Perfect, Perfection – Baker's Evangelical Dictionary of Biblical Theology Online," Bible Study Tools, accessed February 18, 2017, http://www.biblestudytools.com/dictionaries/bakers-evangelical-dictionary/perfect-perfection.html.

2. Brennan Manning, *The Ragamuffin Gospel: Embracing the Unconditional Love of God* (Bletchley: Authentic Media, 2009), 149.

3. Margaret Feinberg, *Fight Back with Joy: Celebrate More, Regret Less, Stare Down Your Greatest Fears* (Brentwood, TN: Worthy Publishing, 2014), 85.

4. "Connection," Merriam-Webster, accessed February 18, 2017, http://www.merriam-webster.com/dictionary/connection.

5. Ina Garten, *Barefoot Contessa: Family Style* (London: Bantam Press, 2012), 21-22.

6. Letitia Baldrige, *Letitia Baldrige's New Manners for New Times: A Complete Guide to Etiquette* (New York: Scribner, 2016), 405-407.

7. "What is beauty," Circe Institute, accessed February 18, 2017, https://www.circeinstitute.org/2009/03/what-is-beauty.

8. "Strong's Greek: 2570. καλός (kalos) -- beautiful, good," Strong's Greek: 2570. καλός (kalos) -- beautiful, good, accessed February 18, 2017, http://biblehub.com/greek/2570.htm.

9. "Research," Brené Brown, accessed February 18, 2017, http://brenebrown.com/research/.

10. Baldrige, *Letitia Baldrige's New Manners for New Times,* 3.

11. "Prescribing Hospitality for Growth in the Christian Life," Biblical Counseling Coalition, accessed February 18, 2017, http://biblicalcounselingcoalition.org/2016/02/07/prescribing-hospitality-for-growth-in-the-christian-life/.

12. Dave Ramsey, *Dave Ramsey's Complete Guide to Money* (Brentwood, TN: Lampo Press, 2012), 29.

13. Paxcenter.org, accessed February 18, 2017, http://paxcenter.org/enneagram/.

14. C. S. Lewis, *Mere Christianity* (New York: HarperOne, 2012), 44.

15. Richard J. Foster, *Celebration of Discipline: The Path to Spiritual Growth* (London: Hodder & Stoughton, 2008), 191.

16. "5. The First Sign: Jesus Turns Water into Wine (John 2:1-11)," Bible.org, accessed February 18, 2017, https://bible.org/seriespage/5-first-sign-jesus-turns-water-wine-john-21-11.

17. Kenneth L. Barker et al., *Zondervan NIV Study Bible: New International Version* (Grand Rapids, MI: Zondervan, 2008), 1629, John 2:11 footnote.

18. *St. Augustine: Books I-X* (Kansas City: Sheed Andrews and McMeel, 1970), 67.

19. Psalm 126:5

20. Romans 5:2 NIV

21. Jennie Allen, *Stuck: The Places We Get Stuck & The God Who Sets Us free* (Nashville: Thomas Nelson, 2011), 53.

22. Allen, Stuck, 15.

23. "The Intern (2015)," IMDb, accessed February 19, 2017, http://www.imdb.com/title/tt2361509/.

24. "Dave and Jon Ferguson," Finding Your Way Back to God, accessed February 19, 2017, http://yourwayback.org/.

25. "The Facts & Statistics: College Women Student Leadership Barriers," College Women Students, Facts, Statistics, Stress, Leadership Barriers, Perfectionism, Eating Disorders, Anxiety, accessed February 19, 2017, http://www.campuscalm.com/women_leadership_barriers.html.

26. "ERIC - Education Resources Information Center," ERIC - Education Resources Information Center, accessed February 19, 2017, https://eric.ed.gov/.

27. "Companion Worksheet Reader Worksheet and Book Club Guide," accessed February 19, 2017, brenebrown.com/wp-content/uploads/2013/09/GOIReadingCompanion.pdf

28. "The Science Behind the Smile," Harvard Business Review, October 08, 2014, accessed February 19, 2017, https://hbr.org/2012/01/the-science-behind-the-smile.

29. Rebecca Strong, "Social Media, FOMO and the Perfect Storm for the Quarter-Life Crisis," The Huffington Post, May 10, 2016,

accessed February 19, 2017, http://www.huffingtonpost.com/
rebecca-strong/social-media-fomo-and-the_b_9880170.html.

30. "Friendships: Enrich your life and improve your health," Mayo Clinic, accessed February 19, 2017, http://www.mayoclinic. org/healthy-lifestyle/adult-health/in-depth/friendships/ art-20044860.

31. Jonah Lehrer, *How We Decide* (Boston: Mariner Books, 2010), 9.

32. John Medina, *Brain Rules: 12 Principles for Surviving and Thriving at Work, Home, and School* (Pear Press, 2008) 247 and 61.

33. Anne Lamott, *Bird by Bird: Some Instructions on Writing and Life* (Melbourne: Scribe, 2009).

34. "Facts," Anxiety and Depression Association of America, ADAA, accessed February 17, 2017, http://www.adaa.org/ living-with-anxiety/women/facts.

35. Linda Dillow, *Calm My Anxious Heart: A Woman's Guide to Finding Contentment* (Colorado Springs, CO: NavPress, 2007), 128.

36. Katherine Bindley, "Women and Prescription Drugs: One in Four Takes Mental Health Meds," The Huffington Post, November 16, 2011, accessed February 17, 2017, http://www. huffingtonpost.com/2011/11/16/women-and-prescription-drug-use_n_1098023.html.

37. Kenneth L. Barker et al., Zondervan NIV study Bible: New International Version (Grand Rapids, MI: Zondervan, 2008), 1848, note under Philippian 4:6.

38. Drayton Nabers, *The Case for Character: Looking at Character from a Biblical Perspective* (Tulsa: Christian Pub. Services, 2006), 48.

39. Dillow, *Calm My Anxious Heart*, 31.

40. "Dan in Real Life" (2007), IMDb, accessed February 19, 2017, http://www.imdb.com/title/tt0480242/.

41. "Bible Weights and Measurements," Bible Weights and Measurements, accessed February 19, 2017, http://biblehub.com/weights-and-measures/.

42. "English Standard Version," Bible.faithlife.com, accessed February 19, 2017, https://bible.faithlife.com/books/esv/Ge18.11.

43. 1 Thessalonians 4:7, The Message.

44. Kenneth L. Barker et al., *Zondervan NIV Study Bible: New International Version* (Grand Rapids, MI: Zondervan, 2008), 1490, Matthew 13:33 reference.

45. "Can Women Have and Do It All?" Propel Women, accessed February 28, 2017, http://www.propelwomen.org/content/can-women-have-and-do-it-all/gjjr11.

46. "Why You're Always Late and How to Be on Time - Improve Time Management," Time, accessed February 19, 2017, http://time.com/106815/stop-being-late/.

47. Ibid.

48. Sumitha Bhandarkar et al., "How to Keep Yourself From Yelling at Kids Even When You are Hopping Mad," A Fine Parent, November 12, 2016, accessed February 20, 2017, http://

afineparent.com/stop-yelling-at-kids/what-to-do-instead-of-yelling-at-kids.html.

49. Baldrige, *Letitia Baldrige's New Manners for New Times*, 3.

50. Elizabeth Newman, *Untamed Hospitality: Welcoming God and Other Strangers* (Grand Rapids, MI: Brazos Press, 2007), 92.

51. Carolyn Gregoire, "Turning 30: 12 Signs You're In Pre-30 Crisis," The Huffington Post, February 20, 2013, accessed February 20, 2017, http://www.huffingtonpost.com/2013/02/20/turning-30-12-signs-youre_n_2724609.html.

52. "Three Major Faith and Culture Trends for 2014," Barna Group, accessed February 20, 2017, https://www.barna.org/barna-update/culture/649-three-major-faith-and-culture-trends-for-2014#VaFxEflViko.

53. Richard Warren, *The Purpose-driven Life: What On Earth Am I Here For?* (Grand Rapids, MI: Zondervan, 2016).

54. Philip Ryken, *The Message of Salvation: The Lord Our Help* (Leicester: Inter-Varsity, 2001), 243.

55. "35 Things I Wish I'd Known in High School," Lies Young Women Believe, April 29, 2015, accessed February 17, 2017, http://www.liesyoungwomenbelieve.com/35-things-i-wish-id-known-in-high-school/.

56. Ryken, *The Message of Salvation*, 245.

57. NewOnNetflix, "Chef's Table - Season 1 | Dan Barber [HD] | Netflix," YouTube, April 16, 2015, accessed February 20, 2017, https://www.youtube.com/watch?v=tqGZKiOLsU8.

58. "Prescribing Hospitality for Growth in the Christian Life," Biblical Counseling Coalition, accessed February 20, 2017, http://biblicalcounselingcoalition.org/2016/02/07/prescribing-hospitality-for-growth-in-the-christian-life/.

59. Emily P. Freeman, "The Bench - Emily P. Freeman," May 27, 2010, accessed February 20, 2017, http://emilypfreeman.com/the-bench-2/.

60. Nabers, *The Case for Character*, 71.

61. "Goodness // Day 2," Undivided Women, accessed February 20, 2017, http://www.undividedwomen.com/whats-in-your-fruit-bowl/goodness-day-2.

62. 2 Peter 1:10–11 NIV.

63. "Philippians 2:14-15 - MSG - Do everything readily and cheerfully - no bicke . . . ," Bible Study Tools, accessed February 20, 2017, http://www.biblestudytools.com/msg/philippians/passage/?q=philippians%2B2%3A14-15.

64. Manning, *The Ragamuffin Gospel*, 111.

65. Christine Hoover, *Naptime Diaries Lent Devotional* (2015, 2016). OOP. See her website: www.GraceCoversMe.com. Accessed February 20, 2017.

66. John 16:21 NIV.

67. "One Marble at a Time," Parent Cue, August 01, 2016, accessed February 20, 2017, http://theparentcue.org/one-marble-at-a-time/.

68. Proverbs 22:6 KJV.

69. Ryken, *The Message of Salvation*, 18-19.

70. Sinclair B. Ferguson, *The Christian Life* (Edinburgh: Banner of Truth Trust, 1997), 16.

For more information about
Christen Price
&
Invited
please visit:

www.christenprice.com
connect@christenprice.com
www.invitedbook.com
www.facebook.com/chris1oprice
@chris1oprice
www.pinterest.com/chris1o

You can also connect with Christen through online Bible studies at www.undividedwomen.com.

For more information about
AMBASSADOR INTERNATIONAL
please visit:

www.ambassador-international.com
@AmbassadorIntl
www.facebook.com/AmbassadorIntl

Christen Price

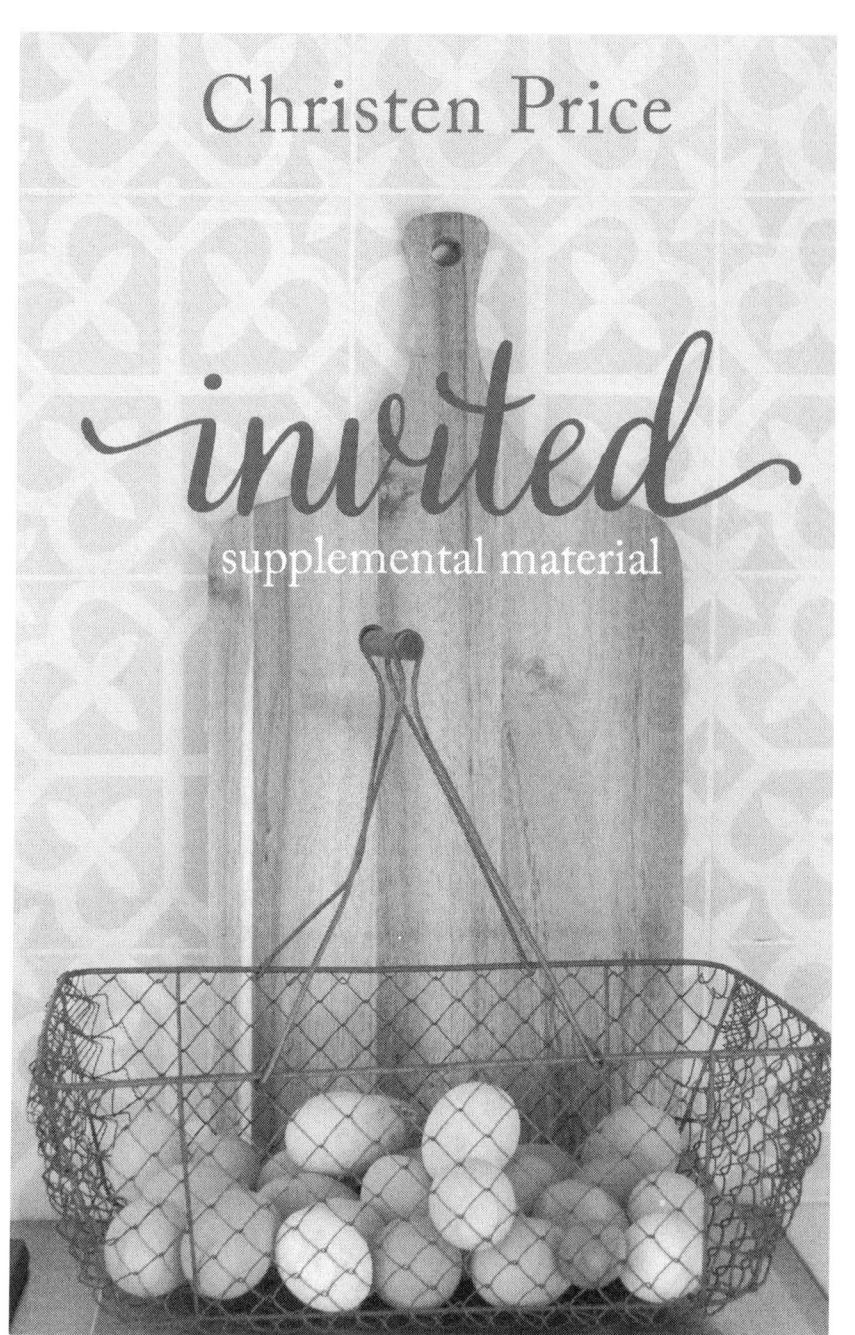

invited
supplemental material

Supplemental Material for *Invited* is available now at www.invitedbook. com, www.ambassador-international and other online retailers now!